THE JOHNSON ECLIPSE

Leonard Baker has been a reporter for the
St.Louis **Globe-Democrat** and for **Newsday,**
a Long Island newspaper. A Washington
correspondent since 1958, his articles
have appeared in many national magazines.

The Johnson Eclipse

A PRESIDENT'S VICE PRESIDENCY

by Leonard Baker

The Macmillan Company

NEW YORK

FIRST PRINTING

TO *Liva*

Contents

1961: The Search for a Role   1

1962: The Shadow of Robert Kennedy   103

1963: The Johnson Eclipse   175

A Note on Sources   271

Index   273

1961

The Search for
a Role

ONE

THIS Friday morning Lyndon Baines Johnson woke at nine o'clock in his home in the fashionable Georgetown section of Washington. He breakfasted from a tray served in his bedroom, then dressed carefully. His costume was striped trousers, a light gray double-breasted vest and a black cutaway morning coat. The outfit was too formal for his own choosing, but this day—as it would be many days in the future—the choice was not his. He looked, however, distinguished and comfortable. A massive man, well over six feet in height and more than two hundred pounds in weight and with a sharply jutting face, he wore his formal clothes with an elegance that belied his poor farm boy youth.

At approximately ten thirty, a black limousine stopped before his door. In it were Carl Hayden, the President Pro Tempore of the Senate, and John W. McCormack, the Democratic leader of the House of Representatives. They were the official escorts for Lyndon and Lady Bird Johnson. They would take them first to the White House and then to the east front of the Capitol. There, on this January 20, 1961, the Texan would be sworn in as Vice President of the United States.

A biting wind from the northwest had struck Washington

the previous afternoon. Eighteen-mile-an-hour gusts enveloped the city in cold and seven inches of snow strangled its traffic arteries. Still, a million people would come to the heart of the nation's capital city today, to stand before the east front of the Capitol and watch the inauguration itself or to line Pennsylvania Avenue and cheer the parade. Other millions would watch the event on television, listen to it on radio, read about it in newspapers. This happening that was about to take place —the inauguration of a President and Vice President—is the nearest thing the United States has to a national festival. Throughout the country there is a universal feeling of good cheer. Men hope the new President will solve the problems that beset the nation even while they know that neither he nor anyone else can. Men regret the retiring of the old President and the passing of his era; at this point of good-bye in a man's career people are charitable and speak only of his successes. The inauguration is also a spiritual triumph. In no other great nation has government been so stable so long, so much the product of rationality rather than barbarism. In no other great nation is the record as long of the transfer of government consistent with the law. In no other nation has civilized democracy succeeded quite so well. The inaugural is, as the new President would call it this day, "a celebration of freedom."

The Johnson car arrived at the White House a few minutes past eleven. John Fitzgerald Kennedy, the President-elect, and his wife already had arrived, to join the retiring President, Dwight David Eisenhower, and Mrs. Eisenhower for a cup of coffee. President Eisenhower had extended the invitations the previous afternoon. It promised to be cold, he had said of the inaugural day, and hot coffee would be welcome. Richard Milhous Nixon, the retiring Vice President, and his wife, Pat, also were there. It could have been a scene in any American home—four couples having hot coffee together before going out on a cold day—except that involved here was great power, which would pass from one set of hands to another. Lyndon Johnson would watch that transfer of power and then, in the coming years, would be an intimate witness to its use, but not a participant. The big Texas hands that had held so much power in past years would now be empty.

At eleven thirty the long line of black limousines pulled away from the White House. Johnson, still then the Vice President-elect, rode with Vice President Nixon. They were a curious combination. Both Johnson and Nixon had been defeated in election contests by the young man who rode in another car, ahead of them, with President Eisenhower. Both men had been born poor, had had to scramble, fight and gouge their way to where they neared the top. Both had to force themselves on what is called the "Eastern establishment," that informal combination of big money and well-placed contacts that can smooth the way for favored young men. The process had hardened both of them; made Nixon, it was said, too hard to be elected President; made Johnson, it was argued, too hard to be nominated for the Presidency. Despite, or because of these similarities, the two men had been political enemies, making the kind of personal remarks about each other that leave bitter memories. In the North during the past campaign Nixon had not debated his Democratic opponent's philosophy but had attacked Johnson personally for his southern origins. And Johnson had retaliated, not by attacking Nixon's campaign promises but by resurrecting the old charge of "McCarthyism" against the Republican. This day, of course, the two men were extremely gracious to each other. The acrimony of the past campaign, if not forgotten, was at least well hidden.

There still was a third reason that they made such a curious pair riding together to the Capitol. Richard Nixon represented Lyndon Johnson's ambition. It had been a "rule" of American politics that the Vice Presidency was the road to political oblivion. Only three men were ever elected from that office to the Presidency—John Adams and Thomas Jefferson at the nation's beginning and Martin Van Buren in 1836. After Van Buren, no Vice President had captured his party's Presidential nomination—until Dick Nixon had done it 124 years later. This meant, or could mean, that the Vice Presidency no longer was the end of a political career but perhaps just another length of the journey leading to the fulfillment of Lyndon Johnson's ambition: to be President of the United States.

That had been one of the chief factors in the making of Lyndon Johnson's decision to become second man. As the Vice Presidency had pulled Nixon from the obscurity of being a California senator with a reputation for ferreting out Communists in government to make him a Presidential candidate after eight years, perhaps it could strip Johnson of the charge of regionalism—a "southern senator" he was called by those who meant the title as an insult—that had dogged his political ambitions and make him a national figure.

The limousines turned into the driveway before the Capitol. Here is where Johnson had made his giant strides. For the previous eight years he had been the leader of the Senate Democrats and the LBJ pennant had whipped in the political breezes storming around the Capitol. If it was never seen, this banner was always felt. It was to Johnson that the senators had come, asking committee assignments, begging favors; sometimes also coming to challenge but never really able to stand up to Lyndon Johnson. Even John Kennedy, from whom Johnson now must take orders and to whom Johnson had promised utmost loyalty, had come to the Texan in years past. Back in 1957, Johnson had been generous, giving this young man an important seat on the Senate Foreign Relations Committee although another senator deserved it from the standpoint of seniority. During the next four years the senator from Massachusetts had used that committee position as one sign that his expertise in foreign affairs qualified him for the Presidency, more so, he argued, than Lyndon Johnson was qualified.

Johnson walked out onto the inaugural platform and the band played a fanfare for him. Johnson smiled and nodded his thanks. When a Texan in the audience stood, waved his ten-gallon hat and shouted "All the way with LBJ!" Johnson turned and waved, a friendly grin on his face. That slogan had once been part of his campaign for the Presidential nomination, a campaign that had ended in humiliating defeat six months earlier. But that humiliation had long since been filed away. There had been much activity in those six months. There had been victory and glory, as well as additional humiliations and hurts.

His daughters Lynda Bird, then sixteen, and Lucy Baines,* then thirteen, already were on the platform when Johnson and his wife, Lady Bird, arrived. The family chatted informally and in a friendly fashion with Chief Justice Earl Warren, who would swear in the new President; with former President Harry S. Truman, who was thoroughly enjoying the triumph of the Democratic Party; and with Nixon, who appeared to be the most relaxed and at ease person on the platform.

A brilliant sun cut through the clouds over the Library of Congress building across the small park from the inaugural stand. But still the temperature hovered at twenty-two degrees. The electric heaters on the open inaugural stand provided little warmth. Mrs. Johnson, wearing a mink coat over an olive green suit and with a matching pillbox hat, sat down first with the collar of her coat thrown back. But as the cold chill began to reach her, she pulled the mink collar closer around her. The men wore their topcoats buttoned, except, that is, for Lyndon Johnson. His was open, as if he did not notice the cold.

---

* In 1964 Johnson's younger daughter changed the spelling of her first name to Luci.

The ceremony began. There were the prayers and the songs. Most of those on the platform, like many in the audience, joined with Marian Anderson in singing "The Star Spangled Banner." But Johnson, it was noticed, did not. To those who knew him well and watched him closely in those few moments, he seemed detached, nervous. The time was now twelve forty, and Sam Rayburn stepped forward. Johnson slipped out of his topcoat and then stood bareheaded across from "Mr. Sam" Rayburn, the Speaker of the House of Representatives, who was now ready to administer the oath of office. It was the first time in the nation's history that a Speaker had sworn in a Vice President, but it was appropriate in this case. The Rayburn-Johnson relationship spanned many years. Although married once years earlier, Sam Rayburn had no children of his own and had come to look upon Lyndon Johnson as the son he might have had. When Johnson had first come to Congress twenty-four years earlier in 1937 as the representative from the Tenth District of Texas, Rayburn already had served in the House twenty-four years. He had guided the gangly young Texan through the intricacies of the House, pushed him ahead when a push would help. Mr. Sam even had nursed Lyndon Johnson when Johnson was ill. They became a political team. In 1940 at the Democratic national convention Johnson had maneuvered the Texas delegation into supporting Rayburn as Franklin D. Roosevelt's running mate. The delegation actually wanted another Texan, Jesse Jones, but Johnson was chairman of the delegation and simply refused to call on the Jones supporters. In the 1950s "Rayburn-Johnson" became almost synonymous with Congress. Then, at the 1960 Democratic convention, Rayburn had given up his traditional role as chairman of the convention to try to win the Presidential nomination for his protégé; Mr. Sam had met defeat at the hands of the Bostonian with the Harvard accent who sat near them now, watching intently.

Johnson raised his right hand and placed his left on a Bible that his mother, Rebekah Baines Johnson, had given him. The oath Johnson was about to take was familiar to him. He had sworn it on nine previous occasions as a member of Congress; on three of those occasions Rayburn had administered the oath as he was about to do now. But familiar with the words or not, Johnson was too nervous this day to say them accurately. Rather than assume his new duties "without mental reservation or purpose of evasion," Johnson took on his position "without any mental reservation whatever." The slip was hardly noticed by the tens of thousands standing in the cold before the Capitol. When the oath was done, Sam Rayburn moved forward and clasped Lyndon Johnson's hand in congratulations, his usually gruff face breaking into one of his rare smiles. Lyndon Baines Johnson of Johnson City, Texas, fifty-two years of age, was officially the thirty-seventh Vice President of the United States.

To most men such a time is success, the fulfillment of a dream. This was not so for Lyndon Johnson. For him this moment was a defeat. He had fancied himself the number one man in the strata of government officialdom and now he was formally stepping down to second place. The leader was becoming a follower. In the Senate, as majority leader during six of the eight Eisenhower years, he had enjoyed thinking of himself as equal to, perhaps even greater than, certainly more influential than, the President himself. Although Eisenhower's control of the Executive branch and the federal bureaucracy was conceded, Lyndon Johnson along with Rayburn claimed control of the Legislative branch and claimed also that the Legislative branch was the part of the federal government that dominated Washington. Now Johnson had no illusions about the new position he was assuming as the second man. "Power is where power goes," he had told his friends who objected to his giving up "a vote for a gavel." But Johnson knew better.

John Nance Garner, a fellow Texan, an equally skilled politician, and like Johnson, a Presidential aspirant who accepted second place, had described to Johnson in trenchant and basic terms the value of the Vice Presidency. "Not worth a pitcher of warm spit" is the way this description usually is reported. Not even that Lyndon Johnson once had shined shoes, run an elevator, worked on a road gang, had known poverty "so common we didn't know it had a name" and had now reached the second highest office in the nation could alter the basic fact: he knew he was stepping down.

But Johnson had made the choice willingly and had accepted the consequences. Shortly after the convention he had explained his relationship to the Democratic Presidential nominee in this manner: "It's just like that old Baptist hymn, 'Where He Leads Me, I Will Follow.'" And so it had been. Lyndon Johnson had given no cause to doubt his loyalty to Kennedy.

His part of the ceremony over, Johnson returned to his seat on the inaugural stand and bowed his head as the Reverend Dr. John Barclay, pastor of the Central Christian Church of Austin, Texas, asked God to "bless Lyndon B. Johnson and add Thy strength to his strength." A few minutes later, the man who was to be Johnson's leader was sworn in as the nation's thirty-fifth President and then began to speak. There were many stirring passages in that inaugural address, the nation's forty-fourth inaugural speech. The most significant, perhaps, came when the forty-three-year-old chief executive said: "Let the word go forth from this time and place, to friend and foe alike, that the torch has been passed to a new generation of Americans." It was not only a new generation, but a young generation. Lyndon Johnson was nine years older than the new President, almost a decade. The other men suddenly come to town as members of the New Frontier—Robert S. McNamara, Lawrence F. O'Brien, Kenneth O'Donnell, Orville L.

Freeman, Theodore C. Sorensen—were much closer than was Johnson to the President's age, to his outlook, his experiences, and his ambitions. Most of these men, like the President, had just finished college when the United States entered World War II; Lyndon Johnson was in his fifth year as a member of Congress on December 7, 1941. Most of these New Frontiersmen had been children, like the new President himself, when Franklin Roosevelt became leader of an economically desolate land. Perhaps, if they struggled with the memories of their youth, they could remember what it was like thirty years earlier when the dry earth and the hungry children raised the question of whether the United States could achieve its promise. But Lyndon Johnson would have no trouble remembering. He had been a part of the Great Depression. The New Deal names he knew—"Tommy the Cork" Corcoran, Benjamin Cohen, Abe Fortas—were unknown along the New Frontier except as references in history books. The political gathering along the Potomac in January 1961 was not one in which Johnson was at home. It was truly, as the President said, "a new generation." It was not Lyndon Johnson's generation.

But Lyndon Johnson could not permit himself to be awed by the difference a decade made. Within this administration he must find a role for himself. It must be a role greater than that of any previous Vice President. First, it must be a role making him vital to the New Frontier so that his selection as the Democratic Vice Presidential candidate in 1964 would be unavoidable. Then it must be a role that would make him a national figure so that in 1968 when he turned sixty, young by political standards, his selection as the leader of his party and as the country's President would be assured.

This meant he must overcome the regional prejudice he believed worked against him as much, if not more, than did religious prejudice work against John Kennedy's Catholicism. Dwight D. Eisenhower was the thirty-third person to serve as

President. Of the first sixteen, from George Washington to Abraham Lincoln, or from the founding of the nation to the end of the Civil War, eight Presidents, one in two, were southerners. Of the next seventeen, not one could accurately be described as "southern." Lyndon Johnson understood why. The labor and liberal factions of the Democratic Party had taught him at his party's convention in July just what standing a southerner, even one who had espoused civil rights as he had done, had with the powers that dominated the selection of the Presidential nominee.

He had begun his appeal against this regional prejudice immediately after being nominated. "This convention," he had said in accepting the Democratic Vice Presidential nomination, "has closed the door on the things which have divided America in the past. We have stepped across boldly into what I believe will be a wholesome, new day of hope and harmony for all Americans regardless of religion, or race, or region." He repeated that theme of ending regional as well as religious prejudice during the next months. He closed his campaign in Austin on November 7, the day before the voting, with the statement that "Americans are ready to lay aside the divisions of the 1860s to meet the challenge of the 1960s. Tomorrow night the world will know that the walls of the past are coming down. We're building a prouder America where opportunity is open to all regardless of their race, or their religion, or the region in which they live." He was to continue this effort as Vice President. "I am aware," he said to a Negro audience early in 1963, "as an heir of Appomattox, that the barriers of bias and prejudice within our society are not all barriers of race and color—or of religion and creed. In our land, as in many lands, men know discrimination for the geography of their birth as well as the genetics of their birth." And to a business group, he said: "Majorities and minorities have relied on stereotypes to mold their opinions of one another. Such stereotypes have been convenient—but they have also been cruel. We can take some measure of satisfaction from the fact that there is progress and that these stereotypes disappear as human understanding spreads. For example, the two highest elective offices in the strongest free nation on earth are held today by men who have overcome the dead hand of the stereotype—for reasons of religion or region of birth."

There was another difficulty—in addition to the decade's difference in age and the regional prejudice—that Lyndon Johnson had to overcome if he was to be the one delivering the inaugural address eight years from this day. This difficulty was the attitude toward Johnson of the men around the President. The "Irish Mafia" the newspapers had dubbed them. These men were skilled technicians, adroit dealers in people and voting blocs, hard-working and brilliant young men. They were not, however, professional politicians. They did not serve the man who had just been sworn in as President because of an attraction to the political world or because of any personal ambition they nursed. Their only motivating factor was their devotion to and admiration for John Kennedy. They were Louis Howes, not Jim Farleys or Len Halls. Some had been with Kennedy for fourteen years, all of his public life. Others were bound to him by family ties. Some had recently joined the intimate circle around him, attracted by his philosophy and his ability to enunciate it. All were loyal to him. His friend was their friend and, more importantly, his enemy was their enemy. They could not forget that Lyndon Johnson had been that "enemy" in the weeks before the Democratic convention in July. Supporters of Lyndon Johnson had encouraged other possible Democratic candidates for the Presidential nomination to battle and perhaps defeat the senator from Massachusetts in the primaries in hopes of leaving a clearer road for Johnson. Supporters of Johnson had challenged whether the New Englander's health permitted him to take on the arduous job of the Presidency. Supporters of Johnson had persuaded other candidates for the nomination to stay in the contest to the last minute to keep needed delegate votes away from the Massachusetts senator. And in the closing days and hours of the campaign for the nomination Johnson personally had intimated—so the Irish Mafia believed—that a "Catholic conspiracy" was behind the Bostonian's drive. Johnson personally had attacked his rival's father, Joseph P. Kennedy, and the young candidate himself; some of these attacks were too strong even to be printed in the newspapers.

Perhaps a more professional group, as professional in their attitudes toward the necessities of politics as was their leader who had just been sworn in as President, could have forgotten or forgiven the Texan. But the group of dedicated, skillful nonprofessionals who made up the Irish Mafia could not. Years later one member of this group, his face darkening, would recall those closing days and hours of the drive for the Democratic nomination in July 1960 and say: "Those attacks by LBJ were the only vicious, personal attacks of the whole campaign."

Lyndon Johnson had been in Washington for almost three decades. He knew how the "palace guard" of men around the President can help or hurt a person by a carefully chosen word, by neglecting to mention a telephone call or "forgetting" to deliver a message. Johnson himself, as a young representative, had basked in the glory of being favored by the men around FDR. Federal funds for Johnson's congressional district had flowed smoothly. Important committee assignments had come easily. He had also seen these men turn against others who then would eventually vanish from political sight. In the struggle for status, the blessings of the men around the President are crucial.

The new President understood this. He also understood that his Vice President was "a proud man with a short fuse" and before the inaugural had determined that the Texan should not be offended. "Just a few months earlier," the President told his aides, "you were clerks on Capitol Hill while he was the most important man there. Johnson's not going to enjoy having to deal with you and you should always take that into consideration." The new President also called in some newspaper friends of Johnson's for background interviews, during which he mentioned that he hoped to make Vice President Johnson a close working partner in the administration and that he would consider it a personal attack if anyone tried to sabotage their relationship. That Presidential "word" was spreading through Washington even as the inaugural ceremonies were droning on.

And now it was over. There was a luncheon at the Capitol, and then the parade back to the White House. Johnson, it was noticed, looked subdued as he sat in the limousine going back up Pennsylvania Avenue. On occasion he smiled or waved a hand, but he seemed without spirit. In contrast, his wife, sitting at his side, had a warm smile at all times. Even more in contrast was the President's younger brother, Robert F. Kennedy, the Attorney General in the cabinet. He rode in the parade sitting on the back of an open convertible, without topcoat or hat, waving and smiling.

At the reviewing stand in front of the White House, Johnson stayed with the President for most of the next four hours to watch the parade go by. Then he and Mrs. Johnson returned to their home for a private family dinner; they had refused all dinner invitations. Later in the evening they returned to the White House to join the President and the First Lady in touring the five inaugural balls.

At the balls, as during the parade and the inaugural ceremony itself, few paid attention to Lyndon Johnson. He was only the Vice President: the second man by title. And the knowledge had begun to spread that—despite any Presidential support he might appear to have—his position would not equal his title. Lyndon Johnson, it was said, was not going to be a very important member of the New Frontier. Forces conspiring against him already had started their work.

TWO

A FTER his election as Vice President in November of 1960, Lyndon Johnson had confidently predicted to his friends that he would continue to be a major power on Capitol Hill. He would be, in fact if not in name, the Senate Democratic leader as he had been for the past eight years. His designated successor, Mike Mansfield of Montana, would occupy the majority leader's position as a figurehead for Johnson. The Texan never framed it in quite those words, but his meaning as he discussed his relationship with the Congress always was clear. Those Washington reporters who were closest to the Texan wrote of this expectation as a coming fact of the New Frontier. And *The New York Times* said in an editorial after the election that "to those who know Lyndon Johnson it is inconceivable that under the circumstances of the new Congress [Johnson] would willingly give up his role as majority leader in anything but name." Within official Washington that prediction was accepted as accurate. No one who had watched the wheeling and dealing of Lyndon Johnson or knew the Johnson reputation as a man who loved power and the use of power in the Senate believed he would ever permit that power to escape him.

John Kennedy did not object to Johnson's continuing to

wheel and deal in the Congress. Kennedy actually welcomed the prospect; having an effective voice among the southerners who controlled the important congressional committees was a reason for placing Johnson on the ticket back in July. "I believe the Vice President-elect," Kennedy said of Johnson, "can be of great assistance in implementing our commitments to the American people." In December, when he still was developing his legislative program and wanted to speak with the congressional leaders, Kennedy had Johnson arrange the meetings with the senators and representatives. In status-conscious Washington this was understood to mean that Johnson would be the Kennedy liaison man with Capitol Hill. John Kennedy, more than some of his aides and supporters, realized that Congress was led by a few powerful men who were more influenced by their own inclinations than they were by the desires of a man whose claim to political position was based on as thin a margin of votes as was Kennedy's.

One such man was Senator Richard B. Russell, Democrat of Georgia. He was chairman of the Senate's Armed Services Committee and chairman of its armed services appropriations subcommittee; he both authorized the spending of money for the military and then appropriated the funds for what he had authorized. If a member of the Senate wanted a military installation located in his state or a defense contract awarded to a firm in his state, it was best that the senator did not cross Richard Russell. Lyndon Johnson was an old friend of Russell's. It was Russell who had made Johnson leader of the Democrats back in 1953 and it was Russell who had always found the additional votes Lyndon Johnson needed when he was pushing a difficult piece of legislation through the Senate.

Another such man was Senator Robert S. Kerr, Democrat of Oklahoma. He was chairman of the Senate public works appropriations subcommittee. If a senator wanted money for a dam or a beach erosion project in his state, it was best that

Bob Kerr think of him in a friendly fashion. Kerr and Johnson were old friends. Both were from oil-producing states and worked to preserve the oil depletion allowance. Their similar interests in using the space program to build up the economy of the South and the Southwest also tied them together.

Sam Rayburn was such a man, of course. Through him could be reached the committee chairmen on the House side: Carl Vinson of the Armed Services Committee and the leader of the moderate southerners, Wilbur D. Mills of the Ways and Means Committee, Clarence Cannon of the Appropriations Committee. Rayburn talked their language; he could deal and trade with them. And Rayburn's ties to Lyndon Johnson were stronger than his ties to any other man in Washington.

All these men on Capitol Hill were powers in their own right. Most came from one-party states or congressional districts. The identity of a Presidential candidate was of little concern to them; they usually gave him strength rather than gaining strength from him. Nor were these men particularly impressed by any party platforms or philosophy as expressed by Kennedy. They had their own philosophies and ideas of what was best for the nation, their own political theories which had been developed over many years. Richard Russell had first come to the Senate when John Kennedy was only fifteen years old and had served in that body almost twice as many years as Kennedy had been in public life; he would be skeptical of anything the new President proposed. And Rayburn and Vinson had come to Congress in 1913 and 1914 respectively; John Kennedy was not born until 1917. And when Kennedy was in grade school, preparatory school and college, they were writing the legislative fabric of the modern nation. They would listen to Kennedy, of course, but somewhat cautiously. Johnson, because of his long-standing relationship with all these congressional powers, could reach them and influence them. He knew how to talk with them, plead with them, and bargain with them and he knew how to do it without offending the esteemed opinion these people had of themselves. Lyndon Johnson would be John Kennedy's chief lobbyist on Capitol Hill.

That at least was the expectation when on Tuesday, January 3, 1961—seventeen days before Kennedy and Johnson took their oaths as President and Vice President—the Eighty-seventh Congress was sworn in. Among its members was Johnson, who had been reelected Senator from Texas at the same time he was elected Vice President. A few minutes after being sworn in for his third senatorial term, Johnson placed his resignation as senator before the presiding officer and sauntered out of the chamber. There was a quorum call to check attendance and most members were moving about, chatting, barely aware of what the Senate as a body was doing. Few, if any, noticed Lyndon Johnson's action in formally severing his tie with the body with which he had served twelve years, and served them boisterously and effectively. Never before had one of Lyndon Johnson's actions on the Senate floor gone so unnoticed.

But Johnson did not intend that this separation be anything more than formal. The Senate had been his home—more so than any other four walls—and he intended to remain a popular and influential guest. That afternoon the Democratic senators held an organizational caucus, at which the senators were to follow a script previously planned by Johnson. First, Mike Mansfield would be elected the new Senate majority leader. Then Mansfield would move that the caucus invite Johnson to attend its future meetings and, more importantly, preside over them. The Vice President-elect's old comrades among the Democratic senators would show their friendship by supporting the move. The few among the Democratic senators who had been critics of Johnson would not embarrass either Johnson or Mansfield by voting against the move. Presiding over the caucus was in itself a task of little responsibility and less power. The Democrats held few such meetings and it was rare that the presiding officer could influence any discussion. But the act of inviting a nonmember of the Senate both to attend regularly and to fulfill the symbolic role of presiding officer would be the significant thing. It would be an acknowledgement by the Democratic senators that Lyndon Johnson remained their leader.

That was the script. Lyndon Johnson, however, was a bad playwright. He did not understand his actors.

The Senate is a curious place and its members curious men. There may be no other institution like it and no other persons like the senators. The senator comes to the seat of national government as an emissary from a local area. He must think of the national good and of the benefit to his home state and sometimes resolve a conflict between them. However he decides, his power cannot be diluted. No matter how small the senator's state in geography and population, his vote is as significant as that of the senator from the largest state. For this reason, each senator must be dealt with equally. Presidents placate him. Pressure groups appeal to him. Lobbyists entertain him. In this atmosphere, the senator begins to reevaluate his importance and in this personal reevaluation his self-esteem rarely goes down. Also, while the final decision—the "yes" or "no" vote—is the senator's, the process leading to this decision is someone else's. An aide must read the dozen newspapers that come into the senatorial office each day and cull from them the stories the senator should read. Another assistant studies the hundreds of bills before the Senate and determines which the senator should explore intimately, which the senator might wish to oppose, which support. Still a third man deals with all those who want some of the senator's time or energy. A senator is a product of a staff—some senators have forty persons working for them—and becomes an institution. The Senate then is an institution made up of one hundred institutions.

As Vice President-elect Lyndon Johnson walked into that Democratic caucus January 3, he did not have that understanding of the Senate. To him, the Senate was made up of a group of men who could be flattered, cajoled and, if necessary, strong-armed. As Senate Democratic leader he had not hesitated to flex his political muscles to produce the votes he wanted. He controlled Democratic committee assignments. Whether a senator got on an important committee often determined if he would become a significant member of the Senate. And getting on an important committee in the 1950s meant asking Lyndon Johnson's permission. Johnson did not use this power viciously. Actually he encouraged younger members of the Senate to move on to important committees. But always the power of yes or no to whether the Democratic member joined the committee he desired remained with Lyndon Johnson. Before challenging Johnson, a senator remembered that some day Johnson might retaliate and that there would be no appeal.

The second source of Johnson's power as Senate leader was his control over the calendar of Senate bills to be acted on. Although the general public's knowledge of the Senate is of major bills affecting the entire nation—civil rights, minimum wage, Medicare—whether a senator is returned after the next election often depends on the small bills such as a new dam, a new erosion control project, a subsidy affecting only the individual senator's state. Whether these bills came to the Senate for a full vote had depended on whether Lyndon Johnson allowed them to move from the calendar to the Senate floor. Again, he did not use this power viciously. Also again, however, he did not hesitate to display this power. Senators were leery of challenging a man with such power and an apparent willingness to use it.*

As Johnson settled into a chair at the caucus beside Mansfield, who was acting as presiding officer, he did not realize that few of the sixty men who faced him were his friends. The blandishments they had showered on him in past years were not the signs of affection he believed them to be but were, instead, the flattery that the wise underling extends to his superior. Johnson did not understand that.

As the caucus was gaveled to order, there was a second reason why hostility was creeping into some of the faces before Johnson. As Senate leader, Johnson had made himself the broker between the southern conservatives and the northern liberals. As with most compromises between sharply divergent views, those Johnson worked out satisfied few people. The southern conservatives believed he gave away too much to the northern liberals. These liberals believed Johnson gave away too much to the southerners. Both were correct. If he could, Johnson avoided a fight. He disliked strife. He would bargain away as much as necessary, add as many provisions as required, to find the consensus he needed for a healthy majority.

The caucus now had elected Mansfield the new Democratic leader. There was no difficulty with this part of Lyndon Johnson's scenario. Well-liked, Mansfield was a genuine liberal who also kept avenues of communication open to the southern conservatives. There was no other man in the Senate around whom the Democrats could muster. Also, Mansfield had been Democratic whip, the party's number two man in the Senate hierarchy. It was becoming traditional that this second man be promoted to the number one spot when it became vacant; Johnson himself had become leader after first being whip.

* The Senate Democratic leadership that succeeded Johnson surrendered these two powers. Committee assignments are made by majority vote of the steering committee, which is now representative of the Senate Democrats, and the calendar is kept clear.

After Mansfield was announced as leader officially, he proposed to the sixty-three member caucus that Johnson be invited to attend its meetings and preside over them. Seated a few feet away from Mansfield, Johnson did not speak but watched the Democratic senators carefully. At this point, the liberals broke away from the script Johnson had written.

What happened then was the third round in what had been a developing dispute between Johnson and the Senate liberals of his party. The dispute began in the late 1950s when northern Democrats in the Senate wearied of Johnson's benevolence. They wanted democracy for the Democrats in the Senate. They suggested to Johnson that the Senate Democrats' steering committee—its formal governing body—be enlarged to give northerners a representation equal to their membership in the Senate. Their intent was quite obvious. Such representation would take control of the steering committee away from Johnson and the southerners he represented and give it to the liberals. The major power Johnson would lose would be that of making committee assignments. The Texan bluntly refused. The northerners did not feel strong enough to challenge him. That was in 1959. It was Round One, and the northern liberals had lost it. It had been a brief skirmish, hardly noticed at the time.

Round Two came up when the Senate convened the next year. Led by Senator Albert Gore of Tennessee, this was much more than a skirmish. Gore was a southerner but a liberal with Vice Presidential ambitions who had been cut out of the tight group of southern Democrats because he had supported civil rights legislation and was not as fiscally conservative as his fellow southerners. Now, as the 1960 election year opened, Gore decided the time had come for revenge. "I am not one of those opposed to Lyndon Johnson. I like to be on his team," Gore explained, "but never on a leash." If the Gore attack succeeded in embarrassing Johnson, it could hurt the Texan's

Presidential ambitions and perhaps send the Democratic convention scurrying around for another southerner to balance the ticket that was to be picked in July, perhaps even another southerner like Gore.

Gore aimed at the Senate Democrats' policy committee. Although a decision or statement of intentions by the policy committee could not bind any senator, the actions and pronouncements of this group set an image and tone by which, theoretically at least, Democrats in the Senate and elsewhere were known: conservative, liberal or moderate. As with the steering committee, this group also was dominated by southerners. As one liberal said at the time, the committee has "only one member from north of the Alabama line and east of the Mississippi River" and that was Theodore Francis Green of Rhode Island, then in his nineties. Although Gore's subject was the policy committee, his target was Lyndon Johnson. "I am concerned," he said, "with a current interpretation of the purpose and role of the Democratic senatorial policy committee, by some, that the committee is merely an arm of the Democratic leadership of the Senate. . . . The Senate Democratic policy committee should represent all the Democrats in the Senate, not merely one." There was no doubt that the "one" Gore referred to was Lyndon Johnson. Johnson did not answer Gore. Instead, because 1960 was an election year and Johnson, hungry for the nomination and not wanting to anger anyone, permitted Gore's formal motion to enlarge the policy committee to come to a vote in a meeting of Democratic senators.

Lyndon Johnson had nothing to fear in that 1960 meeting; he had the votes. Gore was defeated in a secret 51–12 tally. Two of those votes are particularly interesting because of what they indicated about the future political troubles of Lyndon Johnson. Ralph Yarborough, the junior senator from Texas, would be expected to stand behind Johnson. But Yarborough voted with Gore. Yarborough was identified with the liberal wing of the Texas Democrats, the young people of the state, the city dwellers, the supporters of civil rights. Johnson was identified with the conservative wing of the Texas Democrats, the big ranchers, the fast-buck oil boys, the opponents of civil rights legislation. The Yarborough vote against Johnson in 1960 revealed how deep ran the split in the Texas Democratic Party.

The second interesting vote was cast by Hubert H. Humphrey of Minnesota. Although a liberal, Humphrey had become a member of the Senate "club" of southerners who ran the institution, largely through the good offices of his close friend Lyndon Johnson. But Humphrey also voted—by proxy, he was away that day—against Johnson. The Humphrey vote against his close friend and benefactor indicated the seriousness of the northern liberal quarrel with Johnson. This quarrel worked against Johnson at the 1960 convention; almost caused John Kennedy to change his mind about selecting Johnson as his running mate and haunted Johnson through his career as Vice President.

If the significance of those first two rounds in 1959 and in 1960 had been understood as signs of a growing revolt against Lyndon Johnson, the third round in 1961 might never have happened. But Johnson's ego would not allow him to acknowledge that previous attacks on his leadership by liberals in the Senate went any deeper than being spasmodic political aberrations. Nor would the liberals tip off him or Mansfield as to what was about to happen that January day in 1961. If they had privately informed Johnson or Mansfield of the expected opposition, Mansfield would not have made his motion to invite Johnson to attend and preside at the Democratic caucuses. This would have rebuffed Johnson as effectively as what did happen, but it would have done it without publicly embarrassing the Democratic Party, its new leadership in the Senate, its

President- and Vice President-elect. And that's exactly why there was no advance notice of the seriousness of the opposition. The liberals not only wanted to rebuff Johnson, they wanted to slap his face in public.

Mansfield later said he made the motion because he believed the Vice President, a member of the Democratic Party and a former senator, should not be excluded from the party's formal Senate deliberations. But the liberals at the caucus argued it was an unnatural mixing of the Legislative and Executive branches, which the Constitution directs should be separate. "We might as well ask Jack Kennedy to come back up to the Senate and take his turn at presiding," snapped Gore. Although there was some merit to that argument, the main reason for the rebellion was the long-standing dispute over Lyndon Johnson's leadership. He had ridden roughshod too long. This was Round Three, and the liberals wanted to draw blood.

Behind the closed doors the caucus was bitter. Finally, Mansfield threatened to resign from the leadership position he had held only a few minutes unless the caucus backed up his invitation to Johnson. The first vote was on a motion to postpone a decision. The postponement failed 45–18. The next vote was the big one, on the invitation itself. The caucus did agree to extend the invitation to Johnson, but the vote was 46–17. Those seventeen "nay" voters made a larger group than had been expected. They added up to the cold, forceful slap that the Senate Democratic liberals had hoped to administer.

Johnson had sat through the entire caucus, silent, the hurt growing within him. Always an emotional man, he could not shrug off such slaps. He did attend the next caucus as Vice President but only called it to order, then turned the gavel over to Mansfield. Johnson did not show up at other such sessions. He had learned his lesson and he would abide by it. In later years Johnson and his friends would try to rewrite the events of that day to say that Johnson never had planned to exert any continuing authority over the Senate or that he actually welcomed leaving the Senate. But the later fiction could not change the facts of that day.

More importantly perhaps than Johnson's being taught a lesson was his dropping of his plans to become the Kennedy administration's top man on Capitol Hill. "Johnson pulled back somewhat after that caucus," said a Kennedy aide. "He hadn't expected it, and it made him reluctant to approach senators. Kennedy wanted him to go up to Capitol Hill and talk to people and frequently suggested that Johnson do so, but Johnson had to be coaxed somewhat. He would do so, of course, when specifically asked, but rarely otherwise." Johnson also was asked to help round up votes on crucial issues, but so many times he found excuses not to do so that eventually he was no longer asked. Nor did he usually take part in the discussions leading to the development of legislative proposals. He was present at these discussions, but he did not participate.

This Johnson hesitation over helping John Kennedy on Capitol Hill was a disappointment to the White House. Of all the members of the Kennedy administration, it was believed that Johnson could have been the most effective with Congress. "After all," said one Kennedy aide, "who the hell were Kenny O'Donnell or Larry O'Brien? Johnson had much more influence on the Hill than they did, or could have had." Kennedy had hoped very much to have good relations with the members of Congress. As one himself for fourteen years, Kennedy had noticed that the White House, under both a Democrat and a Republican, had limited its approaches on Capitol Hill to the senior members of Congress and the committee chairmen; Kennedy himself never had been contacted by the White House. As President, Kennedy wanted to do better. Reaching the younger members, as well as the seniors, he believed, would give his legislative program a much better chance. He tried such gimmicks as sending a hand-signed and hand-delivered congratulatory note to each member of Congress on his birthday. He had Lawrence O'Brien organize an efficient White House lobbying system. This system not only included White House people but also the legislative liaison people from each agency. At weekly meetings these liaison people provided O'Brien with a report on the progress of legislation in which their agency was involved, how it was doing on Capitol Hill, who was against it and who for it, whose vote might be changed and how and whose vote might not.

Even without Lyndon Johnson the system was a good one. It would have been better with him. He would occasionally show up at one of the periodic White House sessions of these legislative liaison people but would say very little. More often he sent one of his assistants, George Reedy or Bill D. Moyers, to sit in for him. Every so often, however, the White House would have a glimpse of just how helpful Johnson could be on Capitol Hill. Kennedy's first big test in Congress, for example, was the vote to enlarge the House Rules Committee so that it could be stacked with Kennedy supporters. This conservative-dominated committee, established as a traffic cop to regulate the flow of legislation to the House floor, had usurped the power to decide if a bill should be voted on at all. It intended to use that power to block the Kennedy social welfare proposals. Unless the makeup of the committee was enlarged to include some liberals, the Kennedy program was dead. The House vote was set when Lyndon Johnson was tipped off by members of the Texas delegation that some expected "aye" votes were moving into the "nay" column. Johnson reported this to Kennedy and the vote was delayed while additional supporters were rounded up. When the final vote was taken, Kennedy had won, but only by five votes. The tally was 217 for enlarging the committee and 212 against. It had been a squeaker, and Johnson's warning had helped avert defeat.

On other occasions also Johnson showed that his lines to Congress were good. When Kennedy wanted to revamp the income tax system, Johnson advised him to tread lightly on any changes in the oil depletion allowance. For years Johnson and Rayburn had packed the tax-writing committees in Congress with friends of the oil industry just to protect that allowance. The allowance enabled the oil producers, primarily Texans, to pay substantially less of their income to the federal tax collector than did other businesses. Any tax revision bill that included a frontal assault on that allowance would be scuttled in these committees, the Vice President advised. Still later, Johnson advised Kennedy to go ahead with wheat sales to the Soviet Union. Johnson knew that the Midwestern wheat states, like his own Texas, which usually were so anti-Communist, were then so glutted with surpluses of wheat that they would gladly forget ideology if the money involved was solid.

But these incidents were rare, and sometimes, as Lyndon Johnson's separation from Congress grew more pronounced, the advice he did give was bad. In the summer of 1961, when the nation was faced with a crisis over Berlin, Kennedy ordered a military buildup costing $3.2 billion. The New Frontier quickly split into two camps over the advisability of raising taxes to meet that bill. The argument was twofold, political as well as economic. Not only would raising taxes be bad politics, ran one argument, but it would also be bad economics. The point was that an increase in government spending while not raising taxes—deficit spending—would give the nation's economy a needed boost. Johnson, however, took the other side. He argued that a hike of two per cent in taxes should accompany the increased defense spending. This would not only forcibly demonstrate to the nation the seriousness of the Berlin crisis but would also block Republican charges of unwise fiscal policies on the New Frontier, Johnson asserted. He was particularly concerned by this last point. As

Senate majority leader in the 1950s, he had been badly burned by the Eisenhower charges of "budget busters" thrown at the Democrats and did not believe the Democrats should lay themselves open to similar attacks once they were in the White House. But new economic theories had left both Eisenhower and, in 1961, Johnson behind. Taxes were not raised and the extra expenditures did prove the new theories by helping to boost the economy. This made "budget busting" a poor political argument in the early 1960s.

When the Kennedy administration at a later time was concerned about a filibuster by southerners in the Senate blocking a civil rights bill, Johnson again spoke from his experiences in the 1950s. Wear the southerners down was his confidential advice. Use brutal round-the-clock sessions until the southerners, wearied and aged, agree to a deal. It was bad advice. Attitudes toward civil rights in the 1960s were different than those in the 1950s, when Johnson was part of the Senate. Republicans now were ready to go along with breaking a civil rights filibuster just as long as they could have a few concessions and were not abused personally—as they would be if the Johnson suggestions were followed. The problem was to appeal to the Republicans, not browbeat the southerners.

A major difficulty for Lyndon Johnson as Vice President was that he had lost touch with the changing Senate.

One could sense this would happen from the gallery of the Senate the morning of Saturday, January 21, 1961, the day after Johnson was sworn in as Vice President. The Senate was meeting at ten o'clock to confirm the Kennedy cabinet appointees. Precisely on the hour, Johnson strode into the red-carpeted chamber to fulfill the only Constitutional duty he had, presiding over the Senate. He walked to the presiding officer's chair in the well of the Senate and tapped once with his gavel on the desk in front of him. The senators immediately quieted as Johnson called, "The Senate will come to order."

Dr. Barclay of the Central Christian Church in Austin, who had prayed for Johnson at the inaugural the previous day, delivered the opening prayer. During the next twenty minutes the senators made brief speeches congratulating the new Vice President. Johnson smiled when the compliments became too grandiose and occasionally glanced up at the visitors' gallery where his wife and two daughters sat. When the praise of Johnson was done, the Senate went on to confirm the Kennedy cabinet.

This Senate chamber had been the Johnson field of action. Back in that corner is where he had stood with one arm draped around a recalcitrant senator while the fingers of his other hand galloped up the man's arm, cajoling, begging and threatening for a vote. At that chair in the first row by the center aisle Johnson had sat, snapping his fingers and barking commands to his underlings. In the cloakroom at the back of the chamber, he and Richard Russell and Robert Kerr had convened the "club" that ran the Senate to bargain and deal and to emerge at the end with a bill that could pass. This chamber had been Lyndon Johnson's excitement. Now this morning, as the Kennedy cabinet was confirmed, Johnson sat in the chamber with a bored look on his face. He was in the Senate chamber but not of the Senate as he had been for the previous dozen years. One of the roles he anticipated would be open to him as Vice President had been stripped from him.

But he could not allow himself nostalgia or regret about the past. Instead he must turn to the present and the future. He must cut himself off from this body as it had cut him off in the January 3 caucus. He must find himself new roles in Washington outside of the Capitol, new roles as the second man in the Executive branch.

THREE

THE cabinet room adjacent to the President's office in the White House is a cool room, a distinguished chamber. There is a mellowness to its walls, a charm to its decor. There is also in this room the feeling of power. Here, one senses, men sit around the mahogany table, the eight-sided reddish-brown slab that dominates the room, and the climax of their discussion begins events that produce an ever widening circle of repercussions. History begins here.

In the formal cabinet sessions, the Vice President sits across the table from his President. Surrounding the table—a monolith twenty feet long and seven feet at its widest point—sit the cabinet members, or, as with the Ambassador to the United Nations, men of cabinet rank or special guests. When these men gather formally, here is the power of the United States: the diplomatic strength, the missiles, the lines to the business and labor leaders; the men who control the greatest bureaucracy in the world.

But in the informal sessions, there may be even more power. And this was so in the Kennedy administration. John Kennedy chose to operate surrounded by a few loyal men of whose ability he had no doubt. They advised him, suggested alternatives, even at times said "no" to him. Then he made the final decision, picked up a phone and gave the command to one of those who might attend the formal cabinet sessions but not these informal gatherings. The participants in these small informal sessions varied with the problem at hand. But anyone claiming to be part—or who desired to be part—of the power-wielding process had to belong to this group at one time or another. Lyndon Johnson had hoped to be one of its members. "If there is only one man the President can turn to," he said on several occasions, "I want that man to be me."

There were many differences between Lyndon Johnson and John Kennedy. Kennedy was handsome; Johnson hardly so. John Kennedy had, and it was perhaps his greatest charm, the optimism and verve of youth; Lyndon Johnson knew, and it was perhaps his greatest asset, the circuitous routes where experience leads. Kennedy was wealthy, had always been so, so wealthy he could be casual toward the concept of personal wealth; Johnson also was wealthy, but it was new enough to him that he could never be casual toward it. John Kennedy was urbane, sophisticated, charming; Lyndon Johnson was rough, earthy, sometimes so lacking in charm and poise as to be brutal.

But beyond these differences, there were important similarities. Both men belonged to that peculiar breed: the politician. Their styles as campaigners were in blunt contrast. Kennedy was reserved. He avoided the Indian headdresses and the firemen's hats, the hot dogs and the cheese blintzes that are part of the traditional political hoopla. Lyndon Johnson loved the hoopla. He was a baby-kissing, hand-pumping, backslapping politician. During the 1960 campaign, he had eaten Kosher pickles in New York. He had boarded the commuter trains for a quick handshake with the suburbanite. He had held a seven-year-old girl up in the air and wowed her parents when he said, "Honey, come see me in Washington when I'm Vice President." Nor were his speeches as reserved as John Kennedy's.

Johnson had been a real "stump speaker" in the 1960 campaign. He would have been at home on the Chautauqua circuit before radio and television came between the speaker and his audience and when the farmers and their wives drove into town to hear the "speakin'," expecting a show as well as a political pitch, and rarely were disappointed. Lyndon Johnson spoke then emotionally. He did not dwell on statistics but on personalities and alleged outrages. While John Kennedy cited figures in 1960 to prove that the American farmer's income was declining, Lyndon Johnson had shouted that the Republican Secretary of Agriculture, Ezra Taft Benson, was "an anvil strapped to the ankle of American agriculture as it tried to swim through stormy economic seas."

But as politicians, both men were intensely ambitious. Each had been pushed by his father. "Get a move on, Lyndon," Sam Ealy Johnson, Jr. would say as he wakened his young son before dawn, "every boy in town's got a head start on you." Joseph Kennedy, the patriarch of the Kennedy clan, was not so quaint with his children. He was as obvious, however, as he drove his children to compete and, above all, to win. After this initial push from their fathers, both Kennedy and Johnson had developed his ambition on his own. Each wanted to reach the top and so each could understand the other.

Both men also were politically courageous. As a young member of the House of Representatives, John Kennedy almost ended his political career with this remark on the House floor: "The leadership of the American Legion has not had a constructive thought for the benefit of this country since 1918!" The comment was caused by the Legion's leaders' teaming up with conservatives to block housing bills which would have benefited many veterans. Still, aspiring politicians did not attack such large, well-financed pressure groups as the American Legion. Once Lyndon Johnson went before a politically important audience of labor union members. As he walked out on the platform, he was advised not to speak of his vote for the 1947 Taft-Hartley labor bill, a measure that labor unions called the "slave labor" bill. Johnson strode out before the union men and immediately began to speak of his vote for Taft-Hartley.

As political philosophers, both men were middle-of-the-roaders. Early in his Senate career, John Kennedy told a magazine interviewer: "I'd be very happy to tell them that I'm not a liberal at all. I never joined the Americans for Democratic Action or the American Veterans Committee. I'm not comfortable with those people." In later years, as he became a Presidential candidate, Kennedy did not hesitate to embrace ADA people in his cause, but his record through 1960 showed he was not yet ready to embrace the ADA philosophy in full. Lyndon Johnson also was uncomfortable with the Americans for Democratic Action. "We don't want the support of the odd balls on the left or the right," he had said early in 1960, "ADA or KKK."

There was another similarity between the two men and this was perhaps the most important one. It was the belief shared by both that the federal government was a tool to be used, not an ogre to be feared. In January of 1960, John Kennedy told a National Press Club audience that the President should be "a vigorous proponent of the national interest." That was his vision of the national government, an instrument to serve all the people. So it was Lyndon Johnson's. He wrote in 1958:

> Of all endeavors on which I have worked in public life, I am proudest of the accomplishments in developing the Lower Colorado River during the 1930s and 1940s. It is not the damming of the stream or the harnessing of the floods in which I take pride, but, rather, in the ending of the waste of the region.
>
> The region—so unproductive and insignificant in capacity in my youth—is now a vital part of the national economy and potential. More important, the wastage of human resources in the

whole region has been reduced. New horizons have been opened for the fulfillment of young minds, if by nothing more than the advent of electricity into rural homes. Men and women have been released from the waste of drudgery and toil against the unyielding rock of the Texas hills. This is the fulfillment of the true responsibility of government.

Kennedy had reached this point in 1960 by the road of the intellectual. The speech in which he defined the President as the advocate of the national interest was studded with historical references. He spoke of Taft, Harding, Buchanan, Wilson, Coolidge, Grant. He quoted Alexander Hamilton, Theodore Roosevelt, Abraham Lincoln. In contrast, Lyndon Johnson did not find his references in history but in the life he had known as a child—the hunger, the parched land, the dying crops, the mounting debts, the unpainted homes, the ravaged faces.

Still, however, there would be troubles in the working relationship between Kennedy and Johnson. John Kennedy delayed making a decision until it was absolutely necessary. He realized that to decide was to commit one's self and he did not believe it wise to make a commitment until forced to do so. He had not committed himself, for example, to choose Lyndon Johnson as his running mate until after he himself had been nominated for the Presidency. Because Kennedy had been so reluctant to name his choice back at the Democratic convention in July, the liberals who hated Johnson continued to support Kennedy as did Midwestern politicians who hoped the second streak of lightning would hit them. Johnson, however, could not rest if a problem remained unsolved. He lived at a frenetic pace. Incapable of relaxing, not understanding what personal enjoyment was, Lyndon Johnson was out of synchrony with the Kennedy administration.

There was another trouble. Although he had no legal training, Kennedy approached problems like a good lawyer, developing alternatives, turning remote possibilities into solutions; he was a creative person. When he had to confront a problem, he enjoyed the process of building a solution. Johnson, however, approached problems like a good judge. When alternatives were presented to him, he could evaluate them and choose the best one; but he could not create an alternative himself. This was the way he had developed as Senate Democratic leader, constantly seeking a consensus by delving through the various alternatives until he found the one least offensive to the conflicting groups that made up the Senate.

Their circles of acquaintances were different and this was another trouble. The people they called on for advice, the people who had access to them were two separate groups: the Kennedy camp and the Johnson camp. This was more than a social difference, more than a hangover from the days before the 1960 Democratic convention when each camp fought desperately to gain the nomination for its leader. The difficulties became apparent in the period between the election and the inauguration, when Kennedy found himself with five thousand federal jobs to fill, some eighteen hundred of them in important policy positions. After victory was won in November, Johnson bubbled over with ideas for the cabinet. He thought Senator J. William Fulbright of Arkansas, the chairman of the Senate Foreign Relations Committee, should be Secretary of State; and Representative William L. Dawson of Illinois, the political boss of Chicago's Negro section, should be Postmaster General. But the Johnson suggestions did not fare too well. Fulbright was crossed off the list by Kennedy. Partly this was because Fulbright would be anathema to the emerging African nations for his consistent votes against civil rights for American Negroes; unlike Johnson, Fulbright had never changed his public position on the matter of segregation. But more, Fulbright's rejection was due to Kennedy's wanting to be his "own Secretary of State"; Fulbright would be an innovator as John Foster Dulles had been; Kennedy wanted a technician who could implement policies the President made. Dawson was rejected for other reasons. Although the job of heading the Post Office Department long had been a political spoil, Kennedy wanted to give it to a competent business man in hopes of improving service. Another reason against the selection of Dawson was the fear that immediately naming a Negro to the cabinet might appear too crass in view of the promise made during the past campaign by Henry Cabot Lodge, the Republican Vice Presidential candidate, that Nixon would name a Negro to the cabinet if elected President. Other Johnson recommendations were overshadowed by those made by Sargeant Shriver, the President-elect's brother-in-law; Dean Acheson, Robert A. Lovett, David Bruce and others. These were people Kennedy knew and relied on. He believed they understood his thinking and his desires for certain kinds of people.

These people were the "American establishment" people. They had gone to the right schools, principally Harvard. When they needed a bright young lawyer to fill a Washington post, they called one of their old classmates, most likely now a prominent Wall Street attorney, and asked him to recommend a young man from his firm. They themselves had entered public service this way; it was only natural they relied on the same route when it was necessary to seek out other young men. This "establishment," even if informally organized, was a tight group. Bounded on the north by Harvard, on the east by Wall Street, and on the south by the State Department, the triangle formed was an inclusive and exclusive group. It included almost all those who had at least two of the three requisites: Harvard, Wall Street law firm, or government service. It excluded almost all others. It had excluded Lyndon Johnson for years.

In addition to relying on the "establishment," the Kennedy

organization established a regular employment bureau in the weeks before the inaugural. Headed by Shriver, and assisted by such old Kennedy standbys as Kenneth O'Donnell and Lawrence O'Brien, this informal group did not come to Lyndon Johnson for recommendations. Its members didn't know him. They knew a businessman in the Midwest, a retired diplomat living in Virginia, a "boss" in Chicago; to these people the Shriver organization came asking for job recommendations. The process produced one of the most politically balanced cabinets in the nation's history. With only ten positions to fill, Kennedy managed to have a cabinet correctly balanced by politics, religion, business and labor interests, and geography as well as to give the "establishment" adequate representation. Two cabinet members were Republican: Secretary of the Treasury Douglas Dillon, an official in the Eisenhower administration who might easily have been offered a cabinet position if Richard Nixon had been elected in 1960, and Secretary of Defense Robert McNamara. Seven of the cabinet members were Protestants, two were Jewish—Secretary of Labor Arthur J. Goldberg and Secretary of Health, Education and Welfare Abraham Ribicoff—and only one was Catholic—Attorney General Robert Kennedy. Dillon and McNamara, as well as Commerce Secretary Luther H. Hodges, a former textile company executive, and Postmaster General J. Edward Day, a former insurance company official, were representatives of the business world. Goldberg, formerly the nation's leading labor lawyer, represented the unions. That is a four-to-one ratio in favor of business but a necessary balance in an administration that needed to win additional support from the business community. The geographic balance was tipped in favor of the East, where the major political power was. The easterners were Secretary of State Dean Rusk of New York, Dillon of New Jersey, Robert Kennedy, who listed his home state as Massachusetts although he had lived in

Virginia for years, and Ribicoff of Connecticut. The Midwest had three: McNamara of Michigan, Freeman of Minnesota and Goldberg of Illinois. The South and the West fared poorly —Hodges was of North Carolina, Udall of Arizona, and Day of California—but not poorly in relationship to how those two areas had produced for the Democrats in the election. (The South was a peculiar problem. With the exception of Lyndon Johnson and Luther Hodges, few southerners in public life had records that could be described even remotely as pro-civil rights and for that reason they were excluded from consideration as cabinet appointees.) The "establishment" men were Rusk, a former president of The Rockefeller Foundation, and Dillon, a Wall Street lawyer of long standing.

Such a balance did not permit the adding of any additional weights by Lyndon Johnson. He was granted some political appointments at lower levels of his own. His Texas friend and political aide, John B. Connally, Jr., became Secretary of the Navy. Cyrus R. Vance and Kenneth E. BeLieu, both associates of Johnson's from his days as chairman of the Senate Preparedness Subcommittee, were also given Pentagon appointments; Vance as General Counsel in the Defense Department and BeLieu as an assistant secretary of the Navy. A few other Johnson men were scattered throughout the Executive branch. These were jobs allotted to Johnson because he had contributed to the November victory as, for example, the Americans for Democratic Action were allotted Washington jobs in appreciation for their efforts in the November election. The ADA did better, in fact, than did Johnson. At no time did the Vice President have more than a dozen "Johnson men" in Executive branch jobs; there were between thirty-seven and forty-five members or former members of the ADA in the Kennedy administration. Some of these were like Ted Sorensen, a trusted associate of Kennedy's for many years who naturally moved to the White House offices with

Kennedy, or like Orville Freeman, a Kennedy supporter but a man without a job since losing reelection as Governor of Minnesota the previous November. But a good many of the ADA people brought into the administration were like Arthur M. Schlesinger, Jr., Chester Bowles, Mennen Williams and some others who were given appointments to pay off Kennedy's debt to the liberal wing of the Democratic Party.

In the weeks before the inauguration when the major positions were being filled, Johnson spent much of his time at his Texas ranch while Kennedy announced appointments from the front steps of his N Street house in the Georgetown section of Washington or from the porch of his father's Palm Beach home. Before the appointments were announced publicly, however, Kennedy usually telephoned Johnson in Texas to inform the Vice President-elect of the new appointee's name and to introduce them by telephone if Johnson and the man had not met previously. The calls were made as a courtesy to Johnson, so that he would not learn of the appointments first from the newspapers. But there was no mistaking the purpose of the calls; they were to inform Johnson, not to ask his advice. The New Frontier would sometimes be called the Kennedy-Johnson administration or the Democratic administration—that was Lyndon Johnson's preferred phrase—but it was always the Kennedy administration.

But Kennedy was willing to give Johnson the perquisites of important office. In addition to the Vice President's traditional chambers in the Senate Office Building and in the Capitol, so elegant in Johnson's case that they were known as the "Taj Mahal" or "the Throne Room," Johnson was given a six-room suite in the Executive Office Building, across the narrow West Executive Avenue from the President's oval office in the White House west wing. This gave the Vice President a location physically closer to the President than any Vice President ever had before. The President also gave Johnson increased administrative responsibilities as head of the Committee on Equal Employment Opportunity and as head of the Space Council. This last appointment required a change in the law by Congress.

Johnson was invited to all important White House meetings. These included the regular Tuesday morning breakfasts with the Democratic congressional leaders, the regular briefings of Kennedy by government officials before a Presidential news conference and the meetings of the National Security Council, of which the Vice President was a member by statute. At times Kennedy sent Johnson an advance text of a Presidential speech and asked for the Vice President's comments. In discussion with other officials or with persons outside of the government, Kennedy attempted to build up Johnson's importance by using such phrases as "Lyndon and I think . . ." and he told cabinet members to feel free to "Bring your problems to Lyndon or me. . . ."

Still, it became apparent within a few short months after the inauguration of the New Frontier that Lyndon Johnson was not going to be the aide-de-camp that he had wanted to be. Partly it was his fault, partly Kennedy's. "We'd sit around the table," recalled one of the Irish Mafia, "discussing a problem, and LBJ just wouldn't say anything. Everybody would have ideas and want to talk about them, but not Johnson. You'd have to put a direct question to him." Even Johnson's friends concede that this is true, that he carved out a role for himself as a very silent partner. Unless he had a constituent interest involved, such as the depletion allowance that the Texas oil men enjoyed, he kept silent. He followed that practice even when he disagreed with the Kennedy course of action. Partly this was a result of the humiliation he received in the January 3 caucus. It was due partly to the differences between Kennedy and Johnson and partly to the manner in which John Kennedy operated as President.

One of Kennedy's favorite stories of the Presidency was of how Abraham Lincoln, when the question of whether he should issue the Emancipation Proclamation was before him, called his Cabinet together, not to ask the Cabinet members' advice on which course he should take but to tell them instead which decision he had reached. Kennedy believed in making his own decisions. This was demonstrated by the Bay of Pigs affair in the early months of his administration. It was the kind of advice he accepted at that point which showed much of how the New Frontier would be led; it was technical advice. The Joint Chiefs of Staff were asked their opinion about the military feasibility of the operation. Defense Secretary McNamara was asked also about military capabilities. Secretary of State Dean Rusk was asked about diplomatic repercussions. Allen Dulles, the head of the Central Intelligence Agency, which was handling the affair, was asked about the possibilities of an uprising within Cuba once the landing took place. Lyndon Johnson had no such technical advice to offer. Perhaps he could have discussed the rights or wrongs of such an action, if he had been consulted, but no one within the administration seemed concerned at the time with whether such an action was right or wrong.

Johnson knew of the pending invasion, as did almost all of Washington know of one of the nation's worst-kept secrets. But he was not a member of the intimate group of technicians chaired by the President who plotted its course. Johnson was not alone in being excluded from the process that led to the decision to go ahead with the Bay of Pigs. Ted Sorensen, the President's alter ego as much as any man could be, was not officially informed of the pending action; nor did Adlai E. Stevenson, the American Ambassador to the United Nations, know the full details. The exclusion of Johnson, however, was more obvious. The weekend of the invasion, he was far from Washington. Saturday, April 15, he flew to Norfolk, Virginia, to crown his daughter Lynda Bird as queen of Norfolk's Eighth International Azalea Festival. When his Military Air Transport Service plane landed at the Norfolk Naval Air Station at one forty-five that afternoon, eight B-26 bombers already had made the first strike at Fidel Castro's Cuba. After the festivities honoring his daughter had ended, Johnson flew to Texas, where he played host to German Chancellor Konrad Adenauer at a Texas barbecue. The next afternoon, Sunday, as President Kennedy wrestled with the decision of whether to authorize a second strike by the American-controlled planes against Cuba and as nervous young men aboard ships moving silently toward Cuba crushed out their cigarettes because they were so close to their objective, Johnson stood beside Adenauer before seven thousand Americans of German ancestry at Fredericksburg, Texas, to assure "Der Alte" that "You stand up against the Communists and we will stand by your side."

It was late Tuesday, April 18, when the crucial choice of whether to intervene openly in the faltering invasion with American military force was before Kennedy. He slipped from the formal congressional reception at the White House to his office in the west wing. There in the hours that followed, he alone made the decision not to intervene. The Bay of Pigs demonstrated that decision making in the White House was to be a one-man operation, taken after the technical advice of the experts was given. If the experts gave bad advice, as they did in the Bay of Pigs case, then the Kennedy answer was to find better experts, not to junk the system. This was a return to the practice of Harry Truman, who kept a sign on his desk that said: "The buck stops here." But it was a significant change from the era of Dwight Eisenhower, when the authority for making decisions was diffused. It also meant that persons like Lyndon Johnson, who had little or no technical advice to offer, were shut out of the decision-making process.

Months later, when the administration could look at the

Bay of Pigs more calmly, John Kennedy said of Lyndon Johnson: "Lyndon's been in on every major decision, except, that is, for the Bay of Pigs." The President meant the remark as a kindly attempt to absolve his Vice President from any of the blame for the invasion failure. Johnson, however, did not enjoy the public acknowledgement that he had not been a part of the inner circle of the administration in its first great crisis. He would quickly follow up the Kennedy remark with "That's one of the few I was really involved in." That insistence that the public see him as an intimate member of the Kennedy administration stayed with Johnson through his Vice Presidential career. He could not hope to shed his "southern" label unless he was known as a close member of this northeastern administration.

This decision-making process is where the power of the Presidency lies. Anyone who is part of that process, no matter how small his role, is close to power in Washington. This is the power that Johnson missed as Vice President. But while it was a grievous lack for him, it also was a protection. The responsibility of making decisions includes the responsibility of making mistakes. If Lyndon Johnson was denied the first responsibility, he also guarded himself from the second.

In May of 1961, President Kennedy sent Lyndon Johnson on a tour of southeast Asia. The purpose of the trip was to bolster the sagging Diem government in South Vietnam as well as make a goodwill trip to other nations in southeast Asia. A rather remarkable memorandum resulted from that trip. The memorandum was written by Johnson, or at least signed by him, and was directed to Kennedy. Much of it is taken up with an analysis of the political and economic situation in the countries the Vice President had visited, material which had already been readily available to the administration through its ambassadors and others in the field.

Before leaving the United States, Johnson had Kennedy

write the heads of the nations he was to visit explaining the purpose of the trip, the powers assigned to Johnson and the limits of those powers. This protected Johnson in the event a leader sought to pressure the Vice President into making a stronger commitment than he was prepared to give; Johnson could claim his authority was limited by Kennedy's letter. This is spelled out in the Johnson memorandum. Also this memorandum makes clear that "the joint communiques followed item by item the statements in your letters." Where lengthy communiques were involved, they "were cleared through Washington" first. Johnson said he gave no assurances beyond "those you sent me to convey" and no commitments beyond "those authorized in your letters." Rarely had a public figure gone to such lengths to record officially his complete absence of initiative. It is this that makes the memorandum such a remarkable document.

Southeast Asia was then on the verge of becoming the Balkans of the 1960s. The situation in Laos was precarious. In South Vietnam the Diem government controlled barely more than a third of the nation's territory. China was making threatening noises at India. A smart and careful man realized that anyone involved with southeast Asia in 1961 easily could have political troubles in future years as Americans involved with China in the late 1940s had later met trouble at the hand of Senator Joseph McCarthy. But Johnson had his memorandum, carefully preserved to be made available at a later time to friendly newsmen to absolve him of any part in the making of a disaster.

This inclination toward self-protection was not unusual in Washington, particularly among people who do not have the responsibility for decision making. One New Frontiersman, Chester Bowles, was banished because he had carefully informed newsmen that he had disagreed with the decision to launch the Bay of Pigs attack. For Johnson, that inclination combined with his inability to participate in the creativity that Kennedy brought to solving problems, and the Kennedy reliance on persons with technical expertise, combined to separate Johnson from the active members of the administration. There was, in addition, another factor. This was the attitude of the members of the White House staff toward Lyndon Johnson.

The Kennedy assistants still remembered Johnson as the challenger to their man in 1960. They never intentionally slighted him; President Kennedy would not have stood for it. But there were little things that grated on Johnson. Some were real and some were imagined. Sometimes he was called "Lyndon" by the White House staff people when he believed he should have been called "Mr. Vice President." He always addressed John Kennedy as "Mr. President." If he called a staff man at the White House about a government job for a Johnson man, the job, he might be told, would be filled quite suddenly, or the answer would be vague. Johnson thought it best, when he wanted to see the President, to go through the normal channels for setting up an appointment with Kennedy. This meant having a Kennedy aide arrange a time. But the meetings did not always come off. One of the jobs of the White House staff was to protect the President from hundreds of people who wanted to see him. They placed the Vice President among those hundreds. "He just wants to come and talk about a patronage job in Texas," they sneered and found an excuse to postpone the meeting.

Sometimes at the White House sessions, the Presidential aides ignored Johnson. "It was not condescension," said one as he reminisced on the matter in later years. "They just didn't pay any attention to him." Away from both the Presidential and Vice Presidential ears, the young, sophisticated White House staff called Johnson "Uncle Cornpone." Johnson was, of course, "corny" throughout all his political career. But that corn was a mask for a shrewd political operator, as he saw himself, and he did not care to have the young upstarts who made up the "Irish Mafia" ridicule his political prowess.

The men who came to prominence in Washington because of the New Frontier, however, did not think Lyndon Johnson was as good a politician—the standard they used to judge men—as he was reputed to be. They had gone back into his record as Senate Democratic leader and found that it did not really have the luster with which it was credited. During the years from 1953 to 1961, when a Republican was President, Johnson in the Senate and Speaker Sam Rayburn in the House of Representatives worked with President Eisenhower to effect a substantial legislative record. If that record was below what liberals thought adequate, it still was beyond what conservatives considered proper. The picture has since been drawn of Johnson during those years as a "master" strategist who dominated the federal government. And it was said of those years that "what Johnson wanted, Eisenhower usually got."

Not so. What Eisenhower wanted, Johnson usually got.

With power being divided in the 1950s between two political parties, one obviously would have to give and accommodate itself to the other if the country was to be governed. Eisenhower is the one who should have given, considering the political realities. In his second term he was the nation's first "lame duck" President, prohibited by the Twenty-second Amendment to the Constitution from seeking a third term and supposedly without either power or prestige. Also, after the congressional elections of 1958, the Democrats had their strongest majorities in Congress since 1937, 65 to 35 in the Senate and 283 to 153 in the House. With a Presidential election coming up in 1960, it was the proper time for the Democratic leadership to build its record.

But in 1959 Johnson and Rayburn were criticized by Democratic National Chairman Paul M. Butler for "accommodating themselves too much" to Eisenhower. This was not the first criticism the Johnson-Rayburn leadership had received from the national party. In the mid-1950s, liberal Democrats formed the Democratic Advisory Council to offset what its members considered the trend toward the Eisenhower brand of Republicanism being exhibited by Johnson and Rayburn.

The 1959 record of Congress is summarized best by a Herblock political cartoon of the time in *The Washington Post*. It shows a victorious Eisenhower telling a humbled Johnson and Rayburn: "Tell the men they may keep their horses; they will need them for the spring plowing." Eisenhower had won the session hands down. The Republican labor reform bill became law, not the Democratic bill. Democratic proposals for aid to education and aid to depressed areas languished. Liberal proposals with which the Democrats had been associated for years and which were the real challenge to Lyndon Johnson did not pass despite the heavy Democratic margins.

With those proposals that did manage to become law, it was believed Johnson had paid too high a price, that he had gutted them too much in order to win unnecessary votes. "Johnson always won by too big a margin," said a liberal recently of the Texan as Senate leader. "A good legislator wins by just one vote." The year 1959 was also when Eisenhower hurled the phrases "spenders" and "budget busters" as epithets at the Democrats with such good effect that Johnson and Rayburn scurried through the halls of Congress cutting funds from the Eisenhower budget requests—outdoing the Republican President.

At the end of that session, Johnson defended his record by saying that because of the divided government, Democrats were faced with the choice of "creating laws or issues" and chose laws. At the time, however, few believed the Democrats had much of a choice; the Democrats took what Eisenhower allowed them.

The Democratic record in 1960 was no better. This year was particularly significant to Johnson. While other Presidential candidates were wooing the professional politicians by victories in the primaries and personal meetings across the nation, Johnson stayed in Washington, hoping to fashion an outstanding record as a legislative leader. His campaign for the 1960 Presidential nomination was largely based on the premise of his pushing so many liberal programs through Congress that the Democratic convention would be overwhelmed by him and then tap him for its leader. But the Senate that year was an utter failure for Johnson. An increase in the minimum wage and medical care for the aged, the two bills which Johnson needed if he was to impress the big city and labor bosses at the convention, could not be budged. The two-to-one Democratic Senate refused to respond to the man who, it was said, "played on it like a maestro plays on a violin."

The real reason for Johnson's rise to prominence as Senate leader in the 1950s was not his accomplishments in developing, advocating and passing a legislative program; that he simply did not do. Before he became Senate Democratic leader, however, divided government had been the exception for many years rather than the rule. Also, both President Roosevelt and President Truman were strong men who dominated the nation's capital by the force of their personalities. By the time Johnson became Senate majority leader, Washington had forgotten what it was like to have two competent men in powerful positions in government and of opposing political faiths. Johnson's real achievement was making divided government work. He did this by surrendering to the fact of a Republican in the White House.

After this review of Lyndon Johnson as a congressional leader, the Irish Mafia explored Johnson's status as a politician in the national arena. Here again he did not measure up. After all, the Kennedy men were the novices and Johnson was supposed to be the experienced "pro," but they had taken the nomination away from him at Los Angeles. Johnson's biggest mistake in the 1960 drive for the Democratic nomination, the Kennedy men believed, was his refusal to enter the primaries. As Kennedy had to prove that a Catholic could win votes in Protestant areas, Johnson had to demonstrate that a southerner could win votes in the North. But this Johnson refused to do. Instead, he chose to have Hubert Humphrey, a much weaker figure politically, be his stalking horse. This was particularly true in West Virginia. When Kennedy won that primary, he effectively ended the religious issue as far as being a factor in his winning the nomination. The Kennedy camp believed that if Johnson had entered that primary, instead of Humphrey, he would have beaten John Kennedy there, gone on to win the Presidential nomination—and then been defeated by Richard Nixon.

Why had Johnson refused to enter the primaries?

Lyndon Johnson first came to Washington in the 1930s when Congress was the source of political patronage, of the public works projects, of the handouts. A member of Congress in that decade was a political king and held the power to go with that position. But during the 1940s and early 1950s, the sources of this congressional power gradually eroded. Congressmen still wrote the laws, but institutions implemented them. Civil service had dried up federal patronage to a point where the Governor of Pennsylvania had more than ten times as many jobs to fill by appointment than did the President of the United States. Public works still provided "pork" but not unless the Army Corps of Engineers first studied the need for the project in a scientific and nonpolitical manner and then gave its approval. The federal bounty—the welfare distribution, the aid to schools—was administered by a vast bureaucracy. This bureaucracy was too amorphous to be responsive to political pressures; when the congressman pushed at one point, he would find he just sank deeper and deeper into the formless mass, never striking anything that could respond to him. All this meant that the members of Congress were no longer the political bosses of their constituencies.

Lyndon Johnson had not understood this in 1960. He still believed that if Adam Clayton Powell declared himself for Lyndon Johnson, then Negro Harlem would vote for Johnson. He believed that if Carl Hayden was for Lyndon Johnson, then Arizona and the other western states would vote for Johnson. He still believed that if he did a favor for an Ohio senator, then Ohio would do a favor for Lyndon Johnson in 1960. He believed that power still flowed from Washington.

Well before 1960, however, John Kennedy had learned that power moved in the other direction, not from Washington to the states but from the states and cities to Washington. At the 1956 Democratic convention Kennedy had sought his party's Vice Presidential nomination. The members of Congress, representing the power in Washington, backed him. The governors, representing the local power, opposed him. Kennedy lost. At one point in that convention, Robert Kennedy had gone to a southern senator, a close personal friend, to ask him to use his influence with his state's delegates on behalf of John Kennedy. The senator laughed at him, not in a mean way but in a helpless fashion. They won't listen to me, the senator said, talk to the governor. Robert Kennedy did talk to the governor, a man whom he had never met before, and gained no votes for his brother. Because of these experiences, John Kennedy in the second half of the 1950s determined to fashion a campaign for the Presidential nomination in which he and his men would seek support from the people who held the real power.

These were men like Walter Reuther in Michigan. Because of his position as President of the United Auto Workers, his support could swing a substantial labor vote in Detroit. Another such man was William Green of Philadelphia. Although a member of Congress, Bill Green's power came from the patronage his organization controlled in Philadelphia. If he wanted to turn out the votes, the votes turned out. Another was Mayor Richard Daley of Chicago. He too had a tight organization built around patronage and contracts. He too could produce votes. These men were the leaders of the northern city dwellers and these city dwellers were of varied ethnic, religious and racial backgrounds, and with a tradition of liberal thought. They were also older people who required increased assistance from the government and they were young children who needed better schools. During the Eisenhower years, the city bosses had watched as billions of dollars were allotted for highways to crisscross the nation but little was spent to improve life in the cities, as funds went to aid schools in suburban and rural areas but no money was available for schools in the cities, as the subsidy to business increased but the number of federal dollars going to the people of the cities declined. The city bosses had watched also as the Eisenhower administration—and Eisenhower personally—refused to commit itself to solving the problems of civil rights for the Negro. These city bosses then—the Reuthers and the Greens and the Daleys—had come to the 1960 Democratic convention in Los Angeles wanting a Presidential candidate who would be a crusading "liberal," who would fill in all the gaps in the national life left by Dwight Eisenhower. They backed Kennedy there because he had appealed to them with such a "liberal" program. Lyndon Johnson, however, had ignored them; in some cases, insulted them.

Because Lyndon Johnson had not understood this new center of power, had ignored it and offended it, the members of the Kennedy camp discounted his ability as a politician.

There was another reason why the Kennedy men looked with skepticism and some perhaps with distrust upon the Vice

President. They believed they were the vanguard of a new movement in politics in which the young men would take over from the old and tired politicians. "Those guys in their sixties and up," said a New Frontiersman early in 1961, referring to people like Secretary of Commerce Luther Hodges or W. Averell Harriman in the State Department, "are okay because they're too old to be a threat. Whatever political future they have is past. The guys our age, in their forties, are okay because they're like us, the same backgrounds and the same thought processes. But the guys in their fifties," and here the New Frontiersman paused as his mind dwelt on Lyndon Johnson, "are the ones we worry about. They're too old to be part of our group, and they're too young to be crossed off as far as having a political future. In other words, they are a threat to us."

The Vice President never complained to Kennedy. He had nothing specific to complain about, at least nothing that would not sound petty. Publicly, Johnson did not criticize the Kennedy men. Privately, however, Lyndon Johnson often spoke of the "red hots" and "lib-lab boys" in the White House. These men, Johnson let it be known when the Texan's southern or conservative friends mentioned names like Arthur Schlesinger or Chester Bowles or Mennen Williams, were a little too "far out" for him. This attitude crept into print on a few occasions, without Johnson being described as the specific source of the stories. Johnson also talked of unnamed persons at the White House spreading stories about his loss of political power, about supposed disagreements with the President, about his being "out" politically. No one at the White House did spread such stories intentionally, nor did anyone in the upper echelons of the Executive branch do so; President Kennedy had made clear he would tolerate no such backbiting. But at the same time, members of the Kennedy camp did not pretend to be anything they were not. If they never spoke rudely or dis-

respectfully of the Vice President outside of their own small
circle, they also never expressed an affection or respect they
did not feel.

Despite all these negative attitudes toward Lyndon Johnson,
the Texan had been almost the unanimous choice of John
Kennedy's advisers to be the Vice Presidential candidate in
1960. Only Robert Kennedy of the important men around
John Kennedy had another choice; he favored Senator Henry
M. (Scoop) Jackson of Washington. It was not that the Kennedy men were so enamoured of Johnson. They were not. But
they came to him by a process of elimination. Ted Sorensen
and Myer Feldman had prepared a memorandum for John
Kennedy in June of 1960 listing all the Vice Presidential possibilities, describing all their weak points and strong ones, and
then rating them. Lyndon Johnson led that list. This memorandum pointed out that a Kennedy-Johnson ticket would
have geographic as well as religious balance, and also balance
by age. This last point unintentionally echoed a pre-convention
charge leveled by Johnson against Kennedy when the Texan
said the country needed "a man with a touch of gray in his
hair." The memorandum analyzed Johnson's voting record
and concluded that his more recent votes overshadowed his
earlier anti-civil rights and anti-labor record. This was an
intellectual judgment which did not consider the emotions of
the labor and civil rights leaders. Because of this, the Kennedy
forces were thrown off balance when these leaders threatened a
revolt at the Democratic convention rather than accept Lyndon Johnson on the ticket, even in the bottom half. In private
conversations with Kennedy before he had to choose a running
mate, his aides made the same points to him about Johnson
being the best man for the second spot from a political point
of view.

Unlike the other Vice Presidential possibilities, Johnson
would—so it was argued—bring votes to the Democratic

ticket. Senator Hubert Humphrey, for example, because of his extreme liberalism would cost the Democrats support in the South. Senator Stuart Symington, whose chief recommendation was that no one opposed him, might not have cost any votes, but he would not have added any either. Scoop Jackson, Robert Kennedy's favorite, also may not have cost any votes, but he was not well enough known to add any. Only Johnson, because of his southern support, could strengthen the ticket. If anyone could counter the southern fears about a Kennedy administration activism in the civil rights field and calm the southern emotional attitude toward Kennedy's religion, it was Lyndon Johnson.

Also, as much as the Kennedy aides in the early summer of 1960 disliked Johnson and thought he was much less a politician than his friends credited him as being, the Kennedy men also felt—and advised John Kennedy—that Lyndon Johnson was the best man of the Vice Presidential possibilities to walk in the President's shadow, ready to step into the Presidency if that need arose. Kennedy agreed with this estimate.

The "Irish Mafia" was neither Irish nor a Mafia. It was a group of young idealists, politicians and professors of all ethnic backgrounds. In the Kennedy administration the group centered at the White House, but its members were part of most government agencies. They were united by a devotion to John Kennedy and driven by the desire to help make his administration one of the nation's great Presidencies. To them, Lyndon Johnson had been the "southern candidate" at the 1960 convention and was the "southern" member of the administration, just as there were business men and civil rights leaders, labor people and the governor of a southern segregated state in the administration. This influenced their thinking of Johnson and their attitude toward him—as it also influenced John Kennedy. Lyndon Johnson was a power to be dealt with, a fact of political life to be accepted. That is why,

if there was no love between the Kennedy men and Lyndon
Johnson, there was no burning hatred either. Johnson was just
there.

Sometimes there were difficulties that were no one's fault at
the time, but had their roots deep in past events, such as the
first run-in between Lyndon Johnson and Robert Kennedy, the
President's younger brother. This dispute revolved around
Texas patronage. During the Eisenhower years, there had been
little federal patronage for Democrats. Johnson, however, was
able to pick up some gleanings from the White House in the
1950s because his position as Senate leader gave him bargaining power with the Republican administration. As would any
other politician, Johnson used his patronage to shore up his
strength among the Texas Democrats who supported him;
these were largely conservative Democrats. This left the junior
senator from Texas, Ralph Yarborough, without any patronage
to hand out to his supporters, primarily liberal Democrats.

Shortly after the 1960 election, John Kennedy told Lyndon
Johnson that while Johnson might be second in the nation, he
would be first in Texas: no federal appointments would be
made in the state that would be "personally obnoxious" to
Johnson. That was a traditional Senate phrase meaning that
Lyndon Johnson would have a veto over any appointments in
Texas. There were hundreds of important jobs in the state,
most rarely known or discussed outside of a small circle of
affected people but upon which many persons' economic status
depended. The state, for example, had an agriculture stabiliza-
tion committee, as did each agriculture county in the state.
These committees, made up of local people appointed by the
federal government, assigned cotton, rice and wheat acreage
allotments to Texas farmers. For the farmer, his allotment size
determined the extent of the federal subsidy he received and
how much of a crop he would market; whether, in effect, he
survived economically. There were also patronage jobs in the

Texas offices of various federal agencies. The Farm Home Administration is one such agency. It makes loans to farmers and does a big business in Texas. Almost all of these jobs went to men Johnson recommended.

For Ralph Yarborough it was a difficult situation. His supporters came to him seeking patronage and he had few jobs to give them. (One recommendation he successfully made later embarrassed him: Billie Sol Estes.) During all the years of the Kennedy administration, Yarborough often knocked at the door of the White House larder but never received much in the way of goodies. Since most of those jobs did not require congressional confirmation, there was little Yarborough could do to stop them. There were, however, sixteen jobs that did require Senate approval that first year and Yarborough meant to have his say about them. These jobs included four United States attorneys, four custom collectors, four judges and four federal marshals. These sixteen jobs had been given to Johnson to dispense, but Yarborough countered by going to the chairmen of the Senate committees which would consider the appointments and saying the names of the men Johnson wanted were "personally obnoxious." No matter what job Johnson held, no matter what his past association with the Senate had been, that body would not vote to confirm an appointee from Texas if the senator from Texas opposed the appointment. The hassle ended with the jobs being split between Johnson and Yarborough, each receiving eight appointments.

Robert Kennedy was caught in the middle of the Johnson-Yarborough dispute. As Attorney General he headed the Justice Department, which had sent twelve of those sixteen names to Capitol Hill. Also, Robert Kennedy had become what Washington calls the "son-of-a-bitch man." Every administration has one. He is the man who says "yes" or "no" to patronage. His job is to take as much political heat off the President as he can. He is tough, sometimes ruthless. He is the man everyone in Washington—except the President himself—"must see."

This made Robert Kennedy the man Johnson had first to approach about the appointments and it made Robert Kennedy the man who eventually had to say "no" to half the Johnson requests because of Yarborough. "It wasn't so much that Lyndon didn't like Bobby," said one who watched them from a close vantage point and who was a close friend of Robert Kennedy's also, "but Johnson didn't like the idea of having to deal from a secondary position with such a young squirt." There also was the suspicion on Johnson's part that Robert Kennedy enjoyed saying "no" to him. This went back to the confused and turbulent Thursday at the Democratic convention when Lyndon Johnson was tapped as the Vice Presidential nominee. Robert Kennedy made three visits to the Johnson hotel suite to discuss the Texan's withdrawing as a Vice Presidential candidate because of the growing liberal opposition to his choice. In these meetings Robert Kennedy suggested that Johnson become Democratic national chairman instead. Since that day, the premise has been put forward publicly by those involved that Robert Kennedy came to the Johnson suite to advise him of the opposition and to say the national chairmanship would be available if the Texan himself chose to avoid the embarrassment of a floor fight with the liberals at the convention. At the time, however, there was no doubt among those watching the confrontations that Robert Kennedy personally wanted Johnson to withdraw. "Who's the candidate, you or your brother?" John Connally had snarled at Robert Kennedy that Thursday. The younger Kennedy was apparently still smarting from the violently personal attacks Johnson had leveled the previous day at Joseph Kennedy, the father of the Kennedy clan, and at John Kennedy also. Robert Kennedy's pride would not permit him to forget those attacks, nor forgive them. Nor would Lyndon Johnson's pride permit him to forget that Thursday at the convention when he believed he was fighting Robert Kennedy and what the Texan termed a "double cross."

In his first year as Vice President, there was some errand running Johnson could do. After the Bay of Pigs, the President sent Johnson to see former President Truman and gain a statement of support from him as Kennedy gained such a statement from former President Eisenhower. Kennedy tried using Johnson to bridge the growing gulf between the White House and the business world. The corporation leaders did not seem as frightened of Johnson, who was believed more conservative, as they were of Kennedy. "Yesterday is yesterday," Johnson told a business meeting in February 1961. "The idiom of yesterday's politics and yesterday's prejudices no longer applies —not even to the word 'Democrats.'" He substituted for President Kennedy at the fifty-third annual Governors' Conference in Hawaii when Kennedy's bad back kept him from attending. He was a frequent salesman for the New Frontier at the various meetings of clubs and groups that could be of help to the administration's legislative program. He often spoke at Democratic Party fund-raising dinners and tried to take over some of the official entertaining that is the responsibility of the Executive branch. The Johnsons purchased Perle Mesta's rambling French chateau-style home called "Les Ormes." They anglicized the title to "The Elms," installed a swimming pool, music by Muzak, paintings by Texans and were in business.

But that kind of activity could never be a full-time job.

FOUR

I F the expected areas of service—Congressional leader, aide-de-camp—were closing to Johnson, a new area did open up for him, that of "goodwill" ambassador abroad. Because Lyndon Johnson had been a "guts" politician—his philosophy developed from the hurts and anguish he experienced and witnessed—his interests as a member of Congress had been primarily in domestic matters, attempts to heal the wounds that had caused the pain of ravaged land and unproductive fields of which he knew. Because of this background oriented toward the interior of America and also because of his "Uncle Cornpone" demeanor, his attempts at diplomacy were viewed with some alarm by the professional diplomats. Johnson, however, turned out to be a smashing success.

His first trip abroad as a goodwill messenger was to Senegal, an African nation which was celebrating its independence. This trip set the style for future trips of the Vice President, on Kennedy's part and Johnson's. On Kennedy's part, when he sent Johnson to Senegal, he also did his best to give Johnson the appearance of being busy. After Senegal, he told Johnson, stop off at Geneva and find out why the nuclear test ban talks there are stalled. Then go to Paris and talk to the NATO people there, Kennedy added. Oh, and in between would you detour to Spain? McNamara would like you to inspect our defense installations there. Make it back in a week, will you, Kennedy closed. That kind of schedule and its advance release to newsmen indicated an active time for the Vice President. With the exception of the formal visit to Senegal, something demanded by protocol, however, there was little that Johnson was doing on that trip that could not be done by persons on the scene or by telephone calls and written memorandums. When the trip was over—and this became part of the routine also—there was a meeting between Kennedy and Johnson at the White House at which Kennedy told newsmen how valuable the Johnson trip had been. Johnson, the President said, "represented our country with great distinction" and contributed "a great deal to strengthen the support NATO must have if it is going to be an effective shield."

On Johnson's part, he set a style in diplomatic relations that angered the professionals but wowed the people. He proved that "Uncle Cornpone" could be as successful in the jungles of Africa or the dusty streets of Pakistan as he could in the Texas hill country. In Senegal, for example, while the seventeen-man Soviet delegation slept late, Johnson and his wife woke at four thirty one morning, left the capital city of Dakar in an automobile and drove to a small fishing village called Kayar. The per capita income of Kayar then was $100. Johnson told the villagers about his own home state: "The rural per capita income of Texas was only $180 in 1930 and today it is $1,800." Then he went through the streets shaking hands, kissing babies, and just generally having himself a good time. His wife, Lady Bird, looked at the baskets piled high with peanuts and said: "Why, it's just like Texas." When the village chief, Gurtil N'Doye, asked Johnson why he had come to Kayar, the Vice President answered, "I came to Dakar for Independence Day festivities because of President Kennedy's deep interest in Africa, but I came to Kayar because I was a farm boy, too, in Texas. It's a long way from Texas to Kayar, but we both produce peanuts and both want the same thing: a higher standard of living for the people." They loved him in Kayar.

That folksy style was well received in all of Johnson's travels but particularly well in the countries still underdeveloped economically. Johnson understood the poverty the people of these nations knew; he had experienced such poverty himself. He appreciated how a single commodity had a life or death hold on these people. Often he spoke of his own father going broke on cotton, holding onto it in hopes it would go up to twenty-one cents; it always fell at twenty.

In Beirut, Johnson inspected a road crew and was right at home with them. "How much does this truck hold?" he shouted to one of the workers. Five yards was the answer. Johnson nodded, and said, "My first job was on a truck that held only one yard. We loaded it with shovels, then dumped it." He turned to a Lebanese official. "You're going to realize great benefits from work like this," said Johnson. "In my country, one of the most important developments was getting the farmers out of the mud. In my own state of Texas now, no farmer has to drive more than a mile to get to paved road." People responded to that kind of talk; they felt here was a man who understood them.

Johnson also enjoyed meeting people. Without notice he ordered his car stopped and he jumped out of the automobile to greet people personally. When police tried to protect him by placing themselves between Johnson and the enthusiastic crowds, Johnson admonished them for getting between him and "the plain folks." Once in Teheran he shook an estimated three hundred hands in five minutes. One reporter said Johnson hit the city "as though he were running for Shah—and if the warmth of his welcome was an indication, he might be able to get the job." (Some time later, Governor Nelson Rockefeller introduced Johnson at a dinner in New York as "the only American I know of who could be elected mayor of Teheran.") In one city, Johnson shook hands with the fifteen-year-old proprietor of a watermelon stand and said, "Sure good to see you. Tell your mother, brothers and sisters hello for me." This gregariousness also was part of his past. As a poor man himself once, as these people were now, he too had been thrilled at the sight of those who held high office. Years earlier, when Lyndon Johnson worked as an elevator operator, he changed shifts so he could be on duty when the Vice President of the United States visited in that building.

As in many things, Johnson's desire to communicate with the people was sometimes overdone. In the spring of 1961, the Vice President was touring southeast Asia. On a dusty road in Pakistan, Johnson, following his usual routine, jumped out of his car and went among the people who lined the road to shake their hands and speak with them. "Glad to see you," he said, and "Nice of you to come down," and also: "You-all come to Washington and see us sometime." That last was an old familiar line with Johnson; during the 1960 campaign he had advised people, "You-all come down and see us in Washington when we're Vice President." Among those to whom he issued that general invitation to come to Washington that day in Pakistan was a poverty-stricken, bedraggled but bright-eyed camel driver named Bashir Ahmed. In Bashir Ahmed's world, words meant what they said. He was going to Washington, he told his acquaintances later, to visit his friend the American Vice President. He was laughed at and the joke spread. Soon the circle of those who knew of Bashir Ahmed's expectations broadened to include some anti-American journalists in Pakistan. They wrote up the story, thinking it would harm the United States. But they didn't know their man.

Word gradually filtered back through embassy channels to Washington and to Lyndon Johnson about the newspaper stories of Bashir Ahmed and his expectation of coming to the United States to visit Johnson. Nothing would be adequate then, Johnson decided, except that Bashir Ahmed indeed visit the United States. Johnson arranged for the People-to-People program to pay the costs, and on October 15, 1961, when a plane carrying Bashir Ahmed landed at Idlewild International Airport* in New York, Lyndon Johnson was waiting to greet his "friend." Johnson, wearing a dark suit, a white shirt and dark tie, shook hands with and then embraced Bashir. The camel driver wore a traditional Pakistani costume, karakul cap and knee-length sherwani coat. Speaking through an interpreter—Bashir Ahmed spoke only Urdu—the two men chatted for half an hour and then flew together to Texas.

The week's visit of the Pakistani camel driver to the United States had been anticipated with considerable concern at the White House. The worry was that mixing the volatile and often rough Texan with the illiterate Pakistani could not help but result in the camel driver's ending up hurt and embarrassed and the United States' coming under criticism in Pakistan. However, Johnson treated his guest with dignity and with graciousness. He also demanded that others who came in contact with Bashir Ahmed do the same. When he learned that the wire services and some newspapers were assigning their top "funny" writers to cover the visit, Johnson called the heads of these agencies to demand more respect for Bashir Ahmed. Although Bashir was incapable of reading or writing, he turned out to be a true gentleman with an eloquent tongue. When he met John Kennedy at the White House later in the week, for example, Kennedy shook hands with him and said, "You've been the most famous man in America for the last three or four days," and the Pakistani answered, "You have been and will be the most famous man in the world for a long time to come." In Texas, Bashir accompanied Johnson to the

* Later renamed the John F. Kennedy International Airport.

house built by the Vice President's grandfather 104 years earlier and then another house built by Johnson's father fifty-five years earlier. Those two houses plus Lyndon Johnson's ranch with its heated swimming pool and music by Muzak said much of America's history: from pioneer to poor farmer to opulent success.

When the week's visit ended and Bashir Ahmed was ready to fly home from New York, Johnson informed him that the return trip had been routed so that the camel driver could visit Mecca, the spiritual center of his religion. What had begun as a casual remark and which developed as an anti-American campaign and became a cause for concern at the White House ended, eventually, as a diplomatic triumph.

Despite what Johnson considered a record of successes as goodwill ambassador abroad, American diplomats sometimes criticized him for violating the traditional rules of diplomatic conduct—never to his face, however. Johnson was aware of the comments, and they grated on him. He was not always respectful of the career diplomat. Usually the diplomat was a product of America's exclusive eastern private schools and colleges, often out of touch with the average people of the United States as well as those of the nations where they represented the United States. Johnson criticized such diplomats "who would rather keep out of sight under the mistaken impression that our ways of political leadership are a national liability."

There was no criticism, however, of the way Johnson handled himself on one trip: to Berlin in August of 1961, one week after the Communists had begun to build the wall that cut between West and East Berlin. This was the highlight of Lyndon Johnson's first year as Vice President, perhaps of his entire career in that office.

"It is going to be," John Kennedy told Nikita Khrushchev on a somber June day in Vienna, "a cold winter." The remark of the American President was caused by the Russian Premier's insistence that he would sign a separate peace treaty with East Germany by December. Such an act would give the East Germans control over allied access to West Berlin, the western world's outpost one hundred miles behind the Communist border. West Berlin had become a symbol not only of democracy but of America's determination to protect Europe from the military advance of Communism. If West Berlin fell, and control of access routes by the East Germans would be the start of the city's collapse, the result would be either the complete retreat of the United States from its international obligations or war. John Kennedy did not plan to lead his country in retreat.

And so the Berlin crisis of 1961 was underway. America's military force was increased. Additional funds were appropriated. The President spoke on television to the American people, his manner showing the seriousness of the situation. "It was a continuing daily harassment," said one who was part of the intimate circle around Kennedy during those days. "We never knew what was going to happen. We were always afraid that the situation would get out of control, that is, that someone over there would take a shot at someone and that someone would shoot back." Kennedy, this aide remembered, was particularly worried about this last possibility, of an uncontrollable incident beginning a process of military escalation. "If anyone is going to start a nuclear war," Kennedy said several times in explaining his strong insistence on complete control, "it's going to be me."

But on August 13 came an act that was much more than a part of the "continuing daily harassment." Beginning at two o'clock in the morning, a wall began to take form on the East Berlin side of the border between the two halves of the city. *Schandmauer,* the West Berliners called it, the "wall of shame." The title was an accusation thrown at the Communists, but there was a feeling among West Berliners in these first days that the charge also should have been thrown at the Americans. The building of the wall had come as a complete surprise to the Kennedy administration. The President was in Hyannis Port at the time. When he conferred by telephone with his aides and cabinet secretaries, he found that all the contingency plans prepared covered every possible Communist maneuver except this one. Actually there was little that could be done. The wall was built on the East Berlin side of the border and as long as there was no attempt made to stop western access to West Berlin, there was no legal basis for American action. The suggestion that American armed forces move across the border and "knock down" the wall was not seriously considered by the military commanders at the scene. Building the wall was not an act of war: knocking it down was. Besides, the Communists could have countered simply by retreating fifty feet into East Berlin and building another wall.

But the indecision and silence from the White House in the next few days magnified the wall from a shameful barrier into a brilliant Communist coup and the people of West Berlin and of the world wondered about the fate of the city. Would the Americans wait too long before acting? Would they do nothing?

Aggravating the situation further was the political picture in West Germany, where the chancellor, Konrad Adenauer, was being challenged in a coming election by Willy Brandt, mayor of West Berlin. The wall immediately became a political issue in West Germany, with the candidates trying to outshout each other in their demands for the Americans to do something about it. Both Adenauer and Brandt made remarks critical of the United States.

It was against this background that at nine thirty the evening of Thursday, August 17, John Kennedy placed a telephone call to Sam Rayburn's apartment where the Vice President was chatting with his old friend. After a moment Johnson came on the phone. "Lyndon," the President asked, "are you available to go to Berlin?"

Johnson answered that he was available. His only plans for the weekend were a fishing trip on Saturday with Rayburn and a visit to Senator Everett M. Dirksen's farm in nearby Virginia on Sunday. Both could easily be cancelled. The President told him the proposed trip still was up in the air but he would speak with the Vice President again the next day.

Kennedy realized a dramatic gesture was needed, not one that would aggravate the situation but one that would calm it as well as reaffirm the American commitment to West Berlin. Briefly there was thought that the President himself should go to West Berlin, but this, it was believed, would be provocative. "And so Johnson," said a Kennedy aide, "was as high as you could go."

At eleven o'clock Friday morning, Kennedy called Johnson at "The Elms" and asked him to come to the White House. At approximately the same time, Pierre Salinger, the White House press secretary, announced to the press that Johnson would make the trip. Johnson came to the White House and spent that afternoon closeted with Kennedy and State Department advisers. The trip was to have three purposes: (1) keep the United States neutral in the political clash between Adenauer and Brandt, (2) calm the near-hysteria of the West German politicians, and (3) inform the German leaders and the German people of the American position. At the same time that Johnson was preparing for his trip, military planners were starting the process that would send fifteen hundred additional American troops along the Helmstedt Corridor across East Germany to West Berlin. The additional fifteen hundred troops were of little military value; there never was any question that the Communists had the military power to take West Berlin at their discretion. But sending the additional troops across East Germany was a test of the West's access routes, the key to whether the Berlin crisis meant a shooting war. If they were not permitted through . . . and here the words stopped.

The airplane carrying the Vice President arrived in Bonn Saturday morning and immediately Johnson learned that it would be difficult to separate the international scene from local politics. Adenauer was among those meeting Johnson in Bonn and wanted to come to West Berlin with him; he understood the value of being seen with the Vice President at such a moment. Johnson also understood the political repercussions and refused. He did not wish to become involved in the German elections. In the midst of these undercurrents, he said to the people of Bonn: "The American President and the American people are determined to fulfill all our obligations and to honor all our commitments. We are not provocative; neither are we frightened. . . . In our steadfast and unshaken unity [let us] dare to the end to do our duty." On the next leg of the trip Johnson was accompanied by Walter Dowling, the United States Ambassador to West Germany, and Lucius Clay, the retired Army general who was a hero to the West Berliners because of his commanding the city during the Berlin Blockade a dozen years earlier. They boarded an Air Force Constellation for the eighty-minute flight through a twenty-mile-wide access corridor over East Germany. At Tempelhof Airport in West Berlin they were greeted by Mayor Brandt. Johnson inspected an honor guard of American troops and West Berlin police. Then the Vice President was driven to Potsdamer Platz, where the car stopped just ten yards away from the barbed wire and cement barricade that made the *Schandmauer*.

Johnson had had no sleep the night before. The time during the flight across the Atlantic had been taken up by discussions with advisers and speech writing. As tired as he was, however, Johnson could not relax. He had to be careful he made no mistakes. Everything he did must calm the situation rather than provoke it further. A test came for him at this moment as he sat in the automobile before the Wall. A West German cabinet minister tried to persuade Johnson to walk into East Berlin. Johnson refused to be baited. As the West German official increased his arguments, the Vice President remained adamant.

In West Berlin too Johnson found he could not escape local politics. Willy Brandt told the Vice President there that he was particularly angry about the Adenauer visit earlier that year— the weekend of the Bay of Pigs invasion—to the Johnson ranch. Both Brandt and Adenauer had been to the United States earlier in 1961, pulling from the trips as much publicity and political mileage as they could; a close relationship with America was a plus in West Germany. But the publicity Adenauer gained from his trip to the LBJ ranch far surpassed the coverage Brandt's American trip had received. Johnson's temper flared and he "bawled hell" out of Brandt. In addition to saying that this weekend was a particularly inopportune time to try to involve an American Vice President in a German election, Johnson reminded Brandt that Brandt had visited Johnson's ranch back in 1954.

But if Johnson was having troubles with the politicians, he was having no difficulties with the people of West Berlin. As his car moved through the streets of the city, one hundred thousand persons stood on the curbs braving an intermittent rain to cheer him along the eight-mile route. When Johnson, in his usual fashion, ordered the car stopped and jumped out to shake hands with some of the West Berliners, he was nearly mobbed. In the square before the City Hall, where Johnson signed the visitor's Golden Book, a crowd of three hundred thousand cheered him. Later he told the people of the city:

> I have come to Berlin by direction of President Kennedy. . . . To the survival and to the creative future of this city we Americans have pledged, in effect, what our ancestors pledged in forming

the United States: ". . . our Lives, our Fortunes, and our sacred Honor. . . ." This island does not stand alone.

There was no new commitment in Johnson's words, suggested to him the previous day by White House aide Walt W. Rostow, but the city of West Berlin wanted to hear them spoken in that way at that time. The people of West Berlin were groggy, still stunned by the blow of the *Schandmauer*. They needed an extra spurt of energy, an extra hand to lift them up from the depths into which they had been thrown by the events of the past week. It would be said of Lyndon Johnson that he "was a good man in a tight spot." That weekend he was in a tight spot and he was a good man. He provided the energy and the hand the West Berliners needed. His presence and his reiteration of the American pledge to stand by West Berlin brought unashamed tears to the eyes of the people as they watched him go by. Without embarrassment they stretched out their hands to touch him, hoping, so it seemed, that they each could feel the strength of America flow from the Texan to their individual bodies as it flowed to the city as a whole.

And as Johnson moved through the city that day, the fifteen hundred American troops were moving through the Helmstedt Corridor. The Corridor is actually a 104-mile autobahn, a four-lane highway. The shortest land route across East Germany to West Berlin, the road was bumpy in spots; sometimes traffic compressed into one lane. On either side of the road stretched neat farm fields; this weekend the sun was turning the grain a ripe yellow. These fields had a peaceful look about them as did the occasional East German farmer who waved in a friendly fashion to the passing fifteen hundred men of the 1st Battle Group, 8th Infantry. The American trucks rumbled over the bridge that crosses the Elbe River. Thirteen years earlier, a "closed for repairs" sign had gone up on this bridge, starting the Berlin Blockade. Now the 1st Battle Group moved

through the pines and birches of the forests along the Branden-
burg plain, watched each moment by unfriendly eyes. Near
Berlin the trucks passed under the guns of a World War II
Russian tank mounted on a pedestal, a symbolic guard of the
Corridor.

In Washington, President Kennedy had delayed his regular
summer weekend trip to Hyannis Port to wait for word that
the troops had been allowed to pass the Dreilendent checkpoint, two miles outside of the West Berlin border and the last
Communist outpost, and had arrived safely in the city; or word
that they had not.

In West Berlin, the troops—if they were to arrive—would
come sometime Sunday afternoon. Earlier that day, Johnson,
acting on his own initiative, had sent Lucius Clay and Charles
"Chip" Bohlen, a State Department expert on Russia, across
the border between the divided city into East Berlin. They
drove through the city in an unmarked car, making notes of
what they saw. The streets were empty of civilians but filled
with soldiers, tanks and armored cars.

Beginning early Sunday afternoon the people of West
Berlin began gathering along the Helmstedt autobahn just inside the border of their city. They could not see the Communist checkpoint two miles away at Dreilendent, but the road
between the checkpoint and the city was straight. They believed they would see the American soldiers soon after they
moved through the checkpoint, if, that is, they were not
blocked or molested. Soon thousands of West Berliners were
there, standing along the side of the road, sitting on the low
grassy hills that overlooked the highway, leaning against the
railings of the small bridges. Johnson and Clay were there too,
directly inside the border. Like the people of West Berlin, they
waited.

The barbarism of war is so opposed to the standards of a
civilized society that the possibility of its coming is difficult to

accept. And that was why perhaps as the people waited that Sunday afternoon there was somewhat of a picnic air about them. A few brought lunches. Children tossed balls back and forth. Two kilted Scotsmen—no one knew how they had come to be there at that time—entertained the crowd, sporadically playing their bagpipes. But over these few signs of festivity hung a tension. No matter how barbaric, war had come before and could come again; perhaps none knew that better than the people of West Berlin. Despite the constant reports of the progress of the American troops, despite all the arguments voiced that day among the waiting people about why Russia would not block the Americans, no one was sure war would not come that day. No one could be sure until that moment when either the Americans would cross the border or would be blocked from crossing. And so, despite the parents' smiles at the children by their side, the West Berliners frequently turned to the West, to stare apprehensively and troubled at the straight line that was the Helmstedt autobahn.

No one knows who first saw the American column. There was a shout and then another, and finally a roar that moved along the road as the people of West Berlin realized the Americans had arrived. Access to the city had not been blocked. There would be no war that day. Flowers suddenly filled the air. One bouquet fell into the lead jeep, to the surprise of Colonel Glover S. Johns, Jr., the commander of the American column, and his driver, Private James S. Rozelle. An American Army band burst into spirited marching tunes, drowning out the best efforts of the two kilted Scotsmen, who blew into their bagpipes with all their strength, but not drowning out the cries of "Thank you! Thank you!" by the German people. The lead jeep halted and Colonel Johns jumped out to report to the Vice President. The two men shook hands, both smiling. Their weekend as clay pigeons was ended. Colonel Johns, a tough battlefield commander with World War II experience and also a sensitive man, later said of that ride through the crying, shouting and flower-throwing people of West Berlin: "This was the most exciting and impressive thing I've seen in my life, with the possible exception of the liberation of France."

When Lyndon Johnson was leaving West Berlin that night to return to the United States, he said, "I have just seen the soul of a city and a people that will never submit to conquest . . . as I leave for my own country with its traditions of freedom. I salute with honor and gratitude the great-hearted people of West Berlin, the city of unconquerable freedom."

Months later Lyndon Johnson was asked by *The New York Times Sunday Magazine* to choose his favorite photograph of himself. He selected one of him and Lucius Clay taken that weekend in West Berlin. The picture shows the two men in profile, staring ahead, grim-faced, waiting. Johnson said of the photograph, "It captures the dramatic, tension-filled moment at the peak of the Berlin crisis and tells the story of our mission: absolute determination to back West Berlin."

The trip of the Vice President to West Berlin helped quiet some of the anti-American criticism that was developing among the politicians of West Germany. Adenauer, particularly, began to take more care with his remarks. The administration also believed that the trip helped persuade the Communists that a move against West Berlin would meet American resistance. Nineteen months later, in March 1963, in a "background" memorandum Johnson himself summed up his estimate of that trip's accomplishment. The memorandum was prepared for the use of Texas newsmen in the writing of feature stories on Johnson's first two years as Vice President. Johnson was referred to in the memorandum in the third person in case any of the reporters wanted to run the memorandum or parts of it verbatim as their own story, which some of them did. "When the Communists put up the wall in Berlin," read the memorandum, "the immediate reaction was panic on the part of the German people. There was so little will to resist that the Communists could have virtually walked into West Berlin and taken it over. The Vice President went to Berlin, bringing the people the direct pledge of the President of the United States that this country would support West Berlin to the hilt. The visit reversed the depression and today Berlin remains free."

The only discouraging note for Johnson on that trip, excluding the pressures to become involved in West German politics, was the return to the United States. President Kennedy was at Hyannis Port and Johnson wanted to fly there early Monday morning, direct from Bonn, for a dramatic and well-televised hero's return. But the word came back from a Presidential aide that Johnson should fly on to Washington and that the President would meet him at the White House there later at a more respectable if less dramatic hour.

That first year as Vice President, Johnson traveled seventy-five thousand miles to three continents at the request of Kennedy. In all these trips, he was, as he described himself, "the servant of the President." His speeches were always cleared in advance with the White House or the State Department. Secretary of State Dean Rusk went over the more important speeches line by line. In 1962 Johnson made what was described as a "fence mending" tour of the Middle East where American aid was being cut back. He was carefully coached beforehand in the causes of the American cutback and in descriptions of the new approach to American aid. But also he was instructed not to attempt negotiating any details with officials of the countries where he visited. He had no power to do that. It was the impact of his presence—the presence, that is, of the Vice President of the United States—that made his foreign trips valuable rather than anything that men of power can do.

Perhaps because of this or perhaps simply because there

were so many trips abroad, Johnson's role as a foreign emissary of the United States became less and less significant during his career as Vice President. There were no other instances like that of the Berlin Wall in which the electricity of an American Vice President can revive a city. The glowing tributes from the White House at the end of each trip abroad took on a sameness about them. "The Vice President has performed an invaluable service. . . . The Vice President has greatly strengthened the forces of freedom. . . . The Vice President has well represented. . . ." The White House eventually grew tired of the commendations, and the job of dispensing praise was turned over to Dean Rusk at the State Department. Like his other roles as Vice President, that of goodwill ambassador abroad faded in importance.

FIVE

As he moved uncomfortably from role to role, trying to find a niche for himself as Vice President, Johnson was not totally without strength in Washington. There is a belief that the Vice President is completely subject to the whims of the man who is President. This is not as true with a Vice President like Johnson as it would be true with a Vice President like Richard Nixon, for example.

When Nixon was Dwight Eisenhower's running mate, he did not add any appreciable strength to the Republican ticket. It was "Ike" all the way in 1952 and 1956. The only value Nixon had was that he did not take away any votes. Eisenhower could have dropped Nixon in 1956 without the vote that year being altered and it was widely believed in that election that Eisenhower had personally favored the unsuccessful "dump Dick" movement led by Harold E. Stassen. During his entire two terms, Eisenhower could have ignored Nixon, offended him, and it would have done nothing to Eisenhower's own political strength.

Another example of this strength is the relationship between Franklin D. Roosevelt and his Vice Presidents. In 1932 Roosevelt chose John Nance Garner as his running mate because the Texan was needed on the ticket to assure the nomination and then the election. The same considerations kept him on the ticket in 1936. But in that election Roosevelt was returned to office by a stunning margin, making obvious the political fact that he no longer had to rely on Garner for anything. Roosevelt felt free to drop him and did after Garner defied Roosevelt on the "court-packing" plan in 1937. In the same manner Roosevelt dumped Henry A. Wallace in 1944.

Kennedy could not feel so free with his Vice President.

Estimates varied on the value of Lyndon Johnson's presence on the 1960 Democratic ticket. John Kennedy publicly gave Johnson considerable credit. "I think his part in it was most important," said Kennedy shortly after the election. Privately, he said much the same thing. John Kennedy and his aides had understood that only someone like Lyndon Baines Johnson, a product of the South, could have reached below the Mason-Dixon line and come up with needed votes. Kennedy appreciated and admired how Johnson did it.

What impact did Lyndon Johnson have on the 1960 election?

"Ah wish ah could stay and do a little sippin' and whittlin' with you," Johnson told the voters in Rocky Bottom, South Carolina. He was aboard the "LBJ Special," a campaign train traveling south from Washington to New Orleans. This was the fall of 1960. The trees that lined the streets of the small southern towns had just a glint of gold in their leaves. The wind was slightly brisk, enough to relieve the heat still felt from the past summer but not enough yet to chill. Perfect days for the excitement of Presidential politics coming to the local courthouse. At each of the "LBJ Special" stops when the local brass band stopped playing "The Yellow Rose of Texas," Johnson talked of "Mah grandpappy" and "Mah greatgrandpappy." One or the other had lived in that particular community, or had passed through it, or had a brother there, or something—anything would do as long as it established Lyndon Johnson as one of them. "I'd appreciate so much if you-all would come just a little bit closer," Johnson would say. "You make us feel so wonderful to come out here and look us in the eye and give us a chance to press the flesh with you." In the Northeast such an approach would evoke spasms of laughter, but in the small southern communities, the Johnson approach was perfect.

The first stop on that train trip had been Culpeper, Virginia, and it produced a classic line in American politics. Johnson warmed up in his usual way. "I just want to tell you how happy I am that you would come here and howdy and shake hands with us this morning," he said. There was more of the same, such as, in response to a long series of cheers, "God bless you, Culpeper, vote Democratic." Then, as the train was beginning to leave, Johnson shouted: "They tell me we can't carry Virginia. I don't believe it, do you?" The crowd responded perfectly. "No," it shouted. And then over the sound of the band, the puffing of the train, boomed Johnson's voice: "When they tell you that, you just ask 'em, 'What did Richard Nixon ever do for Culpeper?' "

As the "LBJ Special" charged through the South, Lyndon Johnson did much more, however, than just "sip and whittle." He also appealed to the men who influenced the votes. Southern state Democratic organizations differed from those in the North. New York City Democrats, for example, can and usually do exist without reference to other Democrats in New York State. But if a northern state can have several Democratic organizations, the southern state has only one. It was, in 1960, a tight "in-group" of cousins, brothers, old friends, hangers-on. It revolved around a hierarchy of county clerks and judges, sheriffs, the members of the state legislatures. Political strength flowed through these men from those at the bottom to those at the top, and back again. All were tied together; none existed independently. Lyndon Johnson understood this. He also understood that if he could persuade the powers in these organizations to support the Kennedy-Johnson ticket, then he could influence the entire state organization. If the important men were seen on the "LBJ Special," then the lesser men would come aboard the Democratic bandwagon also. They would mention it in the squares in front of the county courthouses as they sprawled on the benches in the shade of the equestrian statues of the Confederate heroes, talk of it in the barbershops across from these squares where the important men of these communities still went to be shaved each day. And those that heard the message would go to their homes and tell their wives and their brothers, the man next door. The word would spread: "Kennedy and Johnson, it's all right."

More than one thousand local Democratic politicians boarded the "LBJ Special" to "press the flesh" with Lyndon Johnson. An expert salesman, Johnson "knew the territory." He spoke of local problems, local politicians, and of how the federal government had provided assistance. It might have been a dam, a military installation, a plant doing defense work or some form of federal subsidy, whether for cotton or schools. These, he insisted, were all made possible by the Democratic Party, and, to a large extent, Johnson argued, by himself. Now, he said, the Democratic Party wanted to be paid back. It wanted support from the South.

Lyndon Johnson has a way of making an appeal that is difficult to resist. Much of his technique is physical. He reaches out and snaps a hand in both of his own. Then the Johnson fingers spring along the other man's arms until the Texan's big hands are pounding him on the back, the arms hugging him, pulling him close. All the time, Johnson breathes out appeals: for a vote in the Senate, for support in the 1960 campaign. Johnson convinces his captive that only he, whether he be governor, senator, county clerk, judge or dogcatcher, can save the election; only he can rescue his party and his country.

"The big story," said Lyndon Johnson to reporters early in October, a few weeks before the 1960 election, "is this: There has not been a single defection in any southern state by an elected Democratic official from the Democratic Party to the Republican Party." And in Winston-Salem, he said: "The turning point of this campaign has been the failure of the Republican campaign in the South." This was important to Johnson, that the southerners not desert, that he fulfill the responsibility assigned to him in the campaign: hold the South.

Despite the absence of defections, however, much of the South still was in the doubtful column in the closing weeks of the campaign. If the important Democratic politicos were not defecting, they were not being very active in behalf of the Kennedy-Johnson ticket. During the campaign weeks, the southern Democrats, senators and representatives, were at their Washington desks or in the House or Senate gymnasiums. "They were hiding out," a Republican explained. "They didn't want to campaign for the Kennedy-Johnson ticket in their home states." But fortunately for the Democrats, Henry Cabot Lodge, the GOP Vice Presidential candidate, came to their rescue. In a speech in Harlem, he promised that a Nixon administration would appoint a Negro to the cabinet. This conflicted with Nixon's attempts to go easy on civil rights in the campaign in hopes of winning southern support. It was also attacked by well-meaning persons who called it discrimination in reverse. Nixon ordered Cabot Lodge to stop such talk. "It didn't gain us one damned vote," lamented a Republican of the Lodge promise. But it gained a number of votes for the Democrats because of Johnson's adroit use of it. "What we see is a Republican Party," Johnson said in the South during the campaign, "trying to talk out of both sides of its mouth at the same time to North and South, to white and black. . . .

Mr. Lodge tells the Negroes in the North that if Republicans get enough of their votes, Negroes can have a cabinet job —and Mr. Nixon tells Mr. Lodge, 'Don't say that so loud, the South might hear you.' "

The Republicans came to the Democrats' help still a second time. This was in Texas, the weekend before the election, a time when Texas was considered up for grabs by both sides. As happened with the Lodge promise of a Negro in the cabinet, Lyndon Johnson caught a live hand grenade and flipped it back. The scene was Dallas.

Because a Presidential campaign is so important to the nation, it can unleash a powerful surge of emotion, a surge that sometimes goes beyond the rational, the polite, the decent. That is what happened Friday morning, November 4, to Lyndon Johnson in Dallas. He had returned to his native state for a last campaign swing, one that would pull the state's twenty-four electoral votes into the Democratic column from which they had strayed in the elections of 1952 and 1956. Johnson had campaigned in forty states, most recently in upstate New York, and had covered fifty thousand miles. It had been a long, hard two months and the outcome was still doubtful. A last break was needed.

Johnson was to speak at a Democratic Party luncheon at the Adolphus Hotel in Dallas that day. His bus pulled up to the hotel after a trip from Fort Worth. There had been several political stops along the way and Johnson was a little tired. In the street a crowd of several hundred people, mostly women, milled around the Johnson bus. They carried signs, shouted and wore red, white and blue ribbons. It looked like any political gathering to welcome a candidate. But this time there was a difference. This crowd was not made up of loyal Democrats. Its members were even more than just pro-Nixon; they were Johnson haters. All the anger in Texas against Johnson for running with a Catholic, for running on a strong civil rights platform, for embracing the social welfare philosophy of the liberal wing of the Democratic Party welled up in these people as they watched the Johnson bus roll to a stop. A prominent Texas Republican said of that crowd: "The women were out on a GOP tag day. It was sheer coincidence they met Lyndon." Whether "coincidence" did bring several hundred Republican campaign workers and two Republican candidates for elected office—many of them carrying anti-Johnson signs—to that particular spot in downtown Dallas at that particular time, the "coincidence" may have been the factor that changed the outcome of the election.

Johnson, his wife, and his aides went to a suite at the Baker Hotel, across the street from the Adolphus. The Baker Hotel is the regular stopping place for the Johnsons when they are in Dallas. The candidate changed his clothes and rested while the talk in the suite was of the crowd below. It was growing larger and nastier. The prudent move would have been to take a circuitous route to the Adolphus. "That's ridiculous," snapped Johnson, "I'm here in my home state. I'll walk across the street."

Crossing from the Baker to the Adolphus Hotel is, normally, a one-minute walk. This day it took Lyndon and Lady Bird Johnson ten minutes. They had to move through a sea of shouting, spitting women. "Nigger lover" was one cry; "turncoat" another. "Judas" said one sign; "We Want Nixon" another. The spit hit Johnson, also his wife. One old-time police reporter, covering the scene, described the women as "Junior League" types—"nice hair-dos, well-dressed." Then he added: "Reminded me of a bunch of chippies held in jail for a while." Through this crowd, Lyndon Johnson and his wife walked slowly, quietly. They smiled faintly, nodded occasionally. He put his arm around his wife to guide her, to protect her, and also, some witnesses thought, to restrain her. Once, as spittle struck Mrs. Johnson, she turned and opened her mouth to answer back, but her husband's hand leaped to her mouth, covering it. As they inched through the crowd, a few of their aides trying to shield them from the pushing and shouting women, the Johnsons' dignity contrasted sharply with the vulgarity of the people surrounding them.

In the lobby of the Adolphus Hotel there was more of the same. Donald Janson, reporting the scene for *The New York Times,* estimated it took Johnson thirty minutes to cross the seventy-five-foot lobby through the one hundred or more people who surrounded them "because the shouting supporters of Vice President Nixon refused to let him through." Johnson declined police assistance, and as he had done outside the hotel, moved calmly through the crowd, his arm around Mrs. Johnson, his face motionless except for a slight smile, an occasional movement of the head. Some of his aides, unable to restrain themselves, shouted at the crowd, but Johnson snapped: "Don't shout back."

Among the crowd of Republicans were at least two prominent GOP officials. One was Bruce Alger, the representative in Congress from Dallas for six years. Alger, then forty-two years old, was a militant conservative. He was seen carrying a sign critical of Johnson and was a member of the crowd, a fact widely publicized. A Republican official who was a leading tactician in the 1960 Presidential campaign said of Dallas and Alger: "I don't know who was responsible. That damned fool we had in Congress should have been one thousand miles away at least, or tried to stop it." The other Republican at the scene was John G. Tower. Then thirty-five years old, Tower was an obscure college professor from Wichita Falls running against Lyndon Johnson for the Senate seat Johnson then held. Johnson was on the Texas ballot twice. He was a candidate for the Vice Presidency and for reelection to the Senate. Tower had come to challenge Johnson to a debate and was not seen to participate actively in the demonstration against him.

During the trip from the Baker Hotel to the luncheon meeting at the Adolphus, Johnson and his wife were not harmed physically, but considering the emotional and hostile nature of the crowd, it was fortunate that nothing happened to tip an angry crowd into a vicious mob. Was it necessary for Johnson to take that walk? Could he have taken a circuitous route to the Democratic luncheon as had been suggested to him? If he had, certainly he would have emerged as a man described as too afraid to walk in the streets of a city in his home state. The GOP probably would have painted him as a man who cowered before "a few women." The potential for danger in that walk would have been so difficult to accept by a civilized society that no one would have believed the situation required security measures. The crowd had given him a challenge he could not ignore. Also, there may have been another reason.

At the Democratic luncheon in the Adolphus Hotel after the demonstration, Johnson acknowledged: "I asked the policemen to stand aside because if the time had come when I couldn't walk unaided through the lobby of a Dallas hotel with my lady I wanted to know it." And Johnson said: "Let everyone see how Nixon runs this campaign." The next day Johnson continued his efforts to link formally the Republican Party to the street demonstration against him. In Houston he charged that Nixon supporters had "hissed and spat upon us while they blocked our way with almost a mob scene for thirty or forty minutes." In Beaumont, Texas, in case his meaning was not coming across, Johnson said: "This demonstration has the approval and the encouragement of high Republican officials. The Republican Party cannot wash its hands of this one. No man is afraid of facing up to such people. But it is outrageous that in a large civilized city a man's wife can be subjected to such treatment. Republicans are attacking the women and the children will probably be next." The next day: "I looked at them and thought of what the Good Book says: 'Forgive them, O Lord, for they know not what they do.'"

In 1960 the South was coming to the end of the legend it had lived by, a romantic legend of Tara and Scarlett O'Hara and Rhett Butler. This legend said that Negroes belonged to an inferior race who enjoyed second-class citizenship, that civil rights movements were like the Civil War: excuses for northerners to pillage the South. In 1960 the legend was dying. The Ross Barnetts and George Wallaces who would occupy so much of the history of the coming decade were only tragic caricatures of a past that had truly gone with the wind. Still, the legend was powerful and the politicians paid homage to it. The South then was like a child clinging to an overprotective but dying parent; the parents' death was inevitable but until it came, it would not be acknowledged. Johnson's difficulty in the campaign had been that he challenged this legend when he ran as the second man to John Kennedy, who promised federal assistance to the Negroes. But the Dallas incident gave Johnson the opportunity to adapt the legend to his purposes. To give the legend legitimacy the South had rationalized that its purpose was to protect the women of the South. In *Gone with the Wind,* Margaret Mitchell has Scarlett O'Hara understand that "there were thousands of women like her, all over the South, who were frightened and helpless. And thousands of men, who had laid down their arms at Appomattox, had taken them up again and stood ready to risk their necks on a minute's notice to protect these women." That this justification had long since ceased to exist, if it ever had, made little difference in the unreal world of the South; it was part of the legend. Johnson understood this. In those last few days of the campaign, he repeatedly emphasized that he and his wife—particularly his wife—had been attacked by an unruly mob and he linked that mob to Richard Nixon. Johnson was trying to convince the South that a vote for him was a vote, after all, to protect the legend by which the South then lived.

The best demonstration of Johnson's resurrection of the legend was the decision of Senator Richard Russell of Georgia to enter, at last, the campaign for the Democratic ticket. Among those who believed the legend in the South, Richard Russell was the modern knight of the Old Confederacy, the one who personified all that is finest of the legend. After the convention, Russell could not bring himself to endorse the Democratic ticket, even when his old friend and protégé Lyndon Johnson was on it. His allegiance to the Democratic Party forbade endorsing Nixon. He sat out the campaign, growing increasingly uncomfortable. He was concerned by the possibility of a Nixon victory. That could turn into a personal defeat for Russell if he was then criticized for not supporting the Democratic ticket. Also, a Democratic victory without Russell's help would mean the Georgian would have much less significance and power in the high councils of his party. Russell needed an excuse to enter the campaign on the Democratic side. Then came the Dallas incident with its attacks on Mrs. Johnson. Russell spoke out for Johnson. "Although we have had our differences," the Georgian said, "I have never been disappointed in Lyndon Johnson." If it was not the most enthusiastic endorsement, it was enough to make voting for the Democratic ticket respectable among those who believed in the legend.

Among the eleven states of the Old Confederacy, 128 electoral votes were at stake in the 1960 election. It was these votes Lyndon Johnson had been sent after. Of these 128, the Democrats won eighty-one in seven states. They won five electoral votes out of eleven possible votes in Alabama, compared to ten votes won in that state in 1956. They made clean sweeps in Arkansas, Richard Russell's Georgia, North Carolina, and South Carolina, all of which had gone Democratic in 1952 and 1956. They regained Louisiana, which had gone Republican in 1956, and Johnson's own state of Texas, which had gone Republican in 1952 and 1956. They lost Florida, Tennessee and Virginia, all of which had gone Republican in 1952 and 1956 and they lost Mississippi, which had gone Democratic in 1952 and 1956. It was a good record but not a spectacular one. Kennedy and Johnson had done about as well in the South as Truman in 1948 and Stevenson in 1952 had done, and only slightly better than Stevenson in 1956. The South had been "held," but there was little gain.

Republicans gave Johnson more credit, however, than those figures indicate he deserved. From the beginning, the GOP considered Lyndon Johnson the strongest running mate that Kennedy could have had. Polls taken for the Republican high command immediately after the Democratic convention in July showed a Kennedy-Johnson ticket beating any Nixon ticket by some four million votes. After the Republican convention and its television exposure of Nixon and Henry Cabot Lodge, and after more voters realized Kennedy was Catholic, the polls showed Nixon regaining a lead, but only a slight one.

Specifically, the Republicans credit Johnson with bringing Texas and the two Carolinas into the Democratic column, especially Texas. "If anyone else had been on the ticket," said a Republican official, "Nixon would have taken Texas." The Republican credited this Johnson feat to the Cabot Lodge promise of a Negro in the cabinet, the Dallas incident and Johnson's political use of both of them, plus the traditional allegiance of the Mexican-Americans in South Texas to Johnson. In the Carolinas, polls taken for the Republicans showed those two states going for Nixon until Cabot Lodge talked of a Negro in a Republican cabinet and Johnson repeated the Lodge promise as loudly as he could.

If that Republican estimate about those three states is correct, then Johnson blocked the election from going to the House of Representatives. With 269 electoral votes needed to win, John Kennedy ended with 303 to 219 for Richard Nixon. Of those 303 votes, forty-six were from Texas and the two Carolinas. If they had gone to Nixon, the final count would have been 257 electoral votes for Kennedy and 265 for Nixon. With neither candidate reaching the 269 figure, the election would have gone to the House of Representatives, where each state would have cast one vote, or the fifteen southern electoral votes that were unpledged would have decided the outcome. In either case, the result would have been reached only after political chaos, with each southern state supporting the candidate who promised to be the most understanding of the southern position on civil rights.

In Texas, out of 2,311,845 votes cast, the Kennedy-Johnson ticket squeaked to victory by only 46,233 votes. Johnson, running on a separate line for senator, topped this by 140,000 votes, indicating his Senate victory may have pulled the Democratic Presidential line ahead of the Nixon-Lodge ticket. In South Carolina, of 386,688 votes cast, the Democratic ticket won by only 9,571 votes. Only in North Carolina, of those three states, did the Kennedy-Johnson ticket amass a respectable lead. Of the 1,368,556 votes cast in that state, the Democrats won by 57,716. The narrowness of the results in those states, particularly in Texas and South Carolina, support the Republican estimate of the Johnson impact on the election outcome.

There is a difficulty, however, with accepting this GOP estimate. Out of 68,836,385 votes cast nationally, the Kennedy-Johnson ticket led by a mere 119,450 votes. With that close a margin, it is difficult to give credit for a final result to any single factor. "We all contributed," said a Democrat who had worked in twenty states to get the people to the polls on election day. "With such a tight margin, you—anyone—might have been it." Statisticians have credited the outcome to the Negro vote in the North, to Kennedy's Catholicism, to television, to Nixon's appearing to need a shave, almost anything.

No national act has been as analyzed as the voting for a President and no such act as much as the 1960 voting for President. One can "explain" why the Catholic and the Jew vote as they do, why the Negro in the North and the white in the South vote as they do, why the factory worker and the factory owner vote as they do. But no one is ever quite sure, not even perhaps the voter himself. Alone in the voting booth, the voter must then decide if his political allegiances will overcome his religious prejudices, if his economic fears can overcome his regional distrust. There is a magic to the moment. The United States by 1960 had become the most powerful nation on earth; its President, the most powerful man. Yet who this President would be was decided not by the wisest men of the land, nor the wealthiest, but by all the men and women—with all their virtues and with all their faults. They lined up before the schoolhouse or the fire station, standing quietly, waiting their turn to decide the fate of their nation and of the world. The magic was that the urge for civilization had triumphed to such a point that this could happen. Like all magical moments, it could not really be explained.

In 1960 then it was impossible to single out one issue, one personality, one factor, one decision responsible for the outcome. Each could have been the ingredient that produced those few extra votes to give John Kennedy a majority of the electoral college. And that was the trouble with the 1960 election. An elected official—who wants to be elected again—must husband his resources. He must placate all those who contributed to his first victory, if it was a narrow one, because the loss of just one contributor can mean defeat the next time. Personally, Kennedy admired Johnson's campaign ability, the Texan's knack of speaking to the South as one of its own; and

Kennedy also admired Johnson's personal courage as evidenced at Dallas. Both factors, Kennedy believed, had contributed to the November outcome. Politically, Kennedy believed he needed Johnson again in 1964.

That was a basic strength of Lyndon Johnson's in the Kennedy administration.

There was a second strength that Lyndon Johnson had, at least in the first year of the New Frontier. This was his remaining tie to Capitol Hill, his relationship with Sam Rayburn, Speaker of the House of Representatives. As the chief elected officer of the House, the Speaker is believed to have great powers. Actually he has very little and had even less in 1961. He cannot force a committee to send a bill to the House floor for debate. He cannot force a member to vote "aye" or "nay"; Rayburn had learned that when his fellow Texans refused to support him in the past. But the Speaker, or at least one like Rayburn, does have the respect and affection of the House members. Also, many of them owe him favors. If he is neither too demanding nor malicious, he can exercise some influence over the House. That Rayburn would use this influence to protect Lyndon Johnson against any slights or attacks was widely accepted as Congress began work on the New Frontier program.

The belief was strengthened in March when the House considered the minimum wage bill. This was an important part of President Kennedy's program; the bill called for raising the minimum wage from $1 to $1.25 and extending the minimum wage law coverage to an additional 4.3 million persons. The proposal ran into some difficulty from Republicans in the House who wanted the hourly increase kept down to fifteen cents instead of a quarter, but it met its strongest opposition from members of Kennedy's own party. The southern Democrats in the House, led by Carl Vinson of Georgia, objected to extending the minimum wage law coverage to an additional four million workers—some of whom were located in the South. These southern workers were primarily Negroes or poor whites who did not vote. Their employers who would have to pay the higher wages were both voters and party contributors. For this reason, the southern legislator was careful to whom he extended minimum wage coverage. The two forces, the GOP and the South, combined. Representative William H. Ayres, a Republican from Ohio, and Representative A. Paul Kitchin, a Democrat from North Carolina, teamed up to produce a substitute bill. It would have raised the minimum wage to the $1.15 figure the Republicans wanted and would have extended the law's coverage to only 1.3 million new workers, a number the South would accept. Then the House entered into a series of three votes that did more to shore up the position of Lyndon Johnson with his political base that first year than perhaps any other action.

The first vote was to substitute the Ayres-Kitchin bill for the administration proposal. This substitution was accepted on a 216–203 roll call vote. Almost all the southern Democrats had joined with the Republicans to vote against the Kennedy proposal.

The second vote came on an administration attempt to recoup its loss. Representative Carl Albert, an Oklahoma Democrat and the third man in the hierarchy of the House Democratic leadership, sat down with Carl Vinson to work out a deal. With Sam Rayburn hovering over them, they agreed to cut out the Republicans. Albert and Vinson compromised on a bill that would raise the minimum wage to $1.25 as the administration wanted, but extended coverage to 3.6 million new workers, a drop of 700,000 from the Kennedy proposal. Those 700,000 excluded would be primarily laundry workers located in the South. Vinson agreed to this and the men went back onto the House floor confident the compromise would be passed. Everyone had a shock. The nonrecord vote was 186–

185 against Albert. By a one-vote margin—a margin so slim as to be difficult to accept as an accident—the Albert compromise had been defeated. Was this because the sentiment in the House was so closely divided or was there another reason? The answer seemed clear a few weeks later when the House voted the third time.

After that second vote, the minimum wage bill that had emerged from the House was the Ayres-Kitchin measure, $1.15 an hour and coverage extended to 1.3 million new workers. The Senate then took up the bill and passed a measure close to that which the administration had originally proposed. A Senate-House conference committee worked out a compromise, $1.25 an hour and coverage extended to 3.6 million workers. This was almost identical to the Albert approach which the House had defeated by just one vote. Since conference reports have to be voted on, this meant the House was going to have another chance at Carl Albert's compromise. Because of the narrowness of the earlier 186–185 vote, there was some suspense when the roll call on the conference report began in the House chamber May 3. But there needn't have been. The conference report was accepted by a vote of 230 to 196. What had been objectionable to the House in March was now overwhelmingly acceptable. People wondered why.

"At the time," explained a Texas Democrat, "Lyndon Johnson was having some troubles with the White House over patronage. He was not getting all the appointments he wanted. When the Albert bill was first defeated by one vote, the White House got the picture. Rayburn had held back, asked a few of his friends to stay off the floor during the vote. That's why the bill was defeated. The White House knew there would be another chance with the conference report, of course. So Johnson's patronage troubles cleared up very quickly. The second time the House voted on the Albert bill, it was passed by a big vote. That's all there was to it. Nobody had any harsh words, no complaints. They all understood the politics of the game. They all stayed friends."

That explanation of the change in the sentiments of the House was widely accepted among Texans, both in Washington and back in the Lone Star State. Conservative Democrats in the state, who coalesced around Lyndon Johnson, understood the story to mean their man still had muscle in Washington where it counted. Liberal Democrats in the state, who more and more were forming around Senator Ralph Yarborough, understood the story to mean Johnson should not yet be challenged as the leader of the Democrats in Texas.

Neither group discussed the story with Johnson, Rayburn or any important member of the White House staff. If they had, they would have learned that the story was completely false. During the first vote on the Albert measure—the one producing the 186–185 vote against the administration—Rayburn was working extremely hard to turn out votes for the Albert compromise. Ironically, the real reason why the Albert compromise was defeated that day was because ten liberals from the industrial states of the North—ten House members whose pronouncements in favor of the administration were the loudest —were in Washington that day, even in the Capitol area, but did not come to the floor for a vote. "It was not a conspiracy," said a House leader, "it was laziness. Three were even in the House restaurant, one floor below the chamber, drinking beer during the vote." The incident produced some positive results. The White House, angry at the liberals, "raised hell," in the words of one of the participants in the scolding that followed. After that, liberals showed up for House votes.

Although the story was false, it was a bonus for Lyndon Johnson because it convinced Texans of his political strength.

But if there was a plus, there also was a minus. If Johnson's strength as Vice President was so dependent upon Rayburn's real or fictional machinations, then he could be quickly stripped of that strength if something happened to Rayburn. Seven months later, Sam Rayburn died of cancer. He was replaced as Speaker by John W. McCormack of Massachusetts, a man with no allegiance to Lyndon Johnson. "The capital is a lonely place without him," Lyndon Johnson said of Rayburn with genuine sadness. That was true. Sam Rayburn had been one of the great figures of American politics. But it was also true that Lyndon Johnson would be a particularly lonely political figure without Sam Rayburn near.

Lyndon Johnson still had a third strength, in addition to that of his constituency—the South—and his ties with Rayburn in 1961. The role of a Vice President in any administration is the product, to a large extent, of the roles played by persons who have held the office previously. And this role has been growing. Some date the growth of the Vice Presidency from John Nance Garner's time, when he attended meetings of the Roosevelt cabinet at FDR's request. Others date the growth of the Vice Presidency from Lauren Bacall, the movie actress. In 1945, shortly after becoming Vice President, Harry Truman was photographed playing the piano at the National Press Club with the attractive Miss Bacall sitting atop the piano. That photograph was used against Truman in the 1948 campaign by Thomas E. Dewey, the GOP Presidential candidate. Referring scathingly to the Truman-Bacall photograph, Dewey promised that his running mate, Earl Warren of California, would be a "full partner" if the Republicans were elected. Truman countered this criticism by promising to do as much with his running mate, Alben W. Barkley. After the election, which Truman won, he had Congress make the Vice President a member of the National Security Council. (A less romantic and less entertaining—but probably as legitimate if not more so—explanation of why Truman had the Vice President made a member of the Council is that Truman, as Vice President under FDR, did not know of the atomic bomb's development and did not wish any future Vice President to be caught so unaware.)

The Vice President's role continued to grow in the Eisenhower years. Because Eisenhower had an understanding with Nixon about the Vice President becoming acting President in the event of a Presidential disability, all future Presidents had to have a similar agreement with their Vice Presidents. Not to do so would mean being open to charges of irresponsibility. And, once such an understanding had been reached, responsibility required that the Vice President be as fully briefed and knowledgeable about his nation, its problems and defenses, as was the President. Also, Eisenhower's illnesses had demonstrated the possibility that the Vice President ignored today may be tomorrow's leader. And because Eisenhower had made Nixon the head of the President's Committee on Equal Employment Opportunity, future Presidents must give that job to their Vice Presidents or risk the politically dangerous charge of slighting civil rights.

This increasing role of the Vice Presidency had become exaggerated in the 1950s because of Nixon. Before he became Vice President, he was just one of ninety-six senators. After serving as Vice President, he was the leading contender for his party's Presidential nomination. For him it was an obvious step up. This was not true for Lyndon Johnson. He had stepped down from a position of power—where he could make decisions that the Senate abided by—to the Vice Presidency, which had grown but not that far. Still, if he was not as strong as he had been, Johnson was not weak. John Nance Garner, Lauren Bacall and Dick Nixon had combined to give the Vice Presidency some strength.

John Kennedy understood these strengths of Lyndon Johnson and he also appreciated Johnson's position and his efforts. If the two men did not get along famously, there was no friction between them. More than most, Kennedy was satisfied with Johnson's performance as Vice President. Between the two men a certain admiration had developed. As that first year ended, Kennedy recalled the phrase "Boston-Austin axis" used to describe the Kennedy-Johnson ticket in the 1960 campaign and said: "The merger of Boston and Austin was one of the last that the Attorney General allowed, but it has been one of the most successful."

Johnson was careful to do nothing to affront the President. It was interesting to watch the two men walk together. Johnson always before had walked with long strides and anyone by his side had difficulty keeping up with him. Now, however, when he was with John Kennedy, he never walked faster than the President and always slightly to the rear of the President, as a good second man should. In all his time as Vice President, Johnson did not hold any news conferences. He did not want to be pushed into saying anything on the record in a spontaneous give-and-take with newsmen that might conflict with administration policy. Occasionally he met with newsmen representing Texas newspapers to discuss local matters with them on an "off-the-record" basis, meaning he could not be identified as the source of the stories. These generally were dull sessions, with Johnson so pressed to make news that he would read aloud random samples of his mail from Texas and with the reporters leaving in disgust. Johnson also advised his staff that there should be no "Lyndon thinks" stories. This was a reference to a typical product of a luncheon meeting between a reporter and an aide to a politician; the newspaper story that emerged ascribed tactics and philosophy to the politician often in conflict with those of his colleagues. Johnson, at the beginning of his Vice Presidency, told some of his Senate friends, as one of them remembered, "People in this town will try to say you and I are at odds. They'll try to separate you and me, the President and me. Don't let them."

In that first year Kennedy and Johnson were trying to avert

any "war" between them from being fought in the newspapers or on the cocktail party circuit that lesser figures in the nation's capital travel. It was difficult because Washington feeds on gossip and Johnson managed it only by submerging himself almost entirely. "He walked willingly but restlessly in Kennedy's shadow," said an employee of Johnson's years later. "Yes, he was unhappy in the Vice Presidency. He's a doer. He's a manager. Not only in the broad sense but in the little things. He put up with it because he wanted to be on the ticket in 1964. He still was aiming at 1968."

Perhaps the most surprising thing the end of that first year was not that Lyndon Johnson had slipped from a position of power, from a position where decisions must be made and from which men and organizations can be manipulated. Despite the predictions of Johnson and his friends at the beginning of the New Frontier that the Texan would continue to reign as he had in the 1950s, the Vice Presidency's only real purpose in the American system is to insure continuity to the American government in the event of the death or disability of the President. Even Johnson acknowledged this privately at the end of the year.

The surprising thing then was that Johnson publicly took his fall from power so gracefully. When reporters came to his Capitol Hill offices, they saw him in his shirt sleeves, a batch of papers before him, a phone at his ear even as he talked with them. His schedule always was heavy. Speaking engagements kept him crisscrossing the country. But those who knew him well understood his frustration and began to appreciate what they came to assume was his regret at having traded a Senate vote for a Vice President's gavel, and his inability to find a role as Vice President.

Whatever his disenchantment with his job, however, Lyndon Johnson did not criticize John Kennedy, even in his most relaxed moments. Once late in 1961, as Johnson was flying across the United States in an Air Force plane, he relaxed with some associates. The subject of John Kennedy came up. "That boy is cool," said Johnson. "If he has to press that button, he will." Then Johnson added what was for him the extreme accolade: "He's tough. I know. He beat me."

Lyndon Johnson did not speak as kindly of himself privately. He was, he sometimes commented to friends, "a cut dog" politically. That is a Texas phrase meaning an animal without potency.

1962

The Shadow of Robert Kennedy

ONE

TED Lewis, a Washington-based columnist for the New York *Daily News,* wrote a piece in July 1962 about the "wacky developments involving people who should know better." The first of about a dozen examples of Washington wackiness he listed read this way: "Eunice Kennedy Shriver, a sister of the President, has seriously chit-chatted about a 'Kennedy-Kennedy' ticket in 1964. This would mean Jack and Bobby, not Jack and Lyndon for a second term."

The night after the column appeared, Walter W. Jenkins, Vice President Johnson's closest aide, went to the home of Kenneth O'Donnell. Jenkins demanded to know if the column item was part of a campaign preparing the public for the dumping of Johnson in 1964. Astonished, O'Donnell insisted that the President's sister, the wife of the Peace Corps director Sargeant Shriver, had been joking, if she had said anything about a Kennedy-Kennedy ticket. As for the column, O'Donnell insisted to Jenkins: "Ted Lewis is just trying to jazz you." And "jazzed" Jenkins was, as were many other persons associated with the Vice President—and to a certain extent as Lyndon Johnson was himself. He did not consider the incident funny. Nor did President Kennedy. He advised his relatives to make jokes on subjects other than the makeup of the 1964 ticket.

Johnson and his aides had become concerned over such "wackiness" because it had become apparent during 1962 that Robert Kennedy, and not Lyndon Johnson, was the number two man in the Kennedy Administration. This was so not only because John and Robert Kennedy were brothers, although that certainly had initiated it. It was due more to the curious political relationship between the two men.

Of all the prominent members of the Kennedy administration, the cabinet level appointees and the Vice President, Robert Kennedy was the only one not restricted in his loyalty to the President by his past political associations. He represented no political power such as the Americans for Democratic Action or organized labor on the left or the conservative South on the right. Instead, his past was tied intimately to the President's. Nor did he become a prisoner of the bureaucracy of the Justice Department as other members of the New Frontier became caught up in their own departments. Other department heads developed their own points of view, influenced by their own departmental experts and bureaucratic interests, guided at times by the members of Congress with whom they dealt, limited often by the restrictions of the past. In contrast, Robert Kennedy intended and succeeded in making the Justice Department a tool for carrying out the policies of the Kennedy administration solely. Other cabinet members, like Abraham Ribicoff, the Secretary of Health, Education and Welfare, quite naturally had their own political ambitions which, consciously or unconsciously, influenced their actions as members of the Kennedy administration. Robert Kennedy, however, had no such personal ambitions. Any political future he might have would be held in abeyance until after his brother's administration had ended.

Robert Kennedy came to the administration with no personal political strength and little or no thought of competing with his older brother to gain any. While other officials might be the South's man or the ADA's man, the Wall Street man or the West's man, Robert Kennedy was only the President's man. There were no restrictions on his service, no bounds to his toughness when toughness was required, no end to his sacrifice when sacrifice was needed. That was why John Kennedy had wanted him in the administration and that was why Robert Kennedy earned his darkest reputation in the Kennedy years. He was finger man, hatchet man, "no" man, man-to-see, man-to-curse. Lyndon Johnson had learned this the previous year when he realized he had to discuss his patronage problems with Robert Kennedy; he learned this again in 1962, only more bluntly. Washington and the rest of the nation became well aware of Robert Kennedy's position in 1962. Because Robert Kennedy took on these responsibilities, he took the brunt of much of the opposition to the Kennedy administration throughout the country. "Bobby," so the saying went, "is the ruthless one."

If Robert Kennedy was the ruthless one, Lyndon Johnson was the forgotten one.

Partly this was the nature of the Vice Presidency. As John Kennedy had shown in the Bay of Pigs affair the previous year, his inclination in times of crises was to seek out the technical advice of experts, persons who could speak knowingly because they represented a constituency. Lyndon Johnson usually had no constituency. He did not have the lawyers, the federal marshals, the ability to bring and to threaten court suits that the Attorney General has. He did not have the thousands of diplomats scattered around the world to pick up any scrap of information, interpret it, and report it to him, and then carry out his orders as does the Secretary of State. He did not have the 2.5 million men in uniform—including national guardsmen in Mississippi—the missiles lined up, the submarines at sea which would permit him to advise the President on possible military alternatives as the Secretary of Defense has. Johnson could not speak of foreign reaction to a possible United States move as well as can the Ambassador to the United Nations, who has daily contact with officials of dozens of foreign countries.

Lyndon Johnson's only constituency was his experience on Capitol Hill and his friendships among southern politicians. The Texan had first come to Washington in 1931, after a brief career as a school teacher, to be secretary to Representative Richard M. Kleberg, a member of the wealthy family that controlled the King ranch in southern Texas. For the next four years Johnson ran the Kleberg office in Washington, learning who on Capitol Hill held the power to help or hurt a member of Congress and also how one ingratiates himself with these people. In 1935 Johnson returned to Texas to head the National Youth Administration, a New Deal agency, there. Two years later he came back to Washington, the winner of a special election to fill a vacancy caused by the death of the incumbent representative of the Austin district. Johnson beat nine other candidates in that election to become Congressman Johnson. In 1941 he made an unsuccessful attempt to move from the House to the Senate: the only election he ever lost. He tried again in 1948, won this time by only 87 votes out of 900,000 cast to earn the dubious accolade of "Landslide Lyndon." In 1953 the southerners who controlled the Democratic Party machinery in the Senate made him party leader there. When the Democrats became the majority party in 1955, Lyndon Johnson then became Senate majority leader.

This experience, if valuable, was not unique. John Kennedy himself had fourteen years' experience in Washington. Robert Kennedy had a decade's. Larry O'Brien and Kenny O'Donnell also had Capitol Hill backgrounds. As for Johnson's friendship with southern politicians, he had learned early in 1961 at the caucus of Democratic senators that some of the relationships he thought were friendships were not quite that way. He was unwilling to test others. This relationship between Lyndon Johnson and the South, whether it was a genuine friendship or something else, was the Texan's basic political strength. To risk it in 1962 would mean perhaps losing it in 1964 or 1968 when he would need the South as a basis for political dealing. John Kennedy understood this and accepted it.

This situation—the growing importance of Robert Kennedy and the dwindling importance of Lyndon Johnson—was heightened during 1962. In the Kennedy administration this was the year of crisis. This year was the crucible of the New Frontier. Those who were the intimates of the President as he faced the challenges of that year would be drawn together by bonds of experience, ties that would pull them into a tight circle. Those who were not intimates of the President would be closed out of that tight circle.

There were three crises that year: one a challenge to the Presidency, one a challenge to the federal union, and one a challenge to the continued existence of man. Lyndon Johnson did not play a significant role in any of the three.

The first challenge came in April when the United States Steel corporation raised its prices six dollars a ton. Because steel is such a basic industry, the price increase would have been reflected in the price of every product that used steel and would have raised prices throughout the economy. This meant inflation. Kennedy had tried to prevent that. Inflation would have priced American products out of world markets and would have brought greater unemployment and less economic growth. For almost a year, working with Secretary of Labor Arthur J. Goldberg, Kennedy had used his power, influence and prestige to prevent that from happening. Because of these Presidential efforts, the steel workers' union had accepted a contract with only modest gains. The contract was widely hailed as noninflationary and as one not requiring an increase in the price of steel. The next week the price of steel was increased.

When Roger Blough, President of United States Steel, informed John Kennedy of the price increase late on Tuesday afternoon, a seventy-two-hour period of crisis began in the White House. It ended only when the price increase was rescinded on Friday afternoon. During those three days, Lyndon Johnson had his nose pressed against the glass. He was an outsider looking in.

He first spoke to John Kennedy about the situation, to offer his support for whatever action Kennedy wanted to take, late Tuesday evening when he happened to meet the President at the White House congressional reception. This was several hours after the President had begun the actions that were to become his counterattack. Again Kennedy relied on Goldberg as he had when the contract between the industry and the union was being drawn up. Goldberg had a constituency. In addition to being Secretary of Labor, he also had broad experience with the industry because he had been counsel to the steel workers' union before joining the cabinet. Kennedy called in Walter W. Heller, the chairman of the President's Council of Economic Advisers. He also had a constituency. He could provide the statistical and economic material to buttress an attack on the industry. The speech writers and the personal aides, like Ted Sorensen and Kenny O'Donnell, were called in to offer technical help. And then there were others like Charles Bartlett, a newspaper columnist, and Clark Clifford, a corporation lawyer. Both men had personal contacts inside the steel industry and could keep open lines of communication between the two governments, that of the country and that of the steel industry, in case a chance for peace came. Obscure administration officials were called in to help because of their friendship with officials of steel companies. Senator Estes Kefauver of Tennessee was telephoned; he promised that the Senate Antitrust Subcommittee he headed would launch an investigation. Defense Secretary McNamara was called; the Pentagon was one of the largest purchasers of steel and McNamara immediately began considering how to shift the Pentagon's purchase orders to companies that did not raise prices. Robert Kennedy was called. Because his constituency was the Justice Department, he was particularly valuable. His department would talk in terms of a grand jury investigation. There could be talk of breaking up United States Steel on the basis that it was so large it violated anti-monopoly laws. Lyndon Johnson had no such constituency.

Most of these people had already been called when the President and Lyndon Johnson briefly discussed the steel price increase together at the congressional reception Tuesday night. The next morning at a White House breakfast, the steel price increase dominated the discussion. This was the regular breakfast meeting of top administration personnel that Kennedy always held the morning of his news conferences. Johnson attended such meetings and was present at that one. But he had little to do with the discussion on steel. His status there was much like that of Secretary of State Dean Rusk, who also attended that particular breakfast meeting as he regularly did the discussions on news conference days, but took no part in the fight against the steel industry because his constituency was not involved. Various assignments were given to administration personnel at that meeting, but Johnson was given none. From that point on, he was effectively out of the fight with Big Steel. He did not attend the small gatherings at the White House Thursday and Friday mornings at which the administration's course was reviewed and plotted.

Two years later Johnson encouraged the view that—if it had been him—he would have effected a price rescission as did Kennedy, but he would have done it in a more conciliatory manner, behind the scenes so as to prevent the head-on clash between the Presidency and the business community. Perhaps such an approach could have succeeded in rolling back the price increase, but it would have done nothing about restoring the position of the Presidency. This had concerned Kennedy during those seventy-two hours as much as the price increase, this feeling that the Presidency itself was under attack. Kennedy believed the steel industry had used his office to gain an attractive contract, then had double-crossed the Presidency by not fulfilling its share of the bargain to keep a lid on prices. It did not help the Presidency to have one segment of the American economy use it, then insult it. If the President was to have any power in the future to deal with either industry or labor, it could not permit that affront to stand. It was this point that Johnson missed when he later spoke of using a more conciliatory approach. Perhaps only those very close to President Kennedy, such as his brother Robert, Arthur Goldberg and Ted Sorensen, could appreciate it.

In the second great crisis of 1962 officials of the state of Mississippi challenged the orders of a federal court and jeopardized the integrity of the federal system. Of all the crises in the Kennedy administration, this is the one—and those similar events related to it but of less significance—in which Lyndon Johnson could have used the power of his own constituency to aid the administration. He did not.

The crisis came at the end of September and involved the attempts of James H. Meredith, an Air Force veteran and a Negro, to enter the University of Mississippi—"Ole Miss"—a "white only" college. Federal court orders demanded that he be admitted; state officials refused to comply. Which was paramount in the United States: state or federal jurisdiction? As Attorney General of the United States, Robert Kennedy was charged with seeing that the federal court orders, including those having to do with the admission of James Meredith to Ole Miss, were carried out. There was no question but that Robert Kennedy's constituency, the Justice Department, required that he be an intimate participant in this crisis.

But Lyndon Johnson also had a constituency involved in this crisis: the South. More than anyone else, he was the "southerner" in the administration. The balanced political ticket, whether it is balanced by geography, race or religion, is one of the more criticized aspects of American life. To place someone on a political ticket because of his religious, racial or geographic appeal, it is argued, is discrimination in reverse. Although that may be true, there is another, a more positive side. As the Negro revolution reached its violent climax in the early 1960s, the problem was to prevent the estrangement of the South from the rest of the nation. Could the South have representation in the highest councils of the federal government? And could the federal government have an emissary to the South? This is the value of the balanced political ticket, to provide a conduit between government and the minority groups (as the South was then on the question of segregated schools). It had worked in the past with the Irish in Massachusetts and with the Jews in New York City. In those two cases there was a dialogue between the minority groups and the government. Such a dialogue was needed between the federal government and the South in the early 1960s.

To John and Robert Kennedy it always was obvious that in any test between the federal and state governments, the federal would win—and that it must win. With that understanding in mind and to avoid violence, the Kennedys were willing to accommodate the southern segregationists as much as they could. If a southern governor, such as Mississippi's Ross Barnett—and Alabama's George Wallace the next year—vowed to block desegregation of his state's schools, the federal government made an agreement with him in private conversations to appear to overwhelm him. Marshals would be used if necessary, so the governor could then tell his people he never willingly gave in to the federal government. The essence of this kind of deal was that the federal court order be carried out.

In the last week of September, as the deadline for Meredith's enrollment at Ole Miss came closer and closer and as the passions of the local segregationists became stronger, the Kennedys tried desperately to arrange such an understanding with Ross Barnett. Robert Kennedy telephoned Barnett and explained the procedure he would use in the registering of Meredith. He tried to sound as convinced as he was that the registration would take place. Burke Marshall, head of the Justice Department's civil rights section, called a Mississippian he knew. This was Tom Watkins, an aide to Barnett. The Justice Department was canvased for lawyers from the South or for attorneys who might have contacts in the South. They were asked to call their friends there to stress that Meredith would attend school that semester and to ask them to use whatever influence they might have to permit Meredith's entry to Ole Miss to come about peacefully.

At times Barnett accepted that Meredith would enter Ole Miss. At other times he did not. There were "deals" made. He would back down if a United States marshal drew his pistol from his holster; there was an argument over how many marshals should draw their guns, whether the guns should be loaded, whether the marshals drawing their guns would push the local segregationists to violence. But in some telephone conversations with Robert Kennedy and other federal authorities, Barnett seemed less inclined to go along with any deal. The truth seemed to be that Barnett, an amiable and kindly man basically, was not capable of coping with power and not capable of coping with the monster of opposition created to counter the possibility of a Negro entering Ole Miss. Barnett vacillated. When the cool logic of the Kennedys came to him over the telephone, he was ready to bargain. When the cheers of the segregationist crowd reached him, however, he became obdurate.

Lyndon Johnson made no contribution to the resolving of this crisis. There were no calls from his Capitol Hill office to his southern friends from his Senate days. There was no attempt by Johnson to work through the informal political structure of the South. He did not approach the "Courthouse Crowd" that he had utilized so well in the 1960 election. When the showdown came the weekend of September 29 and 30, it had been well anticipated. One Kennedy aide was called from a hospital bed to be at the White House for the crucial hours leading up to the climax. Lyndon Johnson, however, was not called. He was not even in Washington. Instead, he was at his Texas ranch, entertaining a group of newsmen who represented Texas newspapers in Washington.

That Sunday night, September 30, the men closest to President Kennedy tightened around him. There was the Attorney General and his aide, Burke Marshall. There were the old standbys, Kenny O'Donnell, Larry O'Brien and Ted Sorensen. In the previous thirty-six hours, the President personally had tried direct appeals to Governor Barnett. He also had tried opening up a circuitous route: the calling of southern Congressmen—Lyndon Johnson's old friends—in hopes they might convey his determined message to the power structure in Mississippi. The Presidential pressures appeared to climax with a nationwide appeal over television. But that "climax" was overshadowed several hours later with the dispatch of federal troops. Dawn came before any of those at the White House finally went to bed.

With everything John Kennedy tried to avert disaster at Ole Miss, he could not succeed. "The South," said one of the men who was associated with Kennedy that weekend, "hated Jack Kennedy." This hatred was evident to newsmen who traveled through the states of the Old Confederacy in those years. The segregationists spoke of "the Kennedys" with a vehemence only surpassed by the tone of their voices as they singled out "Bobby," whom they hated even more as an individual. The Kennedys were called "hoodlums" and "racketeers" and many worse names. Robert Kennedy was a "gestapo-type." The segregationists holding responsible positions—the governors like Barnett of Mississippi and Wallace of Alabama and the senators like James Eastland of Mississippi and William Fulbright of Arkansas—did not utter such phrases themselves. But their more "respectable" talk of defiance when a crisis was developing and, even worse, their silence when a crisis came, encouraged such passion and helped make the ensuing violence acceptable in the South.

Because of this the Kennedys could carry on no meaningful dialogue with the southern segregationists on civil rights. As the legend by which the dual society of the South had flourished was coming to an end, the vocal and violent minority that still believed in it was withdrawing into itself, becoming insular. It had difficulty responding to men with Boston accents who were Catholics and sophisticated urbanites as well. And the Kennedys, for their part, had difficulty understanding the South. John and Robert Kennedy were logical men. Because they appreciated the part that politics plays in public life, they were willing to accommodate the southern segregationists with such things as a show of force by federal marshals—to get people like Barnett and Wallace off the political hook with their constituents—but they were never willing to sacrifice the law. As the last minutes of the Ole Miss crisis ticked by and Ross Barnett begged Robert Kennedy to postpone the showdown, Kennedy refused.

Lyndon Johnson did understand these people of the South. Although he had never sympathized with the violent segregationist, Johnson had at times in his earlier public career played on this emotion. Later, he had battled with it, reasoned with it, bargained with it, and on occasions triumphed over it. He could talk to the people in power below the Mason-Dixon line. Whether this would have had any impact belongs in the category of "what might have been" for it did not happen. Perhaps nothing would have calmed the violent feelings of the South in the early 1960s. Outbursts such as happened at Ole Miss may have been necessary to shock men and women back into decency. But perhaps also efforts by the Texan might have persuaded the South's leaders that their encouragement of violence, whether it be done openly or tacitly, was the great wrong they were doing to their home region. Perhaps also in such crises, Johnson might have broken into the storehouse of intelligence and goodwill that the South had locked up tight within its heart.

But because of the absence of Lyndon Johnson in the dialogue between the federal government and the South, it was up to Robert Kennedy to solve the problem. Sitting in the cavernous office of the Attorney General, usually without his suit jacket and with his tie loosened, sometimes, if it was late at night, dressed in a sport shirt, Robert Kennedy met one civil rights crisis after another. His chief weapons were his tightly controlled voice, which revealed the intensity of his feelings, and the understanding that he was backed completely by the President and had the full power of the federal government at his command.

Why did not Lyndon Johnson assist in these crises?

In such a brutal confrontation between the federal government and the states of the South as happened at Ole Miss, any southerner who even appeared less than completely devoted to the state's cause faced loss of political power. That lesson had been taught southern politicians five years earlier. When President Eisenhower sent troops to Little Rock, Arkansas, in 1957 because of resistance there to school desegregation ordered by a federal court, Representative Brooks Hays made the political mistake of trying to open a dialogue between the President and Arkansas Governor Orval Faubus. A religious man who called himself a "moderate" on racial issues, Hays preached that society should end legal segregation and then that the races should segregate voluntarily. He had represented Little Rock in Congress for sixteen years but was defeated in 1958 by a write-in campaign for a more militant segregationist because of that "mistake." Lyndon Johnson as Vice President could make speeches in favor of civil rights, he could take action in areas where passions had not yet burst into the open, but when the last battle came, he could not become involved in the federal government's efforts. To do so would mean the risk of losing the support of his constituency, the power base that would oblige John Kennedy to tap him again in 1964.

If asked by Kennedy for help, Johnson certainly would have responded. To have refused a Presidential request would have meant being branded as disloyal and that was the one thing Johnson could not risk even at the danger of alienating the South. (One member of the Irish Mafia doubted this, saying later that if President Kennedy had asked Lyndon Johnson for help in events such as Ole Miss, Johnson would have snapped: "What's the matter? You trying to put me on the spot?" But that was a minority opinion.) But Kennedy did not ask for Johnson's assistance in such matters. "Kennedy," said one of his aides who was involved in these civil rights events, "doubted that LBJ could do any more than was being done. Kennedy also believed that as President he was going to get the blame anyhow, so why get LBJ into trouble?" There was also a political plus for Kennedy in keeping Johnson out of the fracas. Kennedy himself could not avoid the hatred of the South, but perhaps Johnson could. This might give Johnson the opportunity to woo and win some of the South in 1964 from the bottom half of the ticket as he was credited with doing in 1960.

That Johnson was at his Texas ranch the weekend of the Ole Miss crisis did not go unnoticed in Washington. One columnist who was read primarily in the North wrote an article about Johnson's lack of involvement. A few days later, the columnist received a telephone call from the Vice President personally. For thirty minutes Johnson argued that he had indeed been intimately involved in the weekend's events. He conceded having been at his ranch with the newsmen in Texas but said he had been in telephone communication with the Presidential office; even when he was out boating for an hour on a nearby lake, Johnson insisted he had a ship-to-shore telephone near his hand.

A similar incident happened the next year, in May of 1963. For some weeks Birmingham, Alabama, had been the scene of growing racial violence. On the night of Saturday, May 11, there were bombings and riots in the Negro part of the city. The next afternoon, Sunday, President Kennedy returned early to the White House from his weekend retreat in the country and called in a few close aides, including his brother Robert. Shortly after, three thousand federal troops were sent to bases near Birmingham, in case they were needed in the city. That afternoon, when the President was making these decisions, Lyndon Johnson was at a cocktail party at the Washington home of Representative Hale Boggs of Louisiana. It was apparent to those at the party that Johnson was not in touch with the White House at all that afternoon. Again, when this was reported by columnists later, Johnson disputed the allegation that he had been left out of the White House proceedings.

Johnson was in a delicate position politically. He could turn only one way, but he wanted to look in two directions. He wanted to look to the South, from which he had drawn his political strength since first being elected a Congressman a quarter of a century earlier. If he did not share all of that region's emotions and prejudices, he did understand its hopes for a greater economic growth and its power to influence the makeup of the national Democratic ticket. Because part of his ambition for the Presidency was to help fulfill some of the South's hopes for a richer life, he was reluctant to challenge its power when the federal and regional interests conflicted brutally. He wanted to remain part of the South to help it as well as draw strength from it. At the same time, Johnson looked to the liberal Northeast. Any political strength he might draw from the South could force the liberal Northeast to consider him, but it would be the powers in that area that would make the final decision about his future. He did not want these powers to believe him an insignificant member of the Kennedy administration. Such a belief would make it easier to pass over Lyndon Johnson when the 1968 Democratic nominee was being decided. He never was able to resolve this conflict as Vice President.

When the third crisis of 1962 confronted the Kennedy administration, Lyndon Johnson was brought into the White House deliberations. This crisis involved the presence of offensive Russian nuclear missiles on the island of Cuba and the possibility that their presence could lead to a nuclear exchange between the United States and the Soviet Union. Lyndon Johnson was a part of the deliberations because he was next-in-line to the Presidency in the constitutional line of succession, an important consideration at a time when the chances of a nuclear war were in President Kennedy's opinion between one and three and even.

The crisis spanned thirteen days, beginning the morning of Tuesday, October 16, when McGeorge Bundy, the White House adviser on foreign affairs, came to the President's bedroom with the aerial photographs that demonstrated conclusively the presence of the missile sites. The President immediately ordered the gathering of the small group that was to be called the Executive Committee of the National Security

Council—nicknamed "Excom." Lyndon Johnson was among this group.

During the first two days this group was in session, that Tuesday and Wednesday, it was concerned more with assessing the threat created by the missiles and determining motives than with seeking solutions. There were, however, wide ranging discussions as the sessions were held in the State Department building, the Pentagon and back in the cabinet room at the White House again. The extent of the Vice President's contribution is in question. "Obviously," said a participant in the Excom sessions, "President Kennedy dominated the discussions. And other people there had constituencies—McNamara, the Defense Department; Rusk, the State Department; McCone, CIA; and the like. But Johnson was there and did voice his opinions." However, another participant said: "I attended two of those Excom meetings when Johnson was there, and, to tell you the truth, I can't even remember what he said, or if he spoke at all."

In the rambling discussions of those two days, Johnson did speak and his comments indicated he leaned toward some form of military action initially as opposed to a diplomatic move first. A good many participants in the sessions that Tuesday and Wednesday leaned the same way. Actually in those talks it was difficult to pin down the views of any of the participants because opinions and comments shifted back and forth from viewpoint to viewpoint. Late Wednesday, Johnson left Washington for a previously scheduled campaign trip to the West, in connection with the next month's congressional elections. To have canceled that trip would have aroused too much suspicion and destroyed the hope of surprising the Russians when the United States unveiled its retaliatory action, whatever it would be. President Kennedy also had campaign trips scheduled and also kept them, but his were not as far from Washington and he returned to the White House at night.

It was during the next few days—when Johnson was away —that the Excom group evolved the plan of beginning the American counteraction with a limited blockade as opposed to an air strike, which had been advocated as the major possible military action. It was during these days that Robert Kennedy emerged as, next to the President, the leader of the administration. He did it simply by stepping into a vacuum. The President had to be away from Washington campaigning. The other members of the Excom group were squabbling among themselves, unable to agree on a recommendation. Tempers shortened. Words grew louder. Robert Kennedy took command. Perhaps anyone else could have done it—Richard Nixon had exercised similar authority on occasions in the previous administration—but only Robert Kennedy did it. He had asserted forceful leadership before in the steel crisis and the Ole Miss crisis, where he had a constituency, the Justice Department, that was intimately involved. But he had no such constituency in the Cuba missile crisis; the Justice Department's responsibility is internal, not external. But he had something that no one else seemed capable of in those crucial days: the ability to assume leadership.

That weekend, as President Kennedy was preparing to go on national television to announce the presence of the missiles to the nation and to outline the plan for a counterattack, Johnson was called back from his campaign tour and again joined the Excom group. During the remainder of that week, the Vice President was an intimate member of the small group that watched and waited at the White House. If he did not play a commanding role, he took orders willingly; he was "watch officer" for the Excom group one night. Perhaps of the group involved, he was one of those who considered war most possible. Still, even as he discussed the prospect in the early morning hours with a small group of aides, he remained composed.

When the Cuban crisis had passed, the inevitable reporting

jobs began. *The New York Times* ran more than five thousand words on the two-week period when peace had seemed so tenuous. Johnson's name was mentioned twice—as among those present. Two reporters did a lengthy article for *The Saturday Evening Post* on the confrontation. Since one of the two writers was Charles Bartlett, the President's close friend, and the other was Stewart Alsop, known to have extremely high sources of information, the opinion in Washington was that the *Post* article represented the administration's viewpoint. The article suggested Adlai Stevenson was an "appeaser" and produced a period of embarrassment, confusion and political tension. During the uproar over Stevenson, however, few noticed that Bartlett and Alsop had not mentioned Vice President Johnson's name at all. The Texan was the only one of the government's officials who made up the Excom group who was not listed.

They had not mentioned his name because Johnson had not been a participant of importance in the confrontation. Their omission was not noted because Lyndon Johnson had ceased to be considered a person of importance in Washington. He had been out of two crises, almost out of the third. By the standards then prevalent in Washington he belonged in the category—as *The Times* had put him—of "among those present."

TWO

AFTER the 1960 election, John Kennedy had made his first visit to the LBJ ranch in Texas. There, the two men discussed for the first time Johnson's role as Vice President in the upcoming administration. The talks were inconclusive, but the President-elect did promise that the Texan would head the Space Council, becoming in effect the White House's chief adviser on space. The appointment was a natural one. Johnson's expertise in space matters went back many years. After the Russians had launched Sputnik I, the first man-made satellite, in October 1957, Republicans had termed the feat "a basketball," but Lyndon Johnson had said: "The real meaning of the satellite is that we can no longer consider the Soviet Union to be a nation years behind us in scientific research and industrial ability." Also he said: "Control of space means control of the world, far more certainly, far more totally, than any control that has ever or could ever be achieved by weapons or by troops of occupation."

Largely through Johnson's efforts the Space Act of 1958 had been written. As chairman of the Senate preparedness subcommittee, Johnson was familiar with the military requirements of space. As an intuitive politician, he sensed how the prestige of apparently being "first in space" would help the

Russians in the political process of wooing allies throughout the world; everyone wants to be with the winner. It was also Johnson who cut through the pressures and the in-fighting of the time to produce acceptable legislation. In the late 1950s, the three American military services were squabbling among themselves. The administration was talking about "massive retaliation," which implied quick wars fought with heavy bombers and missiles. To the military man the problem was clear: his service must have a missile in its arsenal or else it would face extinction. Through the mid-1950s the three services had bickered and hassled over control of the missile program as the members of a gang of juvenile delinquents might struggle for possession of the gang's one knife. When the Space Act was being written, each of the three services lobbied extensively for a commanding position in the space program. But the act as written established a new agency, a civilian agency, to develop America's space effort because, the act said, "activities in space should be devoted to peaceful purposes for the benefit of all mankind." This not only cut out the bickering military services but it also was valuable for propaganda purposes abroad.

This talk of "peaceful" purposes of space exploration was not all for show, but a good bit of it was. Congressional leaders realized Congress never would have bought the program except for its military implications. Although these implications were not discussed extensively, the members understood that the civilian space agency could develop a capacity to send a man into space for peaceful purposes but that the military could use that capacity for other reasons. The bridge between the two, the "peaceful" National Aeronautics and Space Agency and the military services, was the Space Council. Under the 1958 act, the President was this council's chairman. President Eisenhower, however, was never much interested in it, did not convene it and did not fulfill his role as chairman.

At one time he even asked for the Council's dissolution. "Let Lyndon have space," Eisenhower once reportedly cracked, "I want my feet on the ground."

In addition to the military and propaganda value of being first in space, Lyndon Johnson had another reason for promoting the space program. Unlike other industries which must locate near certain natural resources or by railroads, within large cities or among large pools of manpower, a space facility can be located almost anywhere. One pulls the scientists, the technicians, the engineers from all over the United States, places them in an installation and lets them begin work. The only "resource" involved is the intelligence of the men who are working.

The space industry—and that is what the space effort would become under the 1958 act, a multibillion-dollar industry—could be centered then in the backward parts of the United States and open them to an economic, cultural as well as political revitalization. This meant the South particularly. The building of a space installation is not just the erection of buildings. It is the building of roads to the site, roads that make it easier for farmers to travel also. It is the spending of enormous sums of money in the local area to purchase food and supplies for the government personnel. The people brought into the installation are not just scientists and administrators, they also are persons with college educations, persons who are not tied by the prejudices of the past nor committed to the politics of another era. The space program could land a man on the moon; it could also open up and transform the American South.

The $60-million space-flight center near Rice Institute in Houston, Texas, was to Johnson the beginning of that city's becoming a scientific community. He saw it catering to the small but wealthy scientific industries such as those drawn to the Boston area by the presence there of the Massachusetts

Institute of Technology and Harvard. As Vice President, Johnson was accused of using political pull to have the center located in his home state. He vigorously denied the charge, saying he had divorced himself from the site selection so he could not be accused of being "the Vice President of Texas rather than the Vice President of the United States." The site selected was adjacent to the congressional district of Representative Albert Thomas, the chairman of the House appropriations subcommittee that has jurisdiction over funds for the space agency. Thomas's congressional district would derive enormous economic benefits from the space center.

The building of an installation by a federal agency where it will benefit the district of the congressman who has financial power over that agency is not an unusual Washington practice. When such comments were made in reference to the space center at Houston, Lyndon Johnson angrily snapped that the insinuations were "a disservice to the nation."

It was because of this background of interest in space on Lyndon Johnson's part that Kennedy, when still President-elect, announced he would ask Congress to rewrite the Space Act to make the Vice President, rather than the President, chairman of the Space Council. This announcement was public notice of Johnson's responsibilities in the American space effort; everyone seemed to hear it—except John Kennedy himself. The administration's first task to promote the space effort was to pick an administrator for the National Aeronautics and Space Agency. Kennedy did not turn to Johnson for a recommendation initially but to Jerome B. Wiesner. A brilliant scientist, Wiesner later became Kennedy's science adviser. Before the inaugural, he headed a task force for Kennedy studying the space program. This task force report was largely critical of the space effort and intimated the United States was too concerned with "stunts" like placing a man in space when placing technical equipment would be just as valuable. Wiesner wanted the space agency headed by a scientist-administrator who would keep the program from straying outside of scientific limits. At least nine persons, perhaps a dozen, who fitted the Wiesner description were approached and offered the job of being the boss of the American space agency in the Kennedy administration. They turned it down flatly. There was a question in their minds whether they could keep the agency from being taken over by the military, or by Johnson, or from being pushed into the obscurity that dozens of Washington agencies know. Some simply did not want to take on the job of bullying money out of Congress, which at best was lukewarm to the man-in-space program.

Then Lyndon Johnson stepped in.

The problem, as he understood it, was not scientists. Scientists can be hired. The real job was to sell an invigorated space program to Congress. To Johnson, this meant the space agency administrator should be a man who knew the ins and outs of Capitol Hill, one who could talk to the members of Congress in language they knew, one who had respect on Capitol Hill. So Johnson went to the place where a man best fitting that description could be found; he went to Capitol Hill. There he talked to his old friend Bob Kerr. The late Senator Robert Kerr of Oklahoma had succeeded Johnson as chairman of the Senate Space Committee. Did Kerr have a man to head the space agency? It just so happened that he did: James E. Webb. Webb was an associate of Kerr's in the senator's gas and oil interests. Webb was not a scientist, but he was an experienced government official. He had headed the Budget Bureau under President Truman and had also worked at the State Department. Considered a brilliant administrator, he could also work effectively and understandingly with the members of Congress because of his past association with Bob Kerr.

On January 25, 1961, five days after Kennedy had been inaugurated, Webb's name was rising fast among the possibilities to head the space agency, but a final decision had not yet been made. Another name suggested frequently was that of James M. Gavin, a retired military man. "I'm hopeful that before the week is out we will have a director of NASA," said Kennedy publicly, hoping to force the various factions pushing different names to settle their differences. Webb finally won when Wiesner, rather than see a man with a military background take over the space agency, gave his support to Webb.*

Webb was called to the President's oval office and, in the presence of Johnson, offered the job. He would accept it, Webb said, on the condition that he was going to be the agency's actual boss rather than a stand-in for Johnson, who would be heading the Space Council. Webb had been around Washington enough to know that it is best to establish one's authority at the very beginning. You'll be the boss, Kennedy assured him. The selection of Webb was announced January 30. Kennedy kept his word; Webb was the boss of the space agency. Two years later, when Webb decided to close down the Mercury space-flight program, the astronauts told President Kennedy they believed another Mercury flight was needed. Kennedy called Webb to ask him about it. Webb said he understood the astronauts' position but that he had decided against another flight. Kennedy said: You know who's going to make this decision, don't you? Webb replied: I hope I do. Kennedy laughed then and told Webb to proceed as he thought best. The Mercury series was not continued.

The Space Council headed by Johnson included Webb, Defense Secretary McNamara, Secretary of State Rusk and Glenn T. Seaborg, chairman of the Atomic Energy Commission. Its purpose was to keep a dialogue going between the people responsible for the military, peaceful and diplomatic uses of space. Each member would know, theoretically, what

---

* Gavin became Ambassador to France.

the other was doing, what the other's needs were and what he could offer. If there was a dispute between any of the Council members and between their agencies, Lyndon Johnson was to umpire that dispute. Although he had great respect for Mc-Namara, Johnson relied more on Webb for advice on the space programs. Johnson understood constituencies too well to trust McNamara completely in matters of space. "We'll listen to what the generals have to say," Johnson commented privately in 1961, "but the generals aren't going to run space."

After finding an administrator to head the agency, President Kennedy then had to decide whether to speed up America's race for the moon. The schedule established by the Eisenhower administration had called for the landing of an American on the moon after 1970. During the campaign Richard Nixon had said this meant 1971, but the size of the funds allotted to the project by Eisenhower indicated it would be well beyond that year. Kennedy had countered in the campaign with the prospect of landing an American on the moon before 1970. After coming to power, however, making the decision was different than making a campaign speech. Estimates of the cost of placing a man on the moon in the 1960s varied between $20 billion and $40 billion. Kennedy already was stuck with a budget dangerously out of balance. And many prominent scientists and influential Democrats were arguing that $20 billion could be spent for much better purposes on the ground than on reaching the moon.

But it was an easy decision in other respects; the choice in favor of speeding up the moon race may have been inevitable. The moon as well as the other outposts in space had become the military "high ground" of the future. Control of these outposts by one nation meant control of earth. The nation that first placed a space station in orbit around the earth, ready to fire a nuclear missile at any enemy, had military control of the world. That, at least, had been a Democratic claim in the late 1950s when President Eisenhower lacked enthusiasm for space; it would be difficult for the Democrats to switch their position now that they were in office. Also, although specific scientific and monetary gains could not be pinpointed at the time, those involved in the program believed that the race to the moon would pay off in new discoveries, new metals, new perspectives. And the final reason was once expressed by John Kennedy as he walked with an official of the space agency from the White House to the official's car. We can compete with Russia in three ways, the official remembers Kennedy saying. One is by nuclear war. But no one benefits from that. Another is an economic race and we're trying to do that. And the third is in the race for the moon. We can win that, Kennedy concluded. These reasons built up a momentum that carried the decision-making process to a point where only one conclusion seemed possible.

Johnson was among those urging that the United States accelerate its moon exploration. Whatever else you do, he once advised the President, you'll be remembered as the man who put an American on the moon. For the first two months of the New Frontier, Kennedy was willing only to ask for small amounts of additional funds for existing programs. In April 1961, however, the Russians sent the first man into orbit. In a brief, five-paragraph memorandum to the Vice President, Kennedy asked: Can we beat the Russians to the moon? Johnson answered: yes.

But Kennedy did not decide in the affirmative until after McNamara and Webb produced a long memo estimating costs for the project. After studying that, Kennedy then asked Congress for "a firm commitment" to back him as he said "I believe we should go to the moon." Johnson's role in the making of the decision had been minimal. It happened that in endorsing the speedup of the moon race, Johnson had backed a winner; but he was part of a consensus in the New Frontier to do it, not the driving force. Actually, when the decision was made by Kennedy to try for a moon landing by an American in the 1960s, Johnson was not even in Washington. He was on his trip to southeast Asia. Congress sensed that Johnson's role in the space effort was not a significant one. The Vice President had hoped for a one-million-dollar budget for his Space Council. This would have been purely for administrative expenses; the Council did no construction or contract awarding of any kind. The bigger the budget, the greater the empire Johnson could build; Congress cut the Vice President back to a half million dollars for the Council. Bitter and hurt, there was nothing Johnson could do.

As head of the Space Council, Johnson appeared to take his duties seriously, even if his responsibilities were only advisory and minimal. In the fall of 1961 he toured a number of space installations trying to seek out problems and to boost morale. At Ames Research Center in California, Johnson said, "In Washington, it is all too easy a matter to conclude that the work is being done in the nation's capital. Actually . . . we know that a major share of it is being done right here by the dedicated scientists, technicians and workers of America." The remarks were appreciated by the workers, who had never before been visited by a government official of such rank. As he finished his visit to each installation, the Vice President made a point of shaking hands and thanking each government employe who had made any contribution to the visit's success. At Brooks Air Force Base in Texas, Johnson was given a demonstration of pressure-suit functions. A man inside the suit showed how it operated. When he had finished, the Vice President grabbed his gloved hand and shook it vigorously. The man, still totally encased in his pressure suit, could not hear a word as the Vice President shouted his appreciation. The man, his face visible through the clear plastic front of his helmet, was astonished at first by the Vice President's intensity, then finally smiled to signify he understood what the Vice President was saying.

Johnson was concerned about the personnel in the space effort and talked of visiting installations frequently to boost morale as he had done at Ames and also of improving the salaries for the government employes involved in the space effort. Most of them were highly trained scientists who could do considerably better financially in private employment. There was an idea during the last months of 1961, in which the Vice President was interested but to which he did not give his approval, of having the space agency establish a "think factory," a private firm that would handle the space effort under contract to the government. The salaries of the "factory's" employes would not be restrained by civil service standards because the employes would not technically be federal employes. The device had been pioneered by the military services. The idea faded after 1961, however, as did Johnson's zeal for the space program. Additional visits to space installations became less frequent. The financial situation of the space agency was not resolved. It was not that Johnson had lost interest, it was simply that the important decision had been made when it was determined in 1961 that the United States would fight to be first on the moon. After that, the problems were administrative—Jim Webb's business.

The Space Council did have other chores. It recommended the development of what became the Communications Satellite Corporation and also urged that the United States build a supersonic transport. Both recommendations, like that of going to the moon, were natural extensions of work done previously in those two areas and of the political realities of the time. The decision to establish the satellite corporation as a mix of public and private ownership was a natural compromise between the advocates of government control and those of complete private control. It was even more natural for an administration that was striving to strike a position between those two forces. The decision to build a supersonic transport—an airliner capable of zooming between the United States and Europe at between two and three times the speed of sound—was also a natural one. To have decided otherwise would have surrendered the future market for such planes to Europe, which had already started building them. To have decided otherwise also would have meant permitting the airplane builders to die a slow death economically as the Pentagon, previously their chief market, turned to missiles.

These decisions actually were technical matters, made by economists and statisticians; Johnson had very little control over them except to stamp his approval on work done at a lower level. Still, Johnson tried to make much of his job as head of the Space Council. He frequently gave speeches on the importance of traveling into outer space and signed magazine articles about the same subject. At the White House breakfast meetings on Presidential news conference days, when John Kennedy reviewed potential questions to develop answers, Lyndon Johnson was as ready with information about space projects as Dean Rusk was with material about foreign affairs. If Johnson could not produce an answer, he rushed to a telephone to call an aide who could.

Johnson's work in space is the only area where he did not find himself up against Robert Kennedy. In foreign or other domestic affairs, the President's younger brother was developing as the "number two" man in Washington, the man who cut through all the bureaucratic structures to find the needed answers. But he stayed out of space matters. Even without this competition, however, Johnson found it difficult to emerge before the public as the leader of America's space effort. The public was fascinated by the daring exploits of the young, handsome astronauts like Alan Shepard and John Glenn. They overshadowed any government official, even if the official had advocated the correct course a few years earlier before it was the popular course.

The Vice President did gain some publicity because of his work in the space effort. These few occasions were important to him because they were almost the only times he received any national attention and he wanted to keep his name before the public. In 1961 when Alan Shepard made his suborbital flight, America's first manned space flight, the Washington center of attention was the President's oval office. One of the more dramatic photographs taken during the countdown for the Shepard flight was in that office with a grim-faced President Kennedy and his wife watching a television set as the last seconds before blast-off went by. Johnson, because he was head of the Space Council, was invited to be in the President's office. There, he shared in the center of attention; part of that dramatic photograph shows Johnson holding a telephone that has an open line to the blast-off point.

In February 1962, Johnson again gained some publicity because of his role in the space effort. This was after the successful orbital flight by John Glenn. Johnson sought permission to ride with the Glenns in the welcoming parades in Washington and New York. President Kennedy considered the proposals appropriate because of Johnson's involvement with the space effort and granted his permission. The Washington parade was on a Monday afternoon. It rained hard that day, but still thousands stood along Pennsylvania Avenue to cheer the nation's newest hero and his attractive wife Annie. The Glenns sat on the top of the rear seat of an open car while the Vice President sat on the seat in front of them. All wore raincoats, but the men did not wear hats although there had been no letup in the rain. The parade took them to the Capitol, where Glenn addressed a joint session of Congress. Following Johnson's advice to keep his speech simple, humble and short, Glenn spoke for only seventeen minutes. He brought the members of Congress roaring to their feet when he said, humbly: "I know. I still get a real-hard-to-define feeling down inside when the flag goes by." Few even had noticed that Johnson had been with Glenn.

Next the Glenns and Johnson went to New York City for the traditional hero's welcome that city enjoys giving. Here the Vice President was noticed but not in the manner he enjoyed. The New York *Herald Tribune* made great sport with its charge that Johnson was hogging the camera while in New York with the Glenns, trying to usurp some of the glory that belonged to the astronaut. The newspaper ran several photographs of the Glenns in which Johnson also appeared. To buttress its charges further, the paper ran a picture of the city's guest book with Johnson's signature over that of the Glenns'. The newspaper attack, however, had the opposite impact of that which had been intended, at least in Washington. The federal government, as large as it is, is like a family. In the New Frontier, the President often was referred to as "Jack" (except, of course, by those who actually knew him and who always referred to him as "The President"). The Attorney General always was "Bobby."* And the Vice President was "Lyndon." Even the next year there would be no talk in Washington of "dumping Johnson" in 1964; it would be, instead, of "dumping Lyndon." But like a family, Washingtonians draw together when one of their own is attacked by outsiders. Most persons who commented on the *Herald Tribune's* attack while having their lunch in a government cafeteria or while sipping a martini at an embassy function accepted as accurate the charge that Johnson was seeking publicity when he went to New York with the Glenns. But in Washington wanting publicity is not a crime; not getting

---

* Except for the President, who would not break the habit, Robert Kennedy's friends called him "Bob" rather than the more informal "Bobby" at his own request.

it, however, is. Also, there was a general awareness of Johnson's contributions to the space effort while a senator and a
general belief that the Vice President did deserve some
laurels. So for a few days at least, Johnson had the sympathy
and good wishes of government officials to a greater extent
than he had perhaps since his return from Berlin.

It would be the last time in 1962 he would ride so high.

THREE

I N January of 1962, the Democratic Party held a victory
dinner at the D.C. Armory in Washington. For one
hundred dollars a plate the party faithful paid tribute to
President Kennedy and helped the party grow rich enough to
elect more Democrats. Many of the "Democrats" who showed
up at the affair would have shown up also if a Republican
administration had been elected. It was that kind of dinner
and they were that kind of party faithful: businessmen with
government contracts, lobbyists trying to make a contact with
an administration official, status seekers, government employes
coerced into buying a ticket; they were more individuals watching out for themselves than they were loyal members of the
Democratic Party.

Among those at the dinner were several hundred Texans
who had come, some of them, because Lyndon Johnson of
Johnson City, Texas, was Vice President. Also they had come
because they had contracts with the federal government or
hoped to, and when an administration official or a Democratic
Party leader approached them to buy a ticket, or preferably
a batch of tickets, prudence dictated they comply. These
Texans had a special treat. As they sat at their dinner table,
unobtrusive men moved among them passing each a note.

The Vice President and Mrs. Johnson, read the notes, would appreciate their coming by "The Elms" the next afternoon for coffee.

Approximately one hundred and fifty Texans came to the Johnson home the next day for coffee. This kind of coffee hour, like the previous evening's hundred-dollar-a-plate dinner, is also part of politics. The Texan would go home and brag about having had his coffee with "Lyndon and Lady Bird" and it would be that much easier to persuade that Texan to give to the party the next time the collector came around.

Johnson took small groups of the Texans around the grounds, explaining that the house had originally been built in the style of a French chateau, that he had anglicized its name and also had the swimming pool installed. The Texans were suitably impressed when Johnson told them the paintings on the walls were by Texans, although few of the guests recognized the paintings or the artists' names. As Johnson talked with the people from his home state, he tried to call each by his first name. The Vice President knew many of the more prominent Texans by sight. He also had an alert staff to point persons out to him. ("You met the tall man with the mustache six months ago in Austin." "Don't be too friendly with that guy; he's for Yarborough.") But with so many persons there it was easy to make a couple of mistakes and several of Johnson's aides winced as the Texan spoke to a short, chubby Texan with thick, wavy black hair and bright eyes peering owllike from behind horn-rimmed glasses. The Vice President insisted on calling his guest "Willie Joe" and that wasn't his name at all.

It was Billie Sol. Billie Sol Estes.

A few months later Texas politicians were trying to forget that name. Except for one point, Billie Sol Estes was the personification of the fast-buck artist, the epitome of the wheeler-dealer society. The one point was that he got caught. That was enough. To raise cash for his varied financial transactions, he gave mortgages on nonexistent fertilizer tanks and then sold the mortgages at a discount. If he had managed to go undetected a few months longer, his various deals would have paid off, he could have bought back the fraudulent mortgages and perhaps would have been honored by the Junior Chamber of Commerce as one of America's more outstanding young men. But an alert newspaper reporter noticed there were no tanks to be mortgaged. In the very short time it takes to hand a typed story to the printer, have it transformed to part of a front page and then have the newspaper distributed to the public, Billie Sol Estes fell from being the Texas version of the all-American hero to the all-American heel.

Nothing so excites Washington as the smell of scandal. Reporters see Pulitzer Prizes and dig into the political mudflats as deeply as they can. The "out" party sees victory at the polls and talks up the "scandal" as much as possible. Innuendo replaces political debate. Because nobody understood the Estes case, it was perfect for such activity. Charges were hurled back and forth; few could judge their validity because the Estes case itself was so murky. Republicans said the whole trouble was with Secretary of Agriculture Freeman. After all, he had appointed Billie Sol Estes to the National Cotton Advisory Commission, even at a time when Estes had been under investigation. The Democrats charged it was all the Republicans' fault. After all, they said, Estes entered the grain storage business under the Eisenhower administration and was able to succeed only because of the policies of that administration. The specific transaction that tripped Estes, the selling of mortgages on nonexistent fertilizer tanks, was completely incomprehensible. The moral dishonesty of the small farmers who had signed Estes's mortgages, lending their names to obviously shady deals in hopes of making a fast buck, was shocking. Even more shocking, however, was the stupidity of the large corporations that bought up the mortgages and paid out millions of dollars to Billie Sol Estes—for nothing.

Everyone, it seemed, wanted to investigate Billie Sol Estes. Former President Eisenhower suggested the Democrats ask the Republicans to conduct an investigation. Senator John L. McClellan of Arkansas, the supersleuth on Capitol Hill, began an investigation. The House Agriculture Committee wanted its own investigation. Secretary Freeman conducted an inquiry within the department. President Kennedy had seventy-five FBI agents looking into Estes's affairs.

Nothing ever produced by all these investigations seriously altered the original Kennedy claim that the federal government had lost no money because of Billie Sol Estes. Nor did the investigations suggest that Billie Sol Estes had succeeded because of the venality of public servants. It became apparent as the investigations dragged on that Billie Sol Estes had achieved prominence and wealth because the federal government's system of subsidizing agriculture was not capable of helping the small farmer but was capable instead of manipulation by fast talkers who knew how to use a little razzle-dazzle. There perhaps was no easier way of making money, for example, than storing surplus grain. The rents charged the federal government were high. The costs of the storage sites were low. All one needed was a commitment from the government for storage, then the money for the sites and the other expenses would fall into line. The responsibility for the development of such a system lay with both political parties.

But the Democrats bore the brunt of the Billie Sol Estes case because he was a member of their party, had contributed to it and to its candidates, and prominent Democrats had treated him kindly. Ralph Yarborough had walked over to the Agriculture Department with him when Billie Sol was having difficulties there. Sam Rayburn once had written Billie Sol a glowing letter. Autographed pictures of both President Kennedy and Vice President Johnson adorned Billie Sol's house. And, although the Democratic administration took the first government action against Billie Sol as Kennedy repeatedly asserted, it only sought the indictments against Billie Sol after the press had exposed him.

Lyndon Johnson had written Billie Sol Estes a letter also. Dated December 28, 1960, the letter was in response to one from Billie Sol Estes recommending the appointment of W. P. Mattox to the Texas State Agricultural and Conservation Committee, a federal group that supervises farm price support programs in the state. The letter began "Dear Billie" and it read:

> It was certainly good to hear from you. As you can imagine I have been receiving thousands of letters and telegrams in the last few weeks, and I haven't been able to answer them as soon as I would like to have. I do want you to know, however, that I have put your suggestion in the hands of the people who will make the final decision on this matter, and I hope the outcome is favorable. I'll let you know if there is anything else that can be done. With best wishes."

The letter was signed: "Lyndon."

Mattox, the friend for whom Billie Sol Estes had written the letter, did not receive the federal appointment to the state committee, however, largely because Lyndon Johnson did not recommend him. Later, when the Estes scandal broke and the administration was in trouble because Freeman had appointed him to the Cotton Advisory Commission, Johnson telephoned Freeman. If Freeman had consulted Johnson about the Estes appointment, the Vice President angrily asserted over the telephone, as should have been done with matters of Texas patronage, the appointment never would have been made. This was not because Lyndon Johnson could anticipate that the Estes appointment would cause embarrassment; it was simply that Estes was backing the Yarborough wing of the

Texas Democratic Party and Johnson was working hard to block Yarborough Democrats from receiving federal patronage.

As for the letter Johnson had sent Billie Sol Estes in December of 1960, an aide of Johnson's later insisted that it was a form reply sent out by the thousands in response to requests for patronage that poured in on Johnson after the 1960 election. Although the letter had been signed "Lyndon," the aide insisted that Johnson had not personally signed the letter— there are writing machines on Capitol Hill that duplicate senators' signatures—and that the Vice President was not even aware of it when it was sent. Johnson himself never publicly commented on the case. Despite the explanation, it was difficult to convince people in Washington that Lyndon Johnson and Billie Sol Estes were not tied together. The mystery and confusion surrounding the Estes activities were deep enough to cover anything and wide enough to include anyone. Texas was filled with people who didn't like Lyndon Johnson and were happy, at the wink of an eye, to drop hints to inquiring Washington newsmen about "the real story" of the relationship between Johnson and Billie Sol Estes. Each lead was checked out. Nothing was traced back to Johnson. Still, the insinuation continued. Johnson couldn't shake it.

On one occasion, a Texas newspaper man was tipped off that the Billie Sol Estes records showed a payment to an "L. B. Johnson." Because the source was a known political opponent of Johnson's, the reporter treated the tip with skepticism, but it had to be checked out. The Vice President's office in Washington was called. A Johnson aide claimed ignorance about the allegation but promised to check it out and call back. The aide sounded nervous, or so the reporter thought.

Thirty minutes later the reporter was in the midst of a long-distance telephone call when the operator broke in on him. The Vice President's office was trying to reach him and did not wish to wait. The reporter said okay and then heard the excited voice of the Johnson aide. The "L. B. Johnson" listed in the Estes records was not the Vice President but a small farmer. The Vice President's aide had the farmer's address, the name of a banker who could substantiate that that "L. B. Johnson" had indeed received funds from Billie Sol Estes, and several other names of persons who could substantiate the transaction. The information killed any story. It had been a remarkable piece of ferreting out facts in only thirty minutes' time and the reporter was convinced that it must have been done by the FBI, which was investigating Estes then. The Johnson office had realized that if the story had been published, the denial—no matter how strong—would never have caught up with it. The people of Washington who knew Lyndon Johnson were ready to believe he was somehow, in some unknown way, tied to Billie Sol Estes.

Billie Sol Estes was a businessman. But he was not of the world of General Motors and United States Steel, of Henry Ford and the Rockefellers. That world centered in the East, around the great firms and the great industrial leaders who built their empires in the latter part of the nineteenth century and the early part of the present century, when the federal government placed no restraint on what a man could do. That world of business fought every piece of legislation designed to place another restriction on it, pull another tax dollar from it, demand that another form be filled out. That world of business existed despite the federal government.

Billie Sol Estes belonged to the world of business that existed because of the federal government.

This was the new world of business. In this world, oil wildcatters struck it lucky and then devised the depletion allowance and the oil import quotas to protect their new wealth. Construction men wrote their most lucrative contracts with the government rather than with private industry. Businessmen pulled the electric power they needed from the dams and power stations built by the federal government. Farmers made more from the government for not growing crops than the market paid for crops that were grown. Billie Sol Estes had made his original money by taking the crops that were grown and storing them. This was the world that existed because of the federal government. These people used the government.

And one of their chief tools had been Lyndon Johnson.

As Senate Democratic leader, he had protected the depletion allowance. He had fought to keep the big construction projects alive. He pushed for generous farm bills. That had been one of his major roles in Washington; he and the late Bob Kerr, himself an oil man of vast wealth, had been the "fast-buck boys'" men in Washington. It was not improper for Lyndon Johnson to have represented his constituency. Each member of Congress has—as he should have—a constituency that is both geographic and economic. And because the members do have these constituencies, the Congress is a truly representative organization where the North and South, East and West, farmer and city dweller, poor and middle class, the "respectable" wealth and the *nouveau riche* are all heard. It was Johnson's personal misfortune, however, to represent a constituency that was always looked upon with suspicion and distrust, that was always believed to be slightly beyond the realm of honesty. This was why Washington accepted the premise that Billie Sol Estes and the Vice President had been tied together somehow, although there never was any proof of such a link. It was why, also, that Lyndon Johnson stayed supersensitive on the matter.

FOUR

AT the same time that talk of the Billie Sol Estes scandal was spreading through the nation's capital, Lyndon Johnson also was running into difficulties as chairman of the President's Committee on Equal Employment Opportunity. The difficulties started out as racial discrimination by the federal government and by government contractors in their hiring policies; they ended as Robert Kennedy. The clash of these two men in this committee at the end of 1962 destroyed any belief still remaining in Washington that they were on friendly terms.

John Kennedy was serious about increasing job opportunities for Negroes. "He didn't understand civil rights. But he did understand job problems," said one civil rights leader about Kennedy as his Presidential years began. Even members of the Kennedy administration conceded the President cut back somewhat on his pledges for civil rights legislation in hopes of winning southern congressional support for his public welfare legislative proposals (which would largely benefit poor Negroes). To compensate for this retreat, Kennedy stressed improving Negro job opportunities. He started with the federal government.

Shortly after Robert Kennedy became Attorney General,

he walked through the halls of the Justice Department building on Pennsylvania Avenue, poking his head into the offices. He did not see any Negroes except in menial capacities. Most cabinet members could have walked through their departments at that time and seen the same thing. Washington at the beginning of 1961 was a southern-oriented city even though it was the nation's capital. Negroes who did have federal jobs were, largely, crowded into the lower pay scales and kept there by the same curtain of prejudice that kept their homes restricted to certain areas of the city. It was not unusual for a Negro federal employe to train a white person and then watch that white person advance up the civil service scale, leaving the Negro far behind.

John Kennedy broke that tradition. Negroes, some competent and some not so, were given prominent jobs in his administration. The Secretary of Labor, Arthur Goldberg, traveled to Negro college campuses trying to recruit young Negroes for federal jobs. Government personnel directors were informed that if two persons of equal background apply for a job and one of them is a Negro, the Negro gets the job. Even those bastions of segregation, the military services, were forced to speed up their desegregation process. On one occasion, Navy admirals and captains from every naval command in the world gathered at the Marine base at Quantico, Virginia, to plan how they could speed up promotions for Negroes in the service.

But the biggest area for the federal government to break barriers of discrimination was with government contractors. There may not be any corporation of any size that does not have some connection with the federal government, either as a prime or subcontractor or even on the third or fourth tier of contracting. There may not be any union local which does not at one time send its members to work on a federal government project. Since the time of Franklin Roosevelt,

there had been committees in Washington to break through
the barriers of discrimination that existed among private employers and unions working for the government. None had
been very successful. Those failures were not due so much to
the committees themselves or the persons who headed them.
Richard Nixon was in charge of the committee in the Eisenhower era and he had a personal commitment to the cause of
civil rights (Nixon was a member of the National Association
for the Advancement of Colored People) as well as a political
desire to do a good job. But the federal government was just
too big for the committee to police all agencies. The time
needed to process a complaint was too long to provide satisfaction for the complaining Negro.

Under the executive order issued by Kennedy, however, a
new approach was adopted. The Kennedy order was largely
written by Abe Fortas,* a former New Deal lawyer, who had
been recommended for the assignment by Lyndon Johnson, an
old friend. The concept of the order was unique. Rather than
waiting for Negroes to walk in with claims they had been discriminated against, the order directed all federal contracting
agencies to make certain that each private contractor agreed,
when he signed with the federal government, not to discriminate in his hiring. Then if he did so, it would be a breach of
contract, subject to cancellation. This moved responsibility
from the individual to prove he had been discriminated against
to the contractor to prove that he had not discriminated.
Each agency would use its regular contract administration
officer to check the contracts. This was done deliberately to
make certain that nondiscrimination would eventually be considered a routine part of government contracting.

Chairing the committee was a difficult job for Johnson.
He could make no friends but could make considerable ene-

* Fortas was named an Associate Justice of the Supreme Court in the
summer of 1965.

mies. Many of the larger government contractors were in the South and were as segregated on their premises as were the communities in which they were located. In many cases these contractors were the prime source of income for the people of these southern communities. To threaten such a company with a contract cancellation meant threatening a southern community with a heavy economic loss; that was no way for Lyndon Johnson to retain his southern political support for 1964. Leaving the South and going into the North, many of the most segregated institutions were the labor unions. Although the committee could not move against these unions directly, it could use indirect means to compel them to end discrimination. A contractor, for example, could lose a contract unless the union local supplying him with help ended its discriminatory practices. But attacking labor unions meant attacking one of the three pillars of the Democratic Party; the other two were the big city bosses and the South. The labor leaders never had much love for Johnson, bitterly objecting when Kennedy had picked him for a running mate at Los Angeles in 1960. Johnson wanted to woo this group, not alienate it more.

There always was the possibility that Lyndon Johnson could do such an effective job as chairman of the committee that he would become the darling of the civil rights groups—but not much chance. The civil rights groups in the early 1960s were coming under the influence and leadership of men more given to grasping for political power for themselves than interested in improving the lot of the Negroes. All the statistics Lyndon Johnson could amass about the improvement in job opportunities for Negroes would have no impact on these civil rights leaders.

Johnson could not have turned down the job of chairing the committee. Richard Nixon had held it; if Johnson then refused the chairmanship, it would appear that he was surrendering to his southern origins. So he took the job and announced: "We mean business."

The first problem for the committee was a budget. "This was the key to whether the committee would be a success or not," explained one of the committee's members years later. Without funds, he explained, the committee would be unable to check on compliance. But Johnson had problems there. The southern oligarchs on Capitol Hill had decided the best way to stymie the Johnson committee was to deny it a budget. The Vice President alluded to this situation briefly at the committee's first meeting and then announced that the committee would have a budget of over one million dollars, a sum adequate for its purposes. The money would come to the committee from other government agency budgets, with Congress neither being informed nor asked to give its approval. The committee members understood Johnson was saying a congressional fight over the committee budget wasn't worthwhile when the money could be available from other sources. Most committee members were willing to accept Johnson's political judgment, but a few members disagreed. They believed a fight with Congress would have to come sometime and that it was better to have it at the beginning. But they had no opportunity to press their point. Lyndon Johnson never put a question of policy forward for discussion. "He rammed through what he wanted," said a committee member. "He never told us anything." If a question was asked at a committee session about the budget, Johnson would listen intently, nod his head when the question was finished, and then rush on to speak of another matter.

But Johnson had secured working funds for the committee. That was the important point. On Capitol Hill the southerners wondered where the funds came from. Richard Russell and Representative James C. Davis of Georgia, in particular, were hot on blocking the committee's funds; but under Johnson the committee managed to sidestep the southerners' attacks. "He was silent before the Russell attacks," said a staff member later of Johnson, "but he did not bend." That apparently would be the Johnson approach. Stand mute before the attacks against the committee, but while he stood silent the committee would go about its work.

How fast would the committee work?

With Lyndon Johnson's luck, the first contractor about which there would be any question was located in Marietta, Georgia. It was the Lockheed Corporation, which had placed one of its largest defense plants in the same state from which the chairman of the House and Senate armed services committees came. Russell was the chairman of the Senate committee; Carl Vinson of the House committee. Of the two men, Russell was the deadlier enemy of the Johnson committee. Although Carl Vinson had always voted "right" on civil rights for a Georgian—against civil rights bills—he long ago had lost interest in racial segregation and would probably have supported all civil rights legislation if the political realities of his congressional district did not forbid such heresy. Richard Russell, however, was the leader of the southern bloc in the Senate, its generalissimo. Continued segregation of Negroes was equated in his mind with preserving the "glory" of the old South. It was for this reason he was so concerned about the Johnson committee's budget.

The Lockheed plant was completely segregated, in job opportunities as well as in the traditional things such as washrooms and restaurants. The company was waiting for a one-billion-dollar defense contract to build large transport planes when the Johnson committee was organized. A report from the company came to the committee suggesting there were no racial difficulties at the plant. The Johnson committee—actually the staff—rejected the report. A participant summed up the activities of the next few days: "Hell broke loose."

The rejection of the Lockheed report raised the possibility that one of the nation's largest companies, its plant practically supporting a community in the home state of Richard Russell, would lose a contract because of the Johnson committee. Various committee members whose origins were from the South tried to have the committee staff switch its position. Russell "raised hell but in a polite fashion." The fracas was settled amicably when the company, the committee and the Air Force drafted an acceptable agreement. The agreement not only committed Lockheed to a policy of nondiscrimination, but it also committed the federal government to locating and training Negroes for skilled jobs. The Lockheed incident taught the committee something it had not expected to learn: American industry was generally willing to go along with a nondiscriminatory policy. It had been blocked before because the company executives believed they should not violate the habits of the communities where their plants were located. But once the industry men could say the federal government insisted on a nondiscriminatory policy, then they found there was not much opposition from the local communities. Money conquered racial prejudice. The job of the committee would not be as hard as some of its members had anticipated.

Still, the committee did not do as much as it could have done. One member reminisced that "we weren't very effective our first year. The statistics on job improvements for Negroes were just so much mimeographed bunk." Much of this lack of results lies with Johnson. Part of the committee's work was to have regional meetings with contractors, union leaders, public officials, and civil rights leaders, to explain the President's order and how the committee intended to implement it. One of the first such meetings was in St. Louis, Missouri. The session had been poorly planned; too many persons were involved in too many meetings during the one-day session. Also Johnson did not help the session's effectiveness. As one

When Sam Rayburn administered the Vice Presidential oath of office to Lyndon B. Johnson on January 20, 1961, it was the first time in the nation's history that a Speaker of the House had sworn in a Vice President. It was fitting in this case, however, because of the relationship between the two men that had spanned many years. Although Johnson was familiar with the oath, he betrayed his nervousness by repeating it inaccurately. A few seconds after this photograph was taken, "Mr. Sam" Rayburn's gruff face broke into one of its rare smiles. Lyndon Baines Johnson was officially the thirty-seventh Vice President of the United States.

UNITED STATES ARMY PHOTO

On January 21, 1961, the Kennedy cabinet was sworn in by Chief Justice of the United States Earl Warren while President Kennedy and Vice President Johnson looked on. These were the new President's formal advisers. Lyndon Johnson had had little voice in the selection of these men and would have still less when they deliberated. This was partly because of John Kennedy's working procedures and partly because of Lyndon Johnson's practice of not speaking unless called upon.

One of Lyndon Johnson's major problems as Vice President was the attitude of the "Irish Mafia" toward him. The "Mafia" was personified by Robert F. Kennedy, the President's younger brother, who never developed rapport with Vice President Johnson during the New Frontier. Although they appeared friendly before newsmen at the 1960 Democratic convention after the Kennedy-Johnson ticket was selected, the coolness in the relationship between Robert Kennedy and Lyndon Johnson often showed itself in later years.

U.S. NEWS & WORLD REPORT PHOTO

A Vice President has many ceremonial chores. Here Mr. Johnson throws out the first ball of the opening game of two minor-league teams in Nashville, Tennessee, in April 1961. A few days later in Washington President Kennedy threw out the first ball to inaugurate the major-league season.

UNITED PRESS INTERNATIONAL PHOTO

The Vice President enjoyed his trips abroad as a goodwill ambassador. He and Mrs. Johnson arrived in Karachi, Pakistan, on a one-day visit in May 1961. Here they are shown being received at the Karachi airport by Pakistan's minister of health and social welfare, Lt.-Gen. W. A. Burki and Mrs. Burki.

EMBASSY OF PAKISTAN PHOTO

After a dinner in honor of the Vice President and Mrs. Johnson, President Mohammed Ayub Khan of Pakistan presents Mrs. Johnson with a piece of Pakistan brocade and Mr. Johnson with a silver hairdressing set.

Lyndon Johnson's principal value as a foreign emissary for the United States was the rapport he quickly developed with the people, particularly in the under-developed countries. The Vice President traveled through foreign countries as if he were running for office. In his talks with the people, Mr. Johnson stressed his own poor beginnings and convinced his listeners that he understood and sympathized with their problems. He also enjoyed himself immensely, and this too the people seemed to understand. More traditional diplomats sometimes criticized the Vice President's techniques, but he ignored the criticism and won many friends for the United States. Shown in a bazaar in Iran, the Vice President is developing his shirt-sleeves diplomacy. The garland of flowers around his neck was presented to Mr. Johnson by the local people as a sign of their affection.

The Vice President's most dramatic trip abroad was his weekend trip to West Berlin in August 1961 after the Communists built the wall that divides West from East Berlin. What was needed to restore the West Berliners' confidence was a reaffirmation of the American commitment to West Berlin, one given strongly enough to reverse the despair that was engulfing the people of that city. Mr. Johnson succeeded in doing that in what may have been the most brilliant feat of his Vice Presidential career. He is shown among the people of West Berlin.

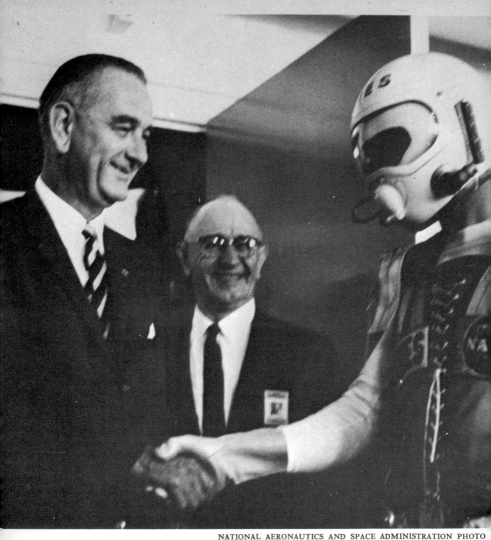

Because of Lyndon Johnson's interests in promoting America's efforts in the field of space, President Kennedy had the 1958 space act rewritten to make the Vice President chairman of the Space Council. Mr. Johnson took his responsibilities in this field seriously. He is shown shaking hands with a National Aeronautics and Space Administration scientist who had just demonstrated the workings of a pressure suit for the Vice President. Mr. Johnson's frequent trips to space installations during his first year in office did much to increase morale among space-agency workers.

Although this was the only field where the Vice President was not in direct competition with Robert Kennedy, Mr. Johnson was unable to attract to himself any of the glamor or the excitement of the American space effort. There was too much competition from the younger men involved who exuded more vitality. Here astronauts Walter Schirra and L. Gordon Cooper are briefing President Kennedy and Vice President Johnson on the Mercury spacecraft.

NATIONAL AERONAUTICS AND SPACE ADMINISTRATION PHOTO

UNITED STATES ARMY PHOTO

The many moods of
Lyndon Johnson.

NATIONAL AERONAUTICS AND SPACE
ADMINISTRATION PHOTO

NATIONAL AERONAUTICS AND SPACE
ADMINISTRATION PHOTO

participant described it: "He spent the first hour and a half of the day, when we should have been started on our meetings, politicking. He made us sit down and watch while he introduced the mayor and the man whom he wanted to be the next mayor." After his morning politicking Johnson flew off to make a luncheon speech in another city and then returned late in the afternoon, again to interrupt the session with additional politicking. Later one of the committee members told Johnson he considered the St. Louis session a fiasco and also reminded the Vice President that politics and principles do not mix in some circumstances. Johnson became very angry and denied he had caused the session's failure. At the next committee meeting, the Very Reverend Francis B. Sayre, dean of the Washington Cathedral, a committee member, reported to the committee on the St. Louis meeting in negative terms. One who attended that session remembered that Johnson then attacked Dean Sayre for ninety minutes, berating him as an ineffective "do-gooder." The tirade shocked those present. It demonstrated Lyndon Johnson not only disliked strife, he also was stung by criticism.

Johnson kept a tight control over the committee. Not only would he dodge controversial questions if they were brought up, he also tried to keep a certain element of surprise in the committee's activities. There was no advance agenda for the upcoming committee sessions and committee members could not prepare themselves with specific questions or statistics with which to challenge Johnson because they did not know what would be discussed at the meetings. Finally, Walter Reuther, the president of the United Auto Workers union and a committee member, complained. As a result, the making of the agenda was turned over to a subcommittee headed by Dean Sayre. This did not solve many problems, however. The Sayre subcommittee had to submit a proposed agenda to Johnson's staff, which then largely reworked it. A committee member

who was part of the minor rebellion that had led to the crea-
tion of the Sayre subcommittee conceded some years later that
Johnson had been correct in wanting to control the agenda.
"He couldn't let the private members push the government
around," this member said. He explained that controlling the
agenda meant controlling what the committee would consider
and what it would do. "The committee couldn't be democratic," this member said. Then he added: "So why did they
pretend that it was."

At the same time there was difficulty within the committee
staff and this conflict also caused Lyndon Johnson some
embarrassment. An early Kennedy backer had been an Atlanta, Georgia, businessman named Robert Troutman. He was
one of the few southerners to support the young senator from
Massachusetts for the Presidential nomination; most southerners then were backing Lyndon Johnson. At the Los Angeles
convention, Troutman was one of those Kennedy men actively
working against Lyndon Johnson. After the 1960 election,
however, Kennedy decided it would be a good idea to have a
southerner working in the area of improving the Negro job
situation. A southerner, assuming he was sincere about helping
Negroes, could speak with other southerners in an understanding manner. Troutman was given an executive position with
the Committee on Equal Employment Opportunity headed by
Johnson. For a southerner just to talk about improving job
opportunities for Negroes required courage and Troutman did
express himself frequently on the need to help Negroes. But
Troutman also was interested in a "go-slow" approach. He
claimed that any legal requirement could always be avoided
by some technical loophole and insisted during his tenure on
the committee that he had accomplished more through voluntary means than others had accomplished through compulsion.

Northern liberals also were interested in the committee's
work and wanted some men they knew and trusted on the staff.

As a result, John G. Feild was given an executive position with the committee. Feild had done similar work in Michigan. An ardent civil rights man, Feild wanted to insure compliance with the Kennedy executive order as quickly as possible. This meant compulsion—threatening to cancel contracts and sometimes carrying through on that threat.

When the agreement had been reached with the Lockheed Corporation in Marietta, Georgia, Feild happened to call the agreement "a plan for progress." Troutman seized on the phrase and developed a "Plans for Progress" program. Dozens of large corporations voluntarily signed agreements pledging themselves to a nondiscriminatory policy in White House ceremonies. As the television cameras recorded the event for the seven o'clock news broadcast, the corporation executives signed "Plans for Progress" promising not to discriminate. It was very impressive, particularly as the Johnson committee began to turn out statistics showing that hundreds of thousands of employes of government contractors were now covered by "Plans for Progress" and showing how many Negroes were finding new and better jobs because of the program.

Many members of the committee remained skeptical of the Plans for Progress; Feild was hostile to them. There was a feeling that signing the papers was becoming a substitute for compliance. No contracts had been cancelled (and none ever were) and there were a few companies, including one in Texas, that obviously were not complying and appeared in no danger of losing their government work. (The Texas company supplied electric power to a military base located within the state. It was argued that cancelling the contract would black out the military base, which had no other source of power.) The statistics were particularly suspect. If a company had three Negroes in its employ, then hired a fourth, it had increased its Negro employment by thirty-three and one-third per cent—an impressive but not significant statistic in this case. If two companies substantially increased the number of Negroes in their employ but eight made no increase, the ten companies could be lumped together statistically and made to appear that all had increased job opportunities for Negroes. (The Plans for Progress program, as originated by Troutman, eventually proved to be a very successful one, but its success came later. Long after Troutman had left the committee, and even after the committee itself ceased to exist, major industries in the United States actively practiced open hiring policies. While some of the companies that proclaimed themselves an "Equal Opportunity Employer" may not really have meant it, there was enough improvement in job opportunities for Negroes by the mid-1960s that the problem became not one of placing Negroes in jobs but the altogether different problem of training Negroes for jobs that were available.)

As the President's Committee on Equal Employment Opportunity was organizing itself its first year, it was pulled between the two philosophies—that of Feild, who wanted strict compliance, even to the extent of actually cancelling contracts, and that of Troutman, who was not ready to go quite that far. Because of his past friendship with John Kennedy, Troutman seemed to be winning the tug of war between the two men. Troutman's credentials as a friend of the President included more than his earlier support for Kennedy. Troutman had been a college roommate of the President's older brother Joseph P. Kennedy, Jr., who was killed in World War II. Troutman also occasionally stopped at the White House to see the President, to discuss casual matters and sometimes to discuss the work of the committee as Lyndon Johnson headed it. The Vice President finally concluded that Troutman was trying an end run around him, wanting to boss the committee without attention to or respect for the position of the Vice President. Lyndon Johnson does not like to be ignored and particularly he does not like to be ignored by his underlings.

Part of the dispute within the committee eventually became public. In June of 1962, *The New York Times* ran a story by Peter Braestrup saying the committee was involved in a fight between the "compulsory" views of Feild and the "voluntary" approach of Troutman. The story quoted Secretary of Labor Goldberg, a committee member, as saying: "I like a little healthy diversity. There is bound to be disagreement in a group as varied as this one." The Vice President wrote a letter to the *Times,* an unusual act for a Vice President, in response to the story. "I do not propose to promote a controversy where in my opinion none exists . . ." said Johnson. "The facts are that people involved in different aspects of a program are quite likely to put heavier emphasis on that with which they are most familiar. . . . The committee operates a compliance program, and, as I have said frequently, we mean business."

The *Times* story did not identify Johnson's position in the Feild-Troutman conflict. It was a difficult one for the Vice President and not many people understood it. He disagreed with the Feild reliance on compulsion. And, although Johnson agreed with the Troutman approach of voluntary compliance, he did not agree with Troutman personally. The solution Johnson devised was to cut out both Troutman and Feild. Johnson had some management experts come in and draw up a new table of organization for the committee staff, one that would make it more efficient. Under this reorganization plan, the staff would be headed by a new executive vice chairman—who would be neither Feild nor Troutman.

At this point Johnson received help from the White House. When President Kennedy learned of the difficulties between Johnson and Troutman, Kennedy agreed that Troutman should resign as a committee staff member. The President did not want any "palace intrigues" against his Vice President. However, the President believed Troutman was a close friend of the two Georgia senators, Richard Russell and Herman Talmadge. Troutman often had left a phone number at the White House where he could be reached: it was Herman Talmadge's home number. Because Kennedy still was trying to avoid angering the southerners in Congress, he was reluctant to ask Troutman for his resignation. Kenneth O'Donnell, the White House aide, had been spending some time on Capitol Hill in recent weeks and did not believe Troutman really was too close to Russell and Talmadge. With Kennedy's okay, O'Donnell asked for Troutman's resignation. He got it and one of Johnson's difficulties was removed.

Johnson next had to take care of Feild. He rammed his reorganization plan through the committee, the one setting up the post of executive vice chairman to head the staff; few of the committee members wanted to challenge Johnson when he insisted efficiency was the cause of the reorganization. Since this made the head of the committee staff much closer to the chairman, it was agreed that the post should be filled with a Johnson choice. Even Feild went along in the agreement. Result: Feild was out. The new man in charge of the committee staff was Hobart Taylor, Jr., a Negro who definitely was "a Johnson man."

Now that Johnson had the committee as he wanted it, however, his troubles were not over. They were, in fact, just beginning. With Troutman and Feild out of the way, Robert Kennedy emerged as Lyndon Johnson's nemesis on the committee.

The reorganization and the leaving of both Troutman and Feild had come in the late summer of 1962, when the committee had been operating more than a year. By that time it had received seventy complaints, settled about sixty of them. It claimed to have created an "equality control" system covering 300,000 manufacturing concerns doing business with the federal government and involving fifteen million workers. The plethora of charts, graphs, booklets and press releases recorded the statistics about Negro employment by area, by industry, showing where it was advancing and where standing still. It almost always seemed to be advancing, rarely standing still. Individual Negroes, however, still found it difficult to get a job. At that time, more than fifty large defense contractors had signed Plans for Progress promising to increase Negro job opportunities. Few, if any of these companies, reported an increase in Negro employment. The committee created a great appearance of effort, but by the end of the summer of 1962 there were very few gains.

President Kennedy became particularly concerned. His interest in improving Negro job opportunities was both genuine and political. If the Johnson committee did not produce, Kennedy would be personally disappointed as well as in political difficulties. And the stories he heard indicated to him that the Johnson committee was not producing. Arthur Goldberg gave him some information, as did Walter Reuther and several other members of the committee. So the President turned, as he was doing more and more, to his brother, Robert Kennedy, the Attorney General. Robert Kennedy always had suspected Lyndon Johnson's sincerity in the field of civil rights; he distrusted him more now that Johnson had the committee staff completely under his control. The younger Kennedy did some investigating on his own. With the help of the Civil Service Commission and some personal friends in the Washington agencies, he amassed a dossier of facts on Negro employment in the federal government and of the efforts being made by federal agencies to increase Negro job opportunities in contracting companies. The record was a poor one.

In the fall of 1962 Robert Kennedy walked into a meeting of the President's Committee on Equal Employment Opportunity, dropped his briefcase on the table before him, yanked it open, looked around at the committee members and announced: "I have just come from the President." In all of Washington there are no seven words with more impact. They imply that the speaker is acting for the President at the President's request. They imply also from their tone that the President is angry, disappointed and about to take action. Robert Kennedy did nothing in that meeting to dispel that impression.

To each head of a federal agency present, Kennedy turned and demanded: "What about your department?" When they stumbled in answering, Kennedy read them statistics about the number of Negroes employed by their departments, the Negroes' civil service status, the improvement or lack of it since the beginning of the Kennedy administration. He was particularly concerned with the number of persons each agency had checking on compliance by private contractors. The Kennedys understood that a private contractor would agree to hire Negroes if necessary to gain a federal contract but then would not hesitate to ignore that agreement if he believed the federal government was not going to check up on him. The real key to the whole Kennedy effort to improve Negro job opportunities was whether federal agencies insisted on compliance. That day Robert Kennedy made clear to the heads of government agencies sitting around the table that they did not have enough people checking compliance.

Diplomacy and tact never had been Robert Kennedy's strong points. He was a direct person. And, if he believed the circumstances warranted it, he was a brutal person. He had shown that several years earlier as counsel to the special Senate subcommittee investigating labor racketeering. Because Robert Kennedy's drive against the hoodlums in the union business was so applauded at the time, few paid attention to what was the dominant facet of his personality: a ruthless determination to achieve what he considered right. In the session with the

Johnson committee that day and in a second session a few weeks later, Robert Kennedy was direct and brutal. As he demanded answers, glared at officials who hesitated in answering him, rattled off statistics, shut off persons protesting they needed more time, he was the embodiment of all the unfavorable adjectives that have been applied to him.

One member of the committee later described the incidents as the President's "using Bobby to build a bushel barrel fire under the committee." The Attorney General, this member said, launched "rip-roaring attacks" in two meetings. And when the attacks were done, "Bobby zipped up his briefcase and walked out." The member then said: "But it was beneficial. It did produce results." This committee member was one of those from outside the government and was not being directly attacked by Robert Kennedy. Other committee members who were members of the federal government were not so generous in their opinions of Robert Kennedy's remarks; they did not care to be treated like labor racketeers. But there was some response. The federal agencies did step up their recruiting and promotion of Negroes. More important, they did insist on more compliance with the nondiscrimination clause of the contracts they signed with private industry.

Robert Kennedy's attack had been leveled at the federal agencies specifically. It hit Lyndon Johnson generally. Although the Attorney General barely spoke to the Vice President in the controversial committee sessions—following his policy of ignoring Lyndon Johnson as much as possible—the attack was really a White House charge that Lyndon Johnson had been ineffective as committee chairman. There was no other implication that could be drawn from the manner and words of Robert Kennedy; the President obviously was using his brother because he did not trust Lyndon Johnson to respond properly to an appeal for stepped-up activity. And Lyndon Johnson could not retaliate. To have done so would have been to retaliate against the President and to have done so in front of a group of top government officials as well as prominent persons from outside the government would have been a public declaration of war. Hobart Taylor made a few faint efforts to answer Robert Kennedy, but the Attorney General barely acknowledged his presence. Lyndon Johnson was so rattled by the Kennedy attacks that for a long time he did not call another committee session.

There always had been rumors of disenchantment between the New Frontier and Johnson, but during the first two years of the Kennedy administration knowledgeable persons had not paid much attention to them, believing them to be the usual rumors that always float around Washington's cocktail party circuit. But after the Robert Kennedy–Lyndon Johnson run-ins in the President's Committee on Equal Employment Opportunity, the rumors gained more credence. Members of the committee, of course, told their friends about it and speculated on the incidents' meaning. For the first time, Lyndon Johnson had been undercut. It had been done in an almost vicious manner and in an almost public fashion.

FIVE

As Lyndon Johnson's second year as Vice President ended, the Texan could survey his possible 1968 competition —and only one name emerged as a serious competitor for the Democratic Presidential nomination that year: Robert Kennedy.

None of the Democratic senators seemed to have the necessary spark that could propel them to the top. Stuart Symington was aging. Henry Jackson had faded into obscurity. Hubert Humphrey remained the intense idealist but political lightweight he had been in 1960. In the governors' mansions were a scattering of Democrats, but only Edmund G. (Pat) Brown of California commanded a large state with a powerful bloc of convention delegates and few ranked Pat Brown as Presidential material. Other persons could flash to the surface in a short time; that was possible but not likely. Even John Kennedy's phenomenal rise to national prominence had begun in 1952, eight years before his nomination and election, when he beat the reputed unbeatable Henry Cabot Lodge to become senator from Massachusetts.

Robert Kennedy had some strikes against him. He was hated in the South because of his civil rights stance. But Lyndon Johnson, more than most people, realized how the South was changing and understood that if a pro-civil rights stance might not be an asset in the South in 1968, it might not be an overwhelming deficit either. Also, Robert Kennedy as a candidate in 1968 could perhaps do so well outside of the South— much better than Johnson could—that the South's attitude toward him might not matter. The younger Kennedy had never run for elected office, meaning he had yet to prove himself as a vote getter. That, however, could be cured easily; there already was talk of his running for Governor of Massachusetts and nobody could beat a Kennedy in Massachusetts. The most talked about of the strikes against Robert Kennedy's having a political future of his own was that he was the President's brother and people might be opposed to him on the basis of "too many Kennedys." But that was a joke. Because a member of a President's family had not immediately succeeded the President to the office before there was no reason to believe it could not happen in the future. Especially when the family was the Kennedys. They already had established several firsts: the first Catholic in the White House, the youngest man elected President, the first senator nominated for the Presidency by a major political party in forty years. Why not the first man to be succeeded by his brother? It was particularly possible because the two brothers were identified so closely together. In 1959 and early 1960, when pollsters had rung doorbells asking persons if they favored John Kennedy to be the 1960 Democratic nominee, they were astonished by the number of persons who said they would vote for "either Jack or Bobby."

There had been a joke in Washington for many years of a "Kennedy dynasty." At a political spoof sponsored by the Gridiron Club in Washington in early 1959, an ersatz Joseph Kennedy sang of his children:

> All of us
> Why not take all of us?
> Fabulous—

You can't live without us.
My son Jack
Heads the procession.
Then comes Bob,
Groomed for succession.

The joke had come alive again in the fall of 1962 when the third brother, Edward M. (Teddy) Kennedy, made a successful try for the Senate seat John Kennedy had given up when he became President. Edward Kennedy was barely old enough to fulfill the Constitution's age requirements for senators when he was elected. After his election, the Kennedy dynasty joke pictured an Orwellian world. "After Jack serves eight years," ran the new story, "then it will be Bobby's turn for eight years; then Teddy's for another eight years. When his term is over, it will be 1984." It was funny only because the prospect of a long line of Kennedys in the White House seemed real; reporters talked of John Kennedy's once saying to his younger brother Robert, "After me, how about you?"

The jokes, however, were not funny to Lyndon Johnson. He seemed unable to compete with the younger Kennedy. Because of Robert Kennedy's special relationship to the President, his roles in the crises of 1962 and his Presidential errand-running such as in the President's Committee on Equal Employment Opportunity, he had emerged as the number two man in the administration. He received considerably more attention from other administration members, the press and the nation than did Lyndon Johnson. Also, in 1962 there were hints that President Kennedy was trying to broaden Robert Kennedy's experience, to make him a more attractive candidate for the White House someday. Early in the year, for example, the President had sent his younger brother on a month-long trip around the world. When the trip ended, the President had his Attorney General make a well-publicized visit to the White House to give a formal report on his findings with Secretary of State Rusk and Vice President Johnson present. In Washington, no one believes the President does anything casually and so it was assumed the President had called that meeting as an expression of the importance he attached to his brother's trip. In the nation's capital persons involved with the government could not remember when an Attorney General, who is primarily a domestic officer, was given such a build-up in foreign affairs.

There was another reason why Lyndon Johnson could not compete with Robert Kennedy. The Kennedys had completely captured the fancy of the American people. Anything they said or did, anything written about them was quickly gobbled up by the American people, who then demanded more, and still more. Respected and dignified political commentators wrote front-page stories about how the President shaved in his morning bath. The movie magazines ran a story about the Kennedys each month; usually it was the same story, repeated with a few slight variations; it made no difference. Newspapers carried stories about how the President eschewed the three-button suit jacket in favor of a more individualized suit jacket with only two buttons. Night club comedians satirized the President. Hollywood glorified him with a movie version of his exploits in the Second World War as a PT-boat commander. There was a Caroline Kennedy comic book. Kennedy was "hot." Partly this was because the first family was more accessible to the different communications media than probably any other family in the White House. Partly it was due to a renewed interest in the Presidency by the American people. Novelists and movie producers had quite suddenly decided to strip the institution of the Presidency of the papier-mâché quality textbooks give it and present the President as a living human being with faults as well as good qualities. But perhaps the most important reason for the public's interest in the Kennedys as individuals was the nature of the Kennedy family itself. Its members are wealthy, handsome, athletic, intelligent and brave. They have a fictional quality about them. But they are real and so if anyone could capture this public adulation in 1968, or so it seemed, it would be the President's younger brother.

Certainly it would not be Lyndon Johnson.

A politician who had known Johnson for some years and watched him intimately on many occasions has described him as "a man of infinite dullness." The phrase is not quite accurate. It should be "a man who gives the appearance of infinite dullness." The Vice President was an exciting person, but he could not communicate a feeling of excitement, particularly when he was before a large crowd. John Kennedy—and his brother Robert—could.

As this second year ended there was little public pretense that Johnson still maintained any significant position in Washington. Members of the White House staff and other Irish Mafia men scattered through Washington joked about the "Judge Crater" in the Vice Presidency. An article in *The Reporter* magazine described the Vice President as one "who chases around continents in search of the duties of his office." And *Time* magazine commented that "although Johnson is often seen, he is not really heard. . . . He is free to speak up, but nobody, really, has to heed him anymore. . . . The Vice Presidency has again become what it was throughout most of the nation's history: a ceremonial office in which a man stands by to take office in case the President dies." Former Vice President Nixon once aptly described how the gloss wears off the office of Vice President. "The first year is the hardest," Nixon said. "You feel you have to accept every single invitation. The second year, you don't have to accept them all. You sort out the most vital and go to those. By the end of the eight years you will be in office, you'll be able to stay home nights and take things easier."

One time a news magazine carried a lengthy story about Robert Kerr's "running" the Senate. The story claimed that Kerr had moved into the vacuum of leadership created by the absence of Lyndon Johnson. The story was erroneous. Mike Mansfield, who succeeded Johnson as majority leader, was filling in a competent and effective manner the job Johnson had held. But because Mansfield's technique of leadership was so quiet and so much in contrast to Johnson's noisier technique, most reporters underrated him and credited the flamboyant Kerr with being the Senate's new "strong man." The day the news-magazine story about Kerr appeared, Johnson was in the Senate chamber chatting with a friend when Kerr ambled in. "I think," said Johnson to his friend, "I'll go kid Bob Kerr about running the Senate." But the friend remembered that Lyndon Johnson did not sound as if he were very amused.

Early in 1963 Johnson appeared on a television panel show on the ABC network in which he was asked about his job. His comments then have a curious ring to them. It is almost a dullness. Did he find the job challenging? "Yes. I have been very gratified at the opportunities that have come my way." Would he describe his job? "The Constitution provides that he [the Vice President] shall preside over the Senate. The law provides that he shall preside over the Space Council, be a member of the Security Council, preside over the Peace Corps Advisory Committee, sit in at the cabinet meetings at the President's invitation. And then, I would say, do whatever the President asked him to do." Would he be capable of assuming the Presidency? "President Kennedy and the members of his staff and his cabinet have given me every opportunity to be aware of all the important decisions that have been made and to participate in them and to make any recommendations I care to make." Reading the words over, as does watching the original program, reveals a defensiveness on Johnson's part. He sounds afraid someone will accuse him of both being unimportant and of trying to be more important than the President. His entire career as Vice President was marked by that double fear. Johnson also said on that program: "I have never felt the Vice Presidency was a comedown from anything, except the Presidency." It was difficult to believe he meant that.

Lyndon Johnson now was making barely any effort to disguise his disappointment in his role as Vice President or his pessimism about his future. To Texas friends he mentioned the possibility of returning to the Senate—running in the 1964 Democratic primary against Ralph Yarborough for Yarborough's Senate seat. There was doubt that Johnson could have beaten Yarborough. Johnson had been growing weaker politically as evidenced by the decrease in his popular vote in his home state between his Senate races of 1954 and 1960. Yarborough's popular vote totals had been increasing. To have entered the primary would have taken Johnson out of the running for the Vice Presidential nomination in 1964. Even if Johnson had lost the Senatorial primary, he would not have been renominated for the Vice Presidency. Nobody wants a candidate who can't carry his home state. At other times Johnson talked of returning to teaching, at a university in Texas; or, perhaps, setting up a library of his papers. The few times he spoke of such a future, there was a despondency to his voice. He sounded like a man reconciled to leaving politics and doing so regretfully, not like one still hopeful of reaching the top.

John Kennedy, however, continued to treat Lyndon Johnson with respect and as if he intended to have him as his running mate in 1964. Kennedy continued his policy of speaking both publicly and privately about Lyndon Johnson in favorable and positive terms. Although a few times now Kennedy wondered aloud what the Texan did as Vice President; Kennedy thought it a dull job. The real clue to Kennedy's attitude toward an individual was whether Kennedy would joke about him; Kennedy only kidded his friends. Early in 1963 the President was speaking at a dinner of newsmen and told this story about Lyndon Johnson:

> Johnson had complained a few days earlier to the President about being strongly criticized by Doris Fleeson, a liberal columnist. Kennedy himself recently had come under attack by Arthur Krock, the conservative columnist in *The New York Times*. Kennedy responded to Johnson's complaint that it was better to be Fleesonized than Krocked.

In the context of relationships between Presidents and their Vice Presidents, the modus vivendi that had developed between Kennedy and Johnson was not a bad one. It may even have been one of the better relationships between the holders of those two offices. Kennedy understood that Johnson could not be an "assistant President," nor did Kennedy want him to be. If Johnson seemed to hold back at times, such as showing reluctance to lobby on Capitol Hill or to become involved in dealings with the South on explosive racial issues, he also never did anything to trouble or embarrass the Kennedy administration. Not all Presidents had been so fortunate.

As the Constitution was first written, it was planned that the Vice Presidency would go to the runner-up for the Presidency. This had produced problems. John Adams, the nation's second President, and Thomas Jefferson, his Vice President, were both personal and political enemies. This was also true of Jefferson, when he became President, and Aaron Burr, his Vice President. As a result, the nation passed the Twelfth Amendment, which, in effect, permitted a Presidential candidate to choose his running mate. From that time on, the Vice Presidency degenerated into an item for barter, offered generally in exchange for regional or philosophical support. And once it was offered in hopes that the recipient would make a large campaign contribution.

Often the system resulted in an embarrassment. The first Vice President named Johnson, Richard M. Johnson (1837–1841), concerned himself primarily with romantic exploits. When his term was finished, his party did not even bother to nominate a successor for him—the office had fallen so low—leaving it to the electors to write in whatever name they chose. The second Vice President named Johnson, Andrew Johnson, elected in 1864, made such an embarrassing show of his inaugural in the Senate chamber that the Senate formally passed a resolution prohibiting the presence of intoxicating liquors on its side of the Capitol. Vice President Schuyler Colfax (1869–1873) probably would have been impeached for personal dishonesty except that his term in office was about to expire. The Vice Presidency was in such disrepute at the turn of the century that it seemed a good place to dump Theodore Roosevelt to prevent him from doing any harm in New York. Thomas R. Marshall, who held the office of Vice President at a time when greatness was demanded of that office, during the illness of Woodrow Wilson, is remembered primarily for having said: "What this country needs is a good five-cent cigar."

And if the Vice President was not an embarrassment, he likely was an opponent. When President Andrew Jackson cried "Our union—it must be preserved," he was speaking directly to and challenging the champion of nullification, John C. Calhoun of South Carolina. Calhoun, at the time, was Jackson's Vice President. And Abraham Lincoln had trouble with his first Vice President, Hannibal Hamlin, because Hamlin opposed Lincoln's policy of conciliation with the South. Theodore Roosevelt was constantly harassed by his Vice President, Charles W. Fairbanks, who went his own way with Congress —which was not Theodore Roosevelt's way. Calvin Coolidge had the same difficulty with his Vice President, Charles G. Dawes. In his first term Franklin Roosevelt and his Vice President, John Nance Garner, worked well together, but this changed in FDR's second term. The split began with Garner's opposition to Roosevelt's plan to enlarge the Supreme Court. The Vice President's opposition spread to include Roosevelt's attempt to purge several Democrats in the 1938 congressional elections and Roosevelt's economic policies in general. After 1938, FDR and Garner rarely spoke to each other; they never saw each other privately. In the early years of the Eisenhower administration, the White House was embarrassed by Vice President Nixon's suggestion that American troops be sent to Indochina to help the beleaguered French there.

It is difficult to be a Vice President. Dwight Eisenhower has stated that the Vice President "is not legally a part of the Executive branch and is not subject to direction by the President."[*] Technically that is correct. But if one hopes to use the Vice Presidency as a pathway to still higher office, one cannot say or do anything that can be construed either as an embarrassment or as opposition to the President. And everything the man holding the office of Vice President does and says, even the most casual of remarks, is tested by newsmen, politicians, members of the President's palace guard, and by the public to determine if it meets that test. Everything Lyndon Johnson said or did passed that test.

His performance was the more remarkable because rarely in American history had there been a combination like Kennedy and Johnson: two men as President and Vice President each representing a large reservoir of political strength. Richard Nixon never brought as much political support to the Eisenhower campaigns and to the Eisenhower administration as Johnson brought to Kennedy. Nixon did gain personal political support at the end of his tenure as Vice President; but the job had given him strength, he had not given political strength to the job. Alben W. Barkley, the "Veep" of the second Truman term, stepped into that position when he had passed the zenith

---

[*] Eisenhower, *Waging Peace*, Doubleday, Garden City, N.Y., p. 6.

of his career, not when he was approaching it as did Johnson. Henry A. Wallace and Harry Truman had been picked as running mates for Franklin Roosevelt in 1940 and 1944 because they did not take support away from him, not because they gave him strength politically as Johnson gave Kennedy strength. When Roosevelt permitted Wallace to be removed from the ticket in 1944, the only complaint came from the liberal wing of the Democratic Party. This was not serious, however, because those liberals never would have supported Thomas Dewey and John Bricker, the Republican nominees.

But Lyndon Johnson represented the South, an area where John Kennedy was not very popular and an area that had voted Republican before and could do so again. In recent years only Garner had a position comparable to Johnson's. A political power in his own right and a possibility for the Presidential nomination in 1932, Garner had strengthened the Democratic ticket and certainly had assured Roosevelt of the Presidential nomination in 1932. But Garner had overplayed his strength and was dumped in 1940. Roosevelt's 1936 victory margin had demonstrated the Texan was no longer needed.

Lyndon Johnson did not overplay his strength. He did as he was told. He kept his complaints to a minimum. When given a specific job, he did it as well as he believed he could. And he watched and he waited.

1963

The Johnson Eclipse

O N E

Millions of years ago a great ocean covered parts of what is the southwestern area of the United States until a table of land thrust itself up from beneath the waters. This plateau faulted in its center, drawing an almost straight line with a jagged clifflike ridge of land from the north to the south. Formally called the Balcones Escarpment, this ridge of land is formidable, frighteningly so, but strangely beautiful also in its primitive power. This is a land of basics; men still watch the sky for water and then the rivers for floods. This is a land that shows the scars of danger; many of the homes are pocked with the bullet hole and arrowhead marks of the Indian raids a century ago, and the graveyards hold the stones of those who met death by the Comanche tomahawk. This is a land tied very much to the past; until the building of the government dams, power lines and irrigation projects, this seemed a land without a future.

This is an arid place of cactus and mesquite spreading out over the high land; below, the land is better and there are orchards of peach trees, acres of alfalfa and great stretches of open grassland for grazing steers. This is a big land. There is no city skyline to limit one's view of the horizon, no smoke of a mechanized society to blot out the sun in the day and the stars at night. Here there is no noise of a million people to deaden the sound of the splash of the icy springs as they flow over their white limestone beds or to hide the snap of a collie chasing a straying goat. Here the world is a larger place.

This land is the hill country of Texas. It is the home of Lyndon Johnson. One cannot understand Johnson, it is often said, unless one visits the soil that nurtured him. Even that may not be enough. Perhaps, instead, one must live in this land, begin to feel its past and understand its people. These people, as one Texan said of them, "opposed slavery, stood up for the Union alongside of Sam Houston, practiced a 'non-conforming' religion and told the authorities to go to hell."* Only a hundred years ago in this land, a short enough time to be remembered by families, Eliza Johnson, Lyndon's grandmother, hid in a cellar with her baby while marauding Indians tramped on the floor above her. Here, many less years ago, Lyndon Johnson shined shoes, rode a jackass to school, shared a bicycle with a cousin because the two boys were too poor to have one each. Here he began. And this land of his beginning is deceptive in its appearance. It indicates an inauspicious place from which to launch a national political career. The men still play dominoes while sitting in the town squares beneath a hot sun. The modern day "cowboy" ambles along the dusty streets, his Stetson pushed back on his head, his plaid shirt open at the neck and pulling around his stomach, his blue jeans tight, his walking boots dusty. He stops in for a cold bottle of beer, which he holds in one hand while he rolls a cigarette with the other. Here the towns are small, only a few hundred people. The visitor may begin to feel this land is weak and its people slothful.

Those who live here beyond the time of the visitor's tour say differently. They agree there is a casualness to both the land

* Former Representative Maury Maverick, Jr., in *The New Republic*, Mar. 14, 1964, pp. 12–13.

and its people, and some will concede when pressed that there is a coarseness in the people that reveals itself in blunt jokes and basic language and there is a ruthlessness when these people are pressed or angered. Within these people also—and one is told this is their most important quality—there is a toughness. This may be the only area within the states of the Old Confederacy where there is a monument to Union soldiers who died in the Civil War. It was built by men tough enough to be a dissenting minority. Here is a land where men watch helplessly while nature does its worst work and then come back to the spot nature has desolated to begin again. (In 1952 a heavy rain—a "gullywasher" it was called here—sent the Pedernales River thundering over its banks, ripping down two hundred pecan trees in the front yard of the LBJ ranch house. Lady Bird Johnson and her mother-in-law were at the ranch house and were rescued by a helicopter as water was lapping at the ranch house steps. Mrs. Johnson was pregnant at the time and suffered a miscarriage. Lyndon Johnson dammed up the Pedernales to control it; the family returned to the ranch.) This is a land that tolerates no subterfuge. A man is strong enough to work this land from before sunup to after sundown or he is not. A man is tenacious enough to hold on in the bad times so he can enjoy the good. A rancher here will say that some years he makes two thousand dollars; other years, twenty thousand. A man is smart enough to outwit nature or nature outwits him. (When goats on the LBJ ranch are sheared for their valuable mohair, a strip of hair is left along their backs untouched. This sheds rainwater and keeps the goats warm. Another rancher not too far from the Johnson place whose goats had been completely shorn lost five hundred goats after one shower and nine hundred after another.)

This is a land, in sum, where a man is well trained for life; for a hard life, that is. Blunt, ruthless, tenacious, smart; such men always are good adversaries. Lyndon Johnson was one of the best. In the year 1963, when all the forces that opposed Lyndon Johnson began to converge into a movement against him, it was time for the man from the Texas hill country to show how tough and tenacious he was.

There never was an organized movement to push Lyndon Johnson off the 1964 ticket. Instead, it was a disorganized collection of wishes of some people, ambitions for other people, misunderstandings by some persons, hopes for revenge on the part of still others. This could be enough. Adlai Stevenson once said of Washington in the early 1960s that "it's all so much personality talk, gossip, and rumor—who's up and who's down. The criticism is sort of brittle now, and there's a lot of malice and mischief." He compared this to the nation's capital in the 1930s "when I first went there . . . the way it used to feel during the long evenings—sitting in the gardens of those Georgetown houses in the hot summers, perspiring, with our visions and with our dreams."*

The difference was more than one of a change in personalities. It represented a change in political philosophy by the country. In the 1930s the young men who flocked to Washington to be part of Roosevelt's New Deal were caught up in developing the philosophy of helping, in Roosevelt's phrase, "the forgotten man at the bottom of the economic pyramid." This was the political revolution in the United States, transferring the federal largesse from the man at the top of the economic pyramid to the man at the bottom, and it largely succeeded. In the eight Eisenhower years the revolution was held in check but it was not reversed. By the time of the New Frontier the philosophical war had been fought and won; the liberalism of the New Deal—meaning the use of the federal government to provide welfare services—was almost universally accepted.

So now the young men come to Washington did not sit in

* *The New Yorker,* July 24, 1965, p. 19.

their Georgetown homes perspiring and talking of their visions and dreams. The dreamers had gone. These new young men were technicians called to implement another's dreams, to fulfill another's vision. Now the homes were air conditioned and the young men talked about people instead of about their hopes for a better tomorrow. This was the stock in trade of the Washington cocktail party circuit. Here, as Stevenson said, the only concern was "who's up and who's down." Each community, not only the political world, has such a place where vituperation passes for sophistication, where one can feel the hot breath of the crowd at a bullfight exulting as the sword flashes into the bull. Few of the habitués of this Washington world actually contributed significantly to the process of governing. But these little worlds can sometimes generate their own power; such often happens in Washington.

A reporter whose sources are ordinarily not very good comes to one of these parties and hears a minor New Frontiersman joke about "Lyndon? Lyndon who?" The reporter makes the crack the basis of a story for his newspaper about Johnson being on the "outs" with Kennedy, which suggests Johnson's political future is bleak. A supporter of Lyndon Johnson's sees the story and figures that only an Irish Mafia man could have been its source. The animosity between the Johnson camp and the Kennedy camp then grows stronger. Gossip has created a political situation.

Or a lower echelon figure in the liberal community comes to one of these parties and hears another popular line early in 1963: "Lyndon Johnson? Say, whatever happened to Lyndon Johnson?" He repeats it among his friends and associates in the liberal community and they spread the story of Johnson's being relegated to obscurity. Soon so many people tell the story, it is believed. This emboldens some liberals to make overt attacks on the Vice President. Gossip has produced a tactic.

This talk had begun in 1962. At a news conference in May of that year a reporter asked President Kennedy:

> Mr. President, there have been rumors in print in and out of Texas that Vice President Johnson might be dropped from the ticket in 1964. I'd like to ask you if you have any reason whatever to believe that either end of the Democratic ticket will be different in 1964?

The President answered:

> Well, I don't know what they'll do with me, but I'm sure that the Vice President will be on the ticket if he chooses to run. We were fortunate to have him before—would again—and I don't know where such a rumor could start. He's invaluable. He not only fulfills a great many responsibilities as Vice President. He participates in all of the major deliberations. He's been in the Congress for years. He's invaluable. So, of course, he will be, if he chooses to be, part of the ticket.

Reporters at that news conference considered Kennedy's remarks to have been offered sincerely. Still, there was a difficulty in accepting them as an unqualified endorsement of Lyndon Johnson for 1964. Whatever President Kennedy's desires, he could not have answered that question any differently in May of 1962 or at any other time up until the convention of 1964. To have given any public support to the "dump Lyndon" rumors would have split the Democratic Party between the northeastern establishment represented by Kennedy and the southern faction of the party represented by Johnson. This southern faction dominated Congress and although Johnson did not control this faction, he had enough support from it that he could not be slighted. Every political realist in Washington understood that if John Kennedy did wish to "dump" Johnson, he could never acknowledge it publicly.

One of the origins of the "dump Lyndon" stories was the belief frequently articulated that John Kennedy never had wanted Lyndon Johnson as a running mate in 1960 but had been either coerced or entrapped into the "Boston-Austin axis." The basis of the belief that Kennedy had been coerced into accepting Johnson was a remark of Robert Kennedy's made in the Kennedy hotel suite at the 1960 convention. He had just returned from the Johnson rooms, where he had warned of a possible fight with party liberals over the nomination of Johnson for the Vice Presidency. He says he's willing to fight for it, Robert Kennedy announced. The meaning of the words was that Lyndon Johnson was willing to join with the Kennedys in fighting the liberals that night, not that he intended to fight against the Kennedys for the nomination. Most persons in that room at the Biltmore understood Robert Kennedy's words correctly. Several, however, misunderstood and passed on to friendly newsmen that Lyndon Johnson had told the Kennedys: either take me as the Vice Presidential candidate or fight me and the South over your choice.

The origin of the entrapment version is more complicated. Although John Kennedy at the convention in 1960 had a memorandum from Ted Sorensen and Mike Feldman that, in effect, recommended Lyndon Johnson as a running mate by pointing out that he would have the most value on the ticket, other members of the Kennedy group were unaware that Johnson was being seriously considered. Kenneth O'Donnell, who along with Robert Kennedy was working with liberals at the convention—who were adamantly against Johnson for the second spot—was unaware that Johnson's name had moved to the top. Five years later O'Donnell told a group of newspaperwomen that Johnson's name was not on any of the "lists I'd seen" of possible Vice Presidential nominees at the 1960 convention. O'Donnell said the choice of Johnson "surprised" him.* Because of this surprise on the part of O'Donnell and

* *The Washington Post,* Apr. 30, 1965, p. C1.

other members of the Kennedy camp, there remained an aura
of suddenness on the part of Kennedy's choice of Johnson.

Also, although Kennedy had reason to believe Johnson
could be persuaded to accept the Vice Presidential nomination
—members of the two men's staffs had discussed it informally;
Johnson himself had dropped some significant hints, and few
people would turn down such an offer if it actually came—
Kennedy anticipated it would require some persuasion. Instead, Johnson readily accepted. His only significant provision
was that Mr. Sam, who had originally opposed his taking the
Vice Presidential nomination, give his assent. Kennedy then
sought out Rayburn. Several southerners had talked with Rayburn a few minutes before Kennedy came to Rayburn's suite,
pointing out to the Texan that only a Kennedy-Johnson ticket
could beat Richard Nixon. That was a powerful argument to
Rayburn and when Kennedy's personal entreaties were added
to it, Rayburn then called Johnson to give his assent. "I am a
damn sight smarter than I was last night," Rayburn said to
Johnson to explain his turnabout. Still, Kennedy's surprise at
Johnson's readiness was obvious and this surprise was inter-
preted by some as an expression of Kennedy's disinclination to
have Johnson on the ticket. According to this theory, Kennedy
made the offer to Johnson only to placate the sensitive Texan
and the party faction he represented and did so with the expectation that Johnson would refuse.*

---

* The most forceful exponent of this theory is the Pulitzer Prize-winning
historian and New Frontiersman Arthur M. Schlesinger, Jr., in his memoir
of the New Frontier called *A Thousand Days* (Houghton Mifflin Co.,
Boston, 1965). He entitles his subsection on the Kennedy choosing of
Johnson "Falling into a Decision." Whether Kennedy did indeed "fall" into
a decision or whether he willingly made the decision will probably be debated by historians forever.

Kennedy came to the 1960 convention without a commitment for a
running mate. One of his political lieutenants at the time has since indicated
to me that this was less a willingness on Kennedy's part to make a deal
and more a refusal by the other major candidates to surrender their chances
for the first spot by tying in with Kennedy. Without making a definite commitment, however, Kennedy had said different things to different people,
usually what they wanted to hear. An official of the Americans for Demo-

These rumors and stories about the selection of Johnson as John Kennedy's running mate always could produce a knowing smile at most Washington gatherings. By the beginning of 1963—after two years of watching Johnson decline in importance, of witnessing the growing impact of Robert Kennedy and the open hostility between the Attorney General and the Vice President—Washingtonians began to give the stories more credence. If they were not believed as a sign that John Kennedy did not want Lyndon Johnson in 1960, they were

---

cratic Action, the liberal group strongly opposed to Johnson, asked Kennedy in June 1960 about his choice for the Vice Presidency. Kennedy replied, as the ADA man remembered: "It will be Hubert Humphrey or another midwestern liberal." On the Monday of the convention week, however, Philip L. Graham, publisher of *The Washington Post,* and Joseph Alsop, the columnist, met with Kennedy to urge him to select Johnson as his running mate. They came away from the meeting strongly believing John Kennedy was inclined to tap Lyndon Johnson. Graham directed his paper, *The Post,* to carry a front-page story the next day, Tuesday, July 12, saying: "The word here tonight is that Sen. John F. Kennedy will offer the vice presidential nomination to Senate Majority Leader Lyndon B. Johnson . . . [and] hopes the Senator will accept." Although *The Post* was the only major newspaper to go so far in predicting a Kennedy-Johnson ticket, Graham's faith never wavered. The next night, Wednesday, July 13, Kennedy was nominated for the Presidency, and *The Post* bureau at the convention filed a story saying: "There was no reason to doubt that Sen. Kennedy's own personal preference is to offer the vice presidential nomination to Senate Majority Leader Lyndon B. Johnson." That story appeared on the front page of *The Post* the morning of Thursday, July 14, a few hours before Kennedy offered the second spot to Johnson. Alsop also predicted a Kennedy-Johnson ticket after that Monday session with Kennedy. In his column appearing Wednesday, July 13, a few hours before Kennedy himself was nominated, Alsop wrote: "A Democratic ticket composed of John F. Kennedy of Massachusetts in first place and Lyndon Baines Johnson of Texas in the second spot cannot be absolutely ruled out, despite the almost universal assumption to the contrary."

Graham and Alsop, in addition to being old friends of John Kennedy, were experienced newsmen. I do not believe they would have gone as far as they did in predicting a Kennedy-Johnson ticket unless they felt almost certain from their Monday meeting with Kennedy that such a ticket would come about. Also, I have talked with many of the members of both the Kennedy and Johnson camps at that convention. In these talks I found nothing to support the thesis that Kennedy "fell" into the decision on the Vice Presidency. Instead, among those with whom I spoke, there was unanimous agreement that Kennedy willingly chose Johnson as his running mate. One of Kennedy's closest political associates described the Kennedy selection of Johnson as "a cold political decision." It is, I think, the most accurate explanation.

suspected of being a sign that he would not want him in 1964. The enemies of Lyndon Johnson then felt emboldened to make their move. If Johnson was to be dumped in 1964, the preliminary work had to be accomplished in 1963; the movement needed time to begin. The formula was simple: Johnson had to be demonstrated to be a political liability to the Kennedys. How could this be done? First, the liberal community had to show its disenchantment with Johnson, raising the possibility of perhaps supporting a liberal Republican ticket in 1964 rather than the Kennedy ticket, or at least encouraging wholesale defections of liberals from the Kennedy line to a Rockefeller or Scranton line. Second, Johnson's own state of Texas had to be demonstrated as being in doubt as to whether it would support a Kennedy-Johnson ticket in 1964; if Johnson could not carry his own home state, his political value would be depreciated immeasurably.

This was the situation Lyndon Johnson faced as 1963 began. It was not a conspiracy masterminded by any single individual or cabal. It was a movement created spontaneously by the situation at the time, consisting of hundreds of persons in Washington, in Texas, in New York City, who didn't like Johnson for a variety of reasons. But it generated its own power as it moved along. And because it was so disorganized it was difficult to oppose. Many men would have surrendered before it, as Lyndon Johnson had indicated on several occasions he was inclined to do. But Lyndon Johnson was a tough man from the Texas hill country. His family had fought Indians, weathered storms and braved floods. He had used the strength, energy and guile he inherited from them to claw his way to the center of Texas politics, long known as one of the roughest arenas in the country. He had then used his inheritance to wile his way to leadership in Washington, also a formidable arena. There never was a time, his friends and associates say, that he proclaimed aloud his defiance of the forces moving against him and vowed to fight them to the death. Instead, within him, it was noticed, there was a growing determination to last through the Vice Presidency, to do a good job as Vice President or as good a job as the position would allow, and to beat his enemies. His heritage from the Texas hill country of tenaciousness had served him well in the past. It did not desert him now. It was not in him to surrender.

TWO

J OHNSON's basic problem was the liberal community. This
was made up of four distinct groups: the northern city
"bosses," labor leaders, civil rights advocates and a loose con-
glomeration of individuals called "intellectuals" for a lack of
a better descriptive title. These intellectuals included professors, Wall Street lawyers and others who dabbled in politics
and largely supported the policies advocated by the first three
groups. The city bosses earned the title of liberal because of
their interest in the social welfare legislation that is part of the
liberal cause. This group always had looked favorably on
Lyndon Johnson. Being politicians themselves, they understood the demands for compromise and finagling that the
political milieu placed on Johnson when he had been Senate
majority leader. They were the same breed of man themselves.
What Lyndon Johnson had done in the cloakrooms of the
Senate during the 1950s, they had been doing in the shadow of
City Hall for decades.

These bosses* actually had favored Lyndon Johnson to be
Kennedy's running mate back in 1960. The weekend before
the Los Angeles convention opened, a group of them gathered

---

* The word "boss" is used here to denote the head of a political organization. There are other definitions. Sorensen, for example, calls ". . . powerful
Kennedy supporters . . . political leaders [while] those in the opposition
camp are called bosses."

in the hotel suite of David L. Lawrence. Former Mayor of Pittsburgh and then Governor of Pennsylvania, Lawrence represented the modern city "boss" in a manner that other bosses envied. As mayor, Lawrence had presided over the re-building of Pittsburgh and then had achieved an equally sub-stantial record as governor. He was considered honest and effective as well as shrewd. Coming to his room that day were Carmine DeSapio of Manhattan, Bill Green of Philadelphia, Matthew McCloskey, the Democratic Party's own financial war chest, as well as other mayors, governors and party leaders. The men at that meeting agreed unanimously on two things: John Kennedy would be nominated in a few evenings to be his party's Presidential candidate and he could only win the following November if Lyndon Johnson pulled in the hard-shell Baptist vote in the South by joining the ticket as the Vice Presidential nominee. Shortly after that meeting ended, John and Robert Kennedy had come to Lawrence's suite. The "bosses," Lawrence reported, agreed Johnson would bring the most strength to the ticket. John Kennedy was non-committal. Robert countered that a running mate from the far West—he still favored Henry Jackson of Washington—would better balance the ticket geographically. Lawrence then re-minded Robert Kennedy of the 1948 election, when Thomas Dewey of New York and Earl Warren of California had lost to Harry Truman and Alben Barkley "who lived across the river from each other" in Missouri and Kentucky. These bosses had stayed with Lyndon Johnson while he was Vice President, were with him still in 1963 and would continue to support him.

The labor leaders, however, were a different matter. They had three strikes against Lyndon Johnson, enough to call him out. The first strike was an old score. In the 1940s, as a mem-ber of the House of Representatives, Lyndon Johnson had supported the Taft-Hartley Act. This law, vetoed by President

Truman and then repassed by two-thirds of Congress over the Truman veto, curbed the power of organized labor. The union leaders counted an "aye" vote on Taft-Hartley as an unpardonable sin. The labor leaders were a power in the party. In 1944 they had demonstrated that although they could not impose their own choice on the Democratic national ticket, they could veto another's choice. James Byrnes, a conservative southerner, was a strong contender to replace Henry Wallace as FDR's running mate that year. But Roosevelt said of the pending nomination, "Clear it with Sidney." This was a reference to Sidney Hillman, a prominent labor figure. When Hillman said "no" to Byrnes, the nomination then went to Harry Truman. As one labor leader explained the situation to a reporter at the time: "We were for Wallace always, but not against Truman." Democrats did not forget this. In 1956 when he was considering a try for the Democratic Vice Presidential nomination, John Kennedy analyzed the assets and liabilities of himself and his competitors. Voting against Taft-Hartley was a prime requisite.

The vote for Taft-Hartley by Johnson, if not forgiven, might have been explained as a youthful indiscretion except for a later move by Lyndon Johnson against organized labor. That had come just a year before the 1960 convention, when Congress was considering the Landrum-Griffin labor reform act. The labor unions considered this even more odious than Taft-Hartley; and Johnson, the union leaders believed, was responsible for its passage.

During the 1950s, a Senate investigation led by John McClellan of Arkansas and starring John Kennedy as an investigating senator and Robert Kennedy as a crusading counsel had produced a long and unsightly record of union corruption. Perhaps the worst aspect of the seamy picture of graft and misuse of responsibility was that labor did not make any serious effort to purge itself of hoodlums and grafters until the

McClellan committee exposures. Nor had the union leaders acknowledged the public demand for corrective legislation. Once, decades earlier, the union leaders were lean, dedicated men who manned barricades against a society grown fat and unfeeling. But in the late 1950s, as officers of the American Federation of Labor and Congress of Industrial Organizations, they had a multimillion-dollar office building across Lafayette Square from the White House, only a block from the headquarters of the Chamber of Commerce. They were chauffered to and from work in limousines, dined at the White House with the President. They could not accept that the public believed union corruption widespread enough to warrant passage of reform legislation. Because they would not acknowledge the need either for a serious cleaning up of their house themselves or for having Congress do it, they lost much of the esteem with which the public had held the labor movement. The enemies of organized labor capitalized on this loss of respect for the labor movement by pushing through a bill in the House that not only included reform measures but which also struck at organized labor's powers. This was the Landrum-Griffin measure. When the bill did pass the House of Representatives, 229–201, the labor leaders looked for a villain. They looked everywhere except at themselves and they found Lyndon Johnson.

Of the twenty Texas members of the House, only four voted against Landrum-Griffin in 1959 although Sam Rayburn had staked his prestige as Speaker of the House on Landrum-Griffin's defeat. Why had the other sixteen deserted Rayburn, their usual leader, at this crucial point? Lyndon Johnson then was considered the most powerful politician in Texas. He knew where campaign funds could be found for a poor candidate. He often could persuade a newspaper editor in Texas to support a candidate or not to support him. More important, he was then considered a big vote-getter in Texas.

In his last election, in 1954, he had won by a three-to-one margin. A pat on the back from him for a congressman in political trouble was considered valuable. Because of this power in Texas, when Lyndon Johnson spoke, the members of the Texas delegation listened. In his private conversations with these members, Johnson had expressed his opinion that a Texas representative must vote for the strongest labor reform bill—Landrum-Griffin. When Texans wrote him asking his opinion of the various labor bills, Johnson replied in the same manner, also in support of Landrum-Griffin. Johnson's comments were gratuitous. Landrum-Griffin was not before the Senate and he never personally was obliged to vote for it or against it. In stating his opinions as he did, he violated a cardinal rule of Congress: never take unnecessary political stands. Simply because his action in voicing his opinion on Landrum-Griffin was so unusual, it had a heavy impact on the Texas members of the House. Organized labor counts votes assiduously. If the sixteen Texans had voted with Rayburn, Landrum-Griffin would have been defeated 213–217.

Johnson had no choice but to take the position he did on Landrum-Griffin. In 1959 he was still representing a constituency of fast-buck oil men and government contractors. Organized labor was the arch enemy of this world. The struggle between them was for the federal dollar, whether it would subsidize this world of business through the oil depletion allowance and other devices or whether it would be used in public welfare to subsidize the working man.

After House passage of Landrum-Griffin, the bill was compromised slightly with a milder measure passed earlier by the Senate. John Kennedy was the chief architect of this compromise and the labor leaders applauded him for doing what they finally came to realize was all that could be done to modify Landrum-Griffin. As for Johnson, when George Meany, the president of the AFL and CIO, came to Los Angeles for the 1960 convention, he declared labor unions against Lyndon Johnson—for both the Presidential and the Vice Presidential nominations.

Besides his own staff from the AFL and CIO, which worked closely with the Democratic Party organization, Meany was joined by a phalanx of labor leaders in opposing Johnson. James B. Carey of the electrical workers union, Walter Reuther of the auto workers and Alex Rose of the hatters were among the more articulate opponents of Johnson. In addition, another anti-Johnson man was Arthur J. Goldberg, the counsel to the steelworkers' union and an adviser to Kennedy at times. Reuther was a political power in Detroit and could influence the turnout in that strategic city for Kennedy on election day. Rose was a vice chairman of the Liberal Party in New York City. This party's endorsement was considered a valuable plus for a political candidate. Goldberg was a respected link between the labor leaders and the intellectuals.

And this gave rise to the third strike labor held against Lyndon Johnson. In picking the Texan, Kennedy was challenging one of the pillars of the Democratic Party. The top officers of the organized labor movement had come to Los Angeles in 1960 believing they held a veto over the Democrats' choice for President and Vice President as they believed they had held such a veto in the past. They came away from Los Angeles feeling impotent. John Kennedy had not listened to them. And they had been helpless to do anything about it. The political power of labor can never be reduced to a complete zero. There is the money and the manpower that unions produce during political campaigns, but even these had been losing their impact. Sources of campaign funds had been widening so that candidates were relying less and less on any single source. As for union manpower in political campaigns having value, this was open to question. A congressman shortly after the 1960 campaign said of the union men who came to "help" him: "They came down to headquarters, and they looked around, and they drank some beer, and they talked about this and that, and they drank some more beer, and they talked some more, and who the hell needs them." The political power of organized labor had declined as its membership lists had grown smaller and its leaders grown more accustomed to the comfortable life. The selection of Lyndon Johnson to be the Democratic Vice Presidential candidate in 1960 was the public acknowledgement by the Democrats that one of the three traditional supports of the party was rotting. Logically, the union men should have been angry at Kennedy: he is the one who defied them. But labor leaders cannot be angry at a Democratic President; they need him too much. Instead they were angry at Lyndon Johnson.

As Vice President, Lyndon Johnson could do nothing to earn the support of organized labor. As chairman of the President's Committee on Equal Employment Opportunity Johnson alienated organized labor even more when he prodded unions as well as industries to end discrimination against Negroes. Labor was a declining political power and by itself would have had little impact on Lyndon Johnson's future, but as part of the vaguely defined but growing sentiment to dump Lyndon Johnson, the opposition of labor was significant.

Members of the third group in the liberal community, the intellectuals, also were not fond of Lyndon Johnson. One observer explained that Johnson's "associations with this group have not been close from his earliest days in Texas politics. Even though he was a New Dealer, intellectuals were not attracted to him. In part this is because Mr. Johnson does not have the earmarks of the intellectual himself. His broad stories, his backslapping, his old style political campaigning are not exactly Ivy League."* That was true; Lyndon Johnson is the opposite of the crewcut, button-down, narrow-lapels, cordovan-shoe Ivy Leaguer. But there was a far deeper reason.

* Anthony Lewis, *The New York Times*, Nov. 23, 1963, p. 1.

If there was anything that distinguished the so-called intellectuals from other members of the political community, it was their detachment from the real world of politics. Secure in their professors' chairs or law offices, they did not have to deal with what John Kennedy described as "the nature and necessity for compromise and balance." This was an advantage to them and also an advantage for the country because it permitted a large group of intelligent, articulate and concerned men to develop and enunciate a political philosophy free from the day-to-day worries of votes and vetoes. And the philosophy they developed pointed the way for the politicians who came behind. Much of the basis of the New Frontier program developed this way; John Kennedy was not a blind follower but he was a learner. In supporting a candidate for office, the intellectuals seek one who is not just a day-to-day trader in the political mart but is also something of a philosopher. With this kind of person they feel at home. It is not necessary that they agree with everything he believes or does, but intellectuals cannot even consider him unless he appears to be governed to some extent by an acceptable philosophy. William Fulbright, chairman of the Senate Foreign Relations Committee, is accepted by the intellectuals, at times he is almost hallowed by them, even though the racist views he has expressed as a senator from Arkansas appall intellectuals. They accept this part of his public posture as a necessary political price that must be paid to continue having the voice of Fulbright available in foreign affairs. Arthur M. Schlesinger, Jr., one of the leaders of the intellectuals in the liberal community, wrote a political tract during the 1960 campaign titled "Kennedy or Nixon: Does It Make Any Difference?" One important reason why Schlesinger insisted it did make a difference is that Kennedy had an identifiable philosophy while, Schlesinger charged, Nixon did not.

Neither did Lyndon Johnson.

In his political career the Texan—or so it appeared, particularly outside Washington—had gone shopping for the best bargains, only motivated by how many pennies he could save. As a technician he believed in saving friendships, in keeping political relationships intact, in avoiding strife; these were his pennies and he hoarded them. But the intellectuals had a Brooks Brothers approach and could never accept Johnson's J. C. Penney manner. It was the difference between the professional, as the Vice President's friends thought of him, and the dilettantes. Each needed the other. The dilettantes can develop a great philosophy and produce outstanding proposals, but these amount to nothing unless the professionals transform them into laws. And the professional can master all the techniques of his trade, but they amount to nothing without the climate for change created by the dilettantes' zealousness. In 1960 the intellectuals were not willing to concede this. Neither was Johnson, nor would he. Five years after that convention he was to speak of this group as those who "like to talk about a lot of things without doing them."

It was this apparent fascination with the mechanics of politics rather than with the purposes of politics on Johnson's part that soured the intellectuals on him, not his backslapping and "Uncle Cornpone" demeanor. The intellectuals were willing to overlook a little corn. They still remembered Harry Truman. He too had been corny, but he turned out to be, in the intellectuals' opinion, a great President. Johnson in the late 1950s had sensed the hostility of the intellectual community and realized he must woo this group if he hoped to win the Presidential nomination in 1960. He met privately with the leaders of the intellectual community. Schlesinger, John Kenneth Galbraith and others were invited to come to his office when they were in Washington or they were asked down to the Texas ranch. The result was that the intellectuals' hostility began to wane. Enough existed in 1960 so that this group opposed Johnson for the Presidential nomination, but there was enough respect to accept the Texan in the second position. If the members of this group never warmed up to Johnson when he was Vice President, they tolerated him without too much difficulty. This tolerance became much easier after the intellectuals observed Kennedy as President using the same penny-pinching techniques in his relations with Congress. This segment of the liberal community then was neutral toward Lyndon Johnson as 1963 began. It would neither oppose him nor support him.

The fourth element in the liberal community was the civil rights group. As with members of the other groups, persons in this group also overlapped into the other three segments of the liberal community. Joseph L. Rauh, an officer of the Americans for Democratic Action and a vigorous fighter for civil rights, had ties to the labor leaders because he was the Washington lawyer for the United Auto Workers. This union was headed by Walter Reuther, who, in turn, had ties to the big city bosses because of his influence on the vote in Detroit. Also, the Washington headquarters of the American Federation of Labor and Congress of Industrial Organizations was providing some of the manpower and funds for the civil rights fight in Washington, although many union locals refused admittance to Negroes. And those big city bosses with large numbers of Negroes among their constituents had to be outspoken on behalf of improving Negro opportunities. But there was a definite group active in the early 1960s that had civil rights legislation as its main cause. When Lyndon Johnson became Vice President this group was almost as much opposed to him as were the labor leaders. Despite his recent actions and statements that tended to place him among those favoring civil rights legislation, Johnson's anti-civil rights record was too long for his conversion to be considered as sincere.

THREE

As Lyndon Johnson tried rising in politics nothing so pushed against him as his civil rights record. The charge that he had first opposed civil rights bills and then "emasculated civil rights bills" was the heaviest obstacle he encountered as a Presidential aspirant in the late 1950s and then as Vice President. In the 1960s, when the racial problem was so demanding of a national solution, his greatest task was to make a commitment to a national solution of the problem rather than the southern solution he had previously espoused and then convince the country that his conversion was sincere.

There is nothing to indicate Lyndon Johnson ever harbored personal prejudices against the Negro or member of any minority. Often he can be moving in his comments against such prejudice. "My first job after college," he was to say in 1965, "was as a teacher in a small Mexican-American school. My students were poor, and often hungry, and they knew, even in their youth, the pain of prejudice. They didn't understand why people disliked them. But they knew it was so. You could see it in their eyes. I often walked home after classes wishing there was more I could do. But all I knew was to teach them the little I knew—hoping it might help them against the hardships that lay ahead. Somehow you never forget what poverty and hatred can do when you see its scars on the hopeful face of a child." As a member of Congress, he had treated Mexican-Americans, Negroes and whites all with equal courtesy.

His congressional district, the Tenth, which he represented from 1937 until 1949, is not of the "old South." Sprawling across ten counties, its shape suggests a map of the United States in miniature. This is the rugged hill country, small farms, the city of Austin. It is not the South with its cotton culture, its slave heritage and its mint juleps. The district was rural primarily. Even as late as 1958 there were only 327 manufacturing companies in the entire district and more than two-thirds—244—of those were small companies employing nineteen persons or less. Only fifteen of the companies employed more than one hundred persons. The farms, however, numbered over ten thousand, each of only several hundred acres. There were Negroes; in 1958 approximately one out of every seven persons in the Vice President's old congressional district was nonwhite, a ratio believed to have been static for some decades. The men worked as laborers in the fields and the women as domestics in the homes of the whites. As late as 1960, of the 14,529 homes in the Tenth district housing Negroes, only 26 per cent—a shade over one out of four—had adequate plumbing facilities. The Tenth actually was typical of many of the southern congressional districts with its segregated schools and its segregated opportunities. It had no racial problem—as long as no one tried to upset the carefully nurtured balance between whites and Negroes. And a politician from such an area would not upset that balance if he wanted to survive as a politician.

But if the Tenth Congressional District in Texas, when Lyndon Johnson represented it, offered the Negro only a second-class citizenship, it was little different in that respect from most other areas of the United States, North and South. It was

different, however, from other areas that had made up the Old
Confederacy in that it had an anti-slavery and anti-Ku Klux
Klan heritage. Germans had settled the area prior to the Civil
War. They were opposed to slavery and remained so when
war broke out, even though they suffered violence at the hands
of their southern neighbors for their position. The descendants
of these Germans also met violence in the 1910s and 1920s
when a reactivated Klan rode through central Texas tar-and-
feathering, threatening and murdering persons of German
descent as well as Mexican-Americans. In 1921 a group of
courageous members of the Texas legislature moved against
the Klan. Among those voting in favor of a resolution that
would have branded the Klan as "un-American" was "Johnson
of Gillespie." This was Sam Ealy Johnson, Jr., Lyndon's
father, himself the son of a Confederate soldier. According
to some Texans with long memories, Sam Ealy Johnson, Jr.,
spoke out several times against the Klan in the legislature in
a "positive" and "courageous" manner at a time when it was
not generally considered politically wise to be against the Klan
in Texas. It was, however, helpful to Sam Ealy Johnson among
his German-American and Mexican-American constituents.

Representing such a district in the House of Representatives
in the late 1930s and 1940s was not made difficult because of
the civil rights problem. The congressman could ignore the
issue entirely except for the few times a year a civil rights bill
was on the floor. Then he must be against it; the whites in his
district were still in the majority and they still preferred that
the Negroes remain as hired hands and servants. And that is
what Lyndon Johnson did as a member of the House. In 1937,
his first year in Congress, he voted against a federal anti-
lynching law and then repeated the vote in 1940. Four times
he voted against a federal law that would have ended state
poll taxes; Texas had a poll tax. Once he voted against establishing a Fair Employment Practices Commission—an FEPC

—and another time he voted against an anti-discrimination rider to a welfare bill. It was a solid anti-civil rights record. It is the basis for the hostility of the civil rights groups toward Lyndon Johnson when he was Vice President.

There is another side to that record, however. It is not as long, not as detailed, but it exists. In those years it was standard during any civil rights discussion for a southern member to rant about the Negro's being responsible for more crime, more illegitimate babies, more welfare, and on and on. Then the congressman made certain his hometown newspaper had a copy of his remarks so that his anti-civil rights stand could be well reported to his white constituents. The member wasn't concerned that the Negroes in his district also read about his remarks; few of them had sufficient schooling to read and even fewer voted. The procedure was degrading and dirty. Few members of Congress felt proud of themselves for engaging in it. On Capitol Hill it was known as "talking Nigra." Every southerner at one time or another was expected to "talk Nigra." No one was considered exempt from the practice; even the most powerful southern politicians followed that rule—and some feel they must still.

Lyndon Johnson, however, never "talked Nigra." Never in his twelve years in the House did he even discuss the issue on the floor of the House; never did he insert an anti-civil rights diatribe in the Congressional Record. Except for his "nay" votes, the issue might not have existed for him. He was the perfect politician for his congressional district. He did as he wanted to do—secured the dams and the public works projects to give the residents of his district the moderately comfortable life they sought, worked in the Congress to make America strong militarily, did nothing to aggravate the racial situation for his white constituents—and he was consistently returned to Congress.

In 1949 Lyndon Johnson entered the United States Senate

and there it was required of him to be a more active foe of civil rights. The House never was the battleground for civil rights in Congress; that always had been the Senate. There, armed with the rule of unlimited debate, the filibuster, the southerners could force liberals to surrender on civil rights by delaying action on all other legislation. But every man who called himself "southerner" was needed. Southern senators numbered only between eighteen and twenty-two and no member who claimed to be from the South could sit on the sidelines. And Lyndon Johnson definitely claimed to be a southerner. He first came to Congress as a seemingly diffident ex-school teacher and House leaders like Sam Rayburn and Carl Vinson of Georgia took him in hand. He learned from them that a few men, a very few men at that, controlled Congress, dictated what bills were to pass and those that were not, how much of his program a President could have and how much he could not have, which young House member could get the "pork" for his district and which could not. And these very few men were largely from the one-party South. Because they ran in districts where they were not challenged, they stayed in Congress many years, building up seniority. This seniority earned them committee chairmanships and the chairmanships gave them life and death power over legislation. When he moved to the Senate, Lyndon Johnson again edged toward the source of power, the southern senators. Men like Richard Russell and Walter George of Georgia liked Johnson right off; he had come highly recommended by Rayburn and Vinson. If they could count on him, Johnson quickly learned, he could count on them. In one of his first Senate speeches Johnson announced that the southern congressional leaders could rely on him as he described himself as "we of the South."

History probably will not be kind to southern senators. It will forget that men like Richard Russell, Sam Ervin, Lister Hill and Walter George fought to make America strong militarily when deriding military strength was popular, that they wrote much of the social welfare legislation now taken for granted. More likely, history will remember only that they were against civil rights legislation. That they were. For a young southerner, as Lyndon Johnson was in 1949, to hope to share their largesse, to profit by their power, it was necessary to join them in that battle. There was the vote outlawing the poll tax, establishing an FEPC, various anti-discrimination riders to welfare bills, and other votes where civil rights was only a peripheral issue, but still an issue. Johnson was against, down the line. But he had voted against civil rights as a member of the House. He must do more in the Senate.

In that first session of the Senate Johnson attended, back in 1949, liberals pressed for a relaxation of the cloture rule, the means of ending a filibuster, in hopes of bringing a broad civil rights bill to a final vote. If the southerners lost the filibuster, civil rights legislation then would be unstoppable. Southern senators liken attempts to weaken the cloture rule to Sherman's marching through Georgia; it must be blocked before the South is ravaged. Each man must do his part; each must take the floor of the Senate with his long oration and help stymie the work of Congress until the liberals surrender their efforts to change the cloture rule. On March 9, 1949, the junior senator from Texas rose to speak. Conceding that "I have been a member of the Senate for only two months," Johnson began a speech that takes up twenty-four columns of small type in the Congressional Record, more than eight full pages. He stated his position unequivocally. On FEPC: "This, to me, is the least meritorious proposal in the whole civil rights program." On the federal government setting standards for voting eligibility: "The framers of the Constitution of the United States were plain, specific, and unambiguous in providing that each state should have the right to prescribe the qualifications of its electorate." On the whole question of race relations: "We in the Senate should learn the facts of life. We cannot legislate love." It was Lyndon Johnson's first civil rights speech in Congress.

Although the speech was unequivocal, it relied on legal arguments rather than demagoguery. This set it apart from many of the other anti-civil rights speeches made in the Senate that year and for more than fifteen years after. Parts of that speech even had the sweetness of reason about them. "Perhaps no prejudice is so contagious," said Lyndon Johnson that March day in 1949, "or so unreasoning as the unreasoning prejudice against men because of their birth, the color of their skin, or their ancestral background. Racial prejudice is dangerous because it is a disease of the majority endangering minority groups. . . . For those who would keep any group in our nation in bondage I have no sympathy or tolerance. Some may feel moved to deny this group or that the homes, the education, the employment which every American has a right to expect, but I am not one of those."

When Lyndon Johnson was Vice President, his friends and his enemies both referred back to that speech. His friends quoted the second section about the "unreasoning prejudice" as proof that Johnson's heart always was behind the Negro movement for equal rights. His enemies quoted the first section that detailed Johnson's opposition to the civil rights legislation. Both sides could find what they wanted. Perhaps the speech was intended that way. Or perhaps Johnson even then was caught in the dialogue between North and South over racial matters as he was to be so caught up in it in later years.

The next year, 1950, Johnson inserted into the Congressional Record an editorial from a Texas newspaper about a pending FEPC bill, written, said Johnson, by "a progressive editor who pulls no punches." The editorial read: "The bill is a phony. The FEPC was conceived in political iniquity and born in political sin." It was the first civil rights insertion

Johnson had made into the Congressional Record since entering Congress thirteen years earlier.

In 1953 Senate Democrats elected Johnson their leader, a position he held until becoming Vice President eight years later. Johnson began his tenure as Senate Democratic leader with these remarks:

> We have all been sent here by our respective states and we all owe a primary allegiance to our constituents. Since this is a nation made up of states, I have never felt any conflict in loyalty between my state and my nation. I have represented Texas to the best of my ability in the past. I shall continue to do my utmost to safeguard the interests of my native state in the future, and I don't think there is another Senator who will disagree with that thought.
>
> I respect and sympathize with the problems of all my colleagues. I know they will be generous and extend the same understanding to me.*

The message came across clearly: Lyndon Johnson remains against civil rights. So there would be no mistaking it, that year he voted against still another attempt to ease the cloture rule. The next year, 1954, the Senate had before it a proposed constitutional amendment to lower the voting age in all states. Southerners opposed the amendment, understanding that if Congress wiped out the age eligibility standard, it could then continue eliminating other standards, including those used by southern states to deny Negroes the vote. Johnson was part of this opposition, saying on the Senate floor: "If the people of

* Lyndon Johnson was wrong about there not being another senator who would disagree with him. A freshman senator, only thirty-five years old, listened to Johnson's words with some misgivings. These misgivings grew into open disagreement. Two years later, this young senator wrote: "In Washington we are 'United States Senators' and members of the Senate of the United States as well as Senators from Massachusetts and Texas. Our oath of office is administered by the Vice President, not by the Governors of our respective states; and we come to Washington, to paraphrase Edmund Burke, not as hostile ambassadors or special pleaders for our state or section, in opposition to advocates and agents of other areas, but as members of the deliberative assembly of one nation with one interest." (John F. Kennedy, *Profiles In Courage*, Harper & Bros., New York, 1956, p. 13.)

Texas ever reach the point where they feel the age limit for voting should be lowered, they are perfectly capable of doing it themselves without any Constitutional amendment."

Lyndon Johnson was following the first rule of successful politics: represent your constituency. As one of a hundred or so southerners in the House, a site where civil rights was not taken too seriously in the 1930s and 1940s, he could afford to ignore the issue, except for the ritualistic "nay" votes. As a senator representing a state that had belonged to the Old Confederacy, however, his responsibilities were different. He must be more active, and so Johnson became more outspoken in his opposition. Much can be said against this first rule of politics. It makes congressmen too parochial. It sets the stage for logrolling; the East can have its federal aid if the South gets some for itself. It harms good men; Lyndon Johnson might have been the Democratic Presidential nominee in 1960 except for his civil rights record, and William Fulbright might have been Secretary of State in 1961 except for his. There is another side, however, to this first rule. Congress, as it has developed, represents not the majority of the people in the nation but, instead, the majority of the people in parts of the nation. This development of the national legislature into a structure of geographical blocs began in the nineteenth century when the South found it necessary to battle the economic domination of the North and the frontier West struggled with the settled East over such lifeblood matters as freight charges and bank rates. The system has not always worked well. In the 1950s and early 1960s, when the South and the farm and western blocs refused to acknowledge the needs of the cities, the Supreme Court had to right the balance with a series of decisions that will strengthen the representation of urban areas in Congress. In the same way the Supreme Court had to move in 1954 with its desegregation decision because the South was unwilling to right the wrong within its own boundaries and the other blocs did not care to move against the South. Anthony Lewis, who reported much of this civil rights struggle for *The New York Times,* wrote in 1964 that "Politicians do not operate in a vacuum. The reason (congressional leaders) pushed no vigorous program of federal action against racial discrimination until recently was that the voters were not, as a whole, demanding such a program." Lyndon Johnson was not alone in not making a commitment to the Negro's cause.

The congressional system works best when the members of one bloc can persuade those in other blocs to join together in a cause. This eventually happened to civil rights legislation. When a bill passed Congress and was signed by the President in the mid-1960s, many persons were surprised at the extent of the legislation and the degree of compliance in the South and other areas of the nation. Civil rights legislation in the mid-1960s represented that national will, not just the philosophy of the "do-gooder" liberals. These liberals had argued their case so long and so passionately and the Negro had dramatized his plight so effectively that the Negro's cause had become the nation's cause. The "vacuum" of which Anthony Lewis wrote had been filled.

After that first rule of represent your constituency, there is a second rule of politics. It is: don't break the first rule until you are strong enough. And strength does not mean honors in Washington. It means votes back home. During his first Senate term, Johnson was not strong. In 1948, when he was first elected to the Senate, he had won the Democratic primary (tantamount to election then) by only 87 votes out of 900,000 cast. The nickname "Landslide Lyndon" he earned rankled, not only because it was a blow to his ego, but also because the fact of his thin margin made him a prisoner of every pressure group and lobbying organization from his home state. He could not defy any prospective voter; he simply was not that rich in votes. But in 1954, when he ran for reelection, he won by a three-to-one margin. Then he began to flex his political muscles.

There were other factors, other trends, other excitements emerging at the same time to influence Lyndon Johnson's stand on civil rights legislation. One was his own ambition. By this time he was seriously considering national office. He came to the 1956 convention as a Presidential candidate, if a weak one, from the South. When the nomination quickly fell to Adlai Stevenson, Johnson sent a message to the Illinois liberal that he would be willing to accept second place. Stevenson was not interested in running with the Texan, however, and threw open the race for the Vice Presidential nominee. Johnson then backed John Kennedy rather than Estes Kefauver, the renegade southerner. Another factor was the growing political power of the civil rights movement. In 1952 Adlai Stevenson could select John Sparkman of Alabama, whose record of voting against civil rights was consistent, as his running mate. But in 1956 Stevenson could not run with an anti-civil rights man. Although the civil rights movement was not then representative of the national will, it was becoming a noticeable force.

Johnson's movements to break away from the southern mold were slow at first. In 1956 the liberals again were trying to pass a civil rights bill. The House had acted favorably and sent the bill to the Senate in July, during the last week of the session. If the bill followed the usual legislative route and went to the Senate Judiciary Committee, controlled by the southern segregationist James O. Eastland of Mississippi, it would die there. But if the bill was brought directly to the Senate floor for debate, bypassing Eastland's Judiciary Committee, there was perhaps a chance for passage, certainly an opportunity for the florid speeches that made good reading for both sides back in their home states. As majority leader, Johnson had to decide how the parliamentary wrangle should be worked out. He insisted the bill go to Eastland's Judiciary Committee for its burial along with the one hundred or so other civil rights bills interred there by the Mississippian over the years. Johnson argued that to bring up civil rights at the last minute would be divisive and threaten other needed legislation waiting to be voted on. "I am not going to take the responsibility for and have the blood on my hands from the killing of the social security bill," he thundered at the liberals in the Senate chamber. (A lengthy civil rights debate also would have threatened the Democratic Presidential convention scheduled to open immediately after Congress adjourned.) In Johnson's negativism, however, some members thought they caught just a hint of changed attitude. If the Democratic policy committee recommends a civil rights bill next year, Johnson said or seemed to be saying to some senators in the cloakrooms, he would make certain it came to the floor.

This subtlety, however, was not caught by the Negro leaders and the ardent civil rights advocates. They believed, and their belief was to haunt Lyndon Johnson as Vice President, that if Johnson had permitted the bill to come to the Senate floor that last week of the 1956 session, it would have passed. They argued that the southerners could not have got away with a filibuster that would have run into the time set for the Democratic convention. Lyndon Johnson was charged with willfully killing chances for civil rights legislation in 1956.

The charge was false.

The bill had been too long in the House. Civil rights leaders there realized so little time remained for action that either the Senate could not act or could act only at the expense of adverse publicity for the Democrats—a reference to the split within the party over civil rights—just as the Presidential nominating convention was to open. These Democrats were all strong advocates of civil rights legislation. They went to Sam Rayburn and asked him to delay the bill in the House even longer before sending it to the Senate, until the last week in July, just as the Senate was about to adjourn. The Senate would be unable to act because of the shortage of time and congressional action on civil rights would then be delayed until 1957. The choice was made deliberately. By postponing action until 1957, it was believed, Congress would have more time to enact a better bill; also the Democrats would be spared the embarrassment of a civil rights fight within their party in a Presidential election year. Lyndon Johnson went along with this strategy, but he had not originated it and had not been consulted when it was being developed. One House member who was a leading author of that strategy said some years later: "Lyndon was not responsible for the delay, but he did take the rap for it. He was much maligned by civil rights groups, wrongly in my opinion."

If his attitude toward a civil rights bill in 1956 was hazy, there was another action that year by Johnson that definitely marked the beginning of his break with the traditional southerners and of his movement toward making a national commitment on civil rights. On March 12, nineteen senators and eighty-two representatives from the southern states presented to Congress a "Declaration of Constitutional Principles." This "Southern Manifesto," as it has since been called, laid down the southern opposition to the 1954 Supreme Court decision calling for the desegregation of schools. It was the grandest moment, the greatest oratory of the southern congressmen, the Pickett's charge of this new North-South conflict. Southerners in Congress flocked to sign as a century before they had rushed to take up arms against the North. There was Sparkman of Alabama, the 1952 Democratic candidate for Vice President. There was Fulbright of Arkansas, a Rhodes scholar and former university president and already a rising voice in foreign affairs. Every southern senator signed the "Manifesto" except one: Lyndon Johnson.

With a Republican in the White House, Johnson and Sam Rayburn (who also did not sign) were the only national elected leaders the Democratic Party had. If they had signed the "Manifesto," which challenged the authority of the Supreme Court, it would no longer have been a document of the South. Instead, it would have become a document of the Democratic Party. The first rule of politics was working on Lyndon Johnson again. The American political system was demanding that Johnson represent his constituency. But now his constituency no longer was that collection of counties in central Texas known as the Tenth Congressional District. Nor was it any longer even the state that once had been part of the Confederate States of America. It was the entire Democratic Party, meaning the entire country. That constituency, Johnson understood, could not go on record as opposing the Supreme Court decision. His broadening constituency was moving him toward the moment of commitment.

In 1957 Johnson, at first, gave little indication there was any change on his part. He voted against an attempt to bypass the Senate Judiciary Committee with a House-passed civil rights bill. Northerners could also oppose such an attempt—as John Kennedy did, for example—and escape criticism by explaining they were against violating the traditional procedure of the Senate. Because of his anti-civil rights record, however, an explanation of that kind on Johnson's part would not have been accepted. Despite the Johnson and Kennedy "nay" votes, the attempt to bypass the Judiciary Committee succeeded and the bill was placed directly on the Senate calendar. The next procedural step was a vote on whether to take the bill off the calendar and bring it to the floor for debate. Seventy-one senators voted "aye" and the bill came to the Senate floor. Lyndon Johnson was in that "aye" column. For the first time in his public career he had supported a civil rights bill. The process of making a commitment had advanced a second step.

Why Johnson changed his position has intrigued both his friends and his enemies. One suggested explanation is that Johnson had learned at the Democratic convention of 1956 that he could never hope to be President or Vice President if he continued to oppose civil rights legislation. As for possible difficulties in Texas for favoring civil rights, these appeared to be not so serious after the election in April of 1957 of Ralph Yarborough to the Senate. Yarborough had been a perennial candidate for statewide office in Texas. But always he had lost, primarily, it was believed, because he was too liberal, particularly on civil rights, for Texas. But when he bucked the state Democratic leaders to win a special election to replace Price Daniel (who was switching his Senate seat for the governor's chair), it led Texas politicians to the belief— largely mistaken, it turned out later—that civil rights might not be quite the verboten area it once had been. Barry Goldwater of Arizona, the leader of the Republican conservative faction in the Senate, also charged that Johnson's transformation on civil rights was purely one of political expediency. In 1964 the Arizona senator described Johnson on civil rights as "the phoniest individual who ever came around." Johnson himself has publicly described his earlier votes against civil rights bills as "mistakes." He was to say in 1965 that "I think all of us realize at this stage of the twentieth century that there's much that should have been done that has not been done. . . . I am particularly sensitive to the problems of the Negro. . . . I did not have that responsibility [to help the Negro] in the years past and I did not feel it to the extent that I do today."

Johnson also has his defenders. One Negro leader who lobbied for civil rights in the Senate cloakrooms during the 1950s and who had many discussions with Johnson commented in the mid-1960s: "Johnson was not against these things [civil rights bills]. It was a question of strategy with him. His position, as he described it to me in the past, was that he believed there was a tremendous need for welfare legislation to benefit the common man. And it would be difficult to enact such legislation if the chief proponents were hopelessly divided on civil rights." With the passage of time and the opening of a greater and calmer dialogue between the North and the South on the issue, there is much to indicate that whatever Lyndon Johnson's personal feelings on civil rights, the Negro lobbyist was accurate when he suggested that emphasis on strong civil rights legislation in the mid-1950s would have killed other legislation. Tom Wicker of *The New York Times* found a parallel for Johnson's development on the civil rights issue in a passage of Joseph Conrad's—about a white man who moved among colored natives of an island "as if he were passing through the shadow of a tree upon his path." Wicker then equated this with "the awakening of the American people to the rejected and forgotten, who had been casting the unnoticed shadow on the path." In the 1950s there was no great national urge on the part of white America, in the North or South, to help the Negro overcome the past wrongs he had suffered. There existed a minority viewpoint, growing increasingly stronger and articulately stated, true, that white America should do something to redress the wrongs of decades, but this was far from enough to persuade the members of Congress to act.

At this time most members of Congress considered civil rights strictly a "political" issue, one to be treated as housing or agriculture is treated. The members traded housing programs for city dwellers for farm price support programs for the rural areas. Civil rights was thought of in the same manner; the essential morality of the issue had not yet swept through the chambers on Capitol Hill. As late as 1960, for example, when John Kennedy had just launched his campaign for the Presidential nomination, he met with a group of Negro civil rights leaders in his Georgetown home. A liberal had brought the Massachusetts senator together with the Negroes in hopes that Kennedy could quell their suspicions of his sincerity on civil rights. Instead of proclaiming that sincerity, Kennedy asked the Negroes to list the two or three legislative requests they wanted most. The implication was that he would try to give them that much. The request was one that a politician makes to a power bloc. The Negroes were surprised; they did not believe their rights should be traded back and forth like so many units of public housing.

Kennedy was not alone in his attitudes in 1960. Despite all the avowals in support of civil rights by the louder liberals in the Senate, most were willing to compromise significantly when it came down to details of legislation. They had shown that when the 1957 bill was being written. Three changes were made in that measure by the Senate after the bill had passed the House. The first deleted the power of the President to use troops to enforce civil rights laws. This was actually a repeal of an 1875 law and it was sponsored on the Senate floor by a man whose pro-civil rights standing never had been questioned, Hubert Humphrey. The second change tore from the bill the Attorney General's authority to initiate cases for preventive relief in civil rights matters. The deletion of this section meant that the Negro himself must initiate the court suits, that the responsibility would be thrown on the person who was too poor and too afraid of physical violence. This authority is the famous "Title III" that became a rallying cry for civil rights advocates for the next seven years. The deletion of this section from the 1957 bill was sponsored by a man who for years renewed his pro-civil rights credentials by continually fighting to strip the southerners of their filibuster power, Clinton P. Anderson of New Mexico. The third change was to add a guarantee of jury trials in criminal contempt cases arising from the bill. This guarantee meant that a white southerner who violated the bill's provisions would be tried by a jury of his fellow white southerners. To the Negro leaders the provision was anathema because they did not believe a white jury in the South would convict a white person for a crime against a Negro. This guarantee was originally proposed for the bill when it was on the House side. Civil rights strategists there were willing to accept it, realizing it was basically correct law. One of them, however, advised keeping the guarantee out of the House bill so the southerners in the Senate "could have something to chew on." This is a classic example of congressional strategy, give your opponent an out. If the southern senators could add the jury-trial guarantee, they could then permit a civil rights bill to pass and return to their constituencies and announce they at least had saved the South from the worst of the evils by forcing the inclusion of the jury trial amendment. That is just what happened. That jury-trial guarantee, more than the other two changes, was the price paid by the Senate liberals to obtain passage of a bill. In addition to Johnson, John Kennedy supported the inclusion of this guarantee. Kennedy, Humphrey and Anderson—like Johnson— understood the Senate demands compromise to operate. Because they prevented a southern filibuster, they were able to pass a bill. Even Senator Jacob K. Javits of New York, a Republican and an ardent civil rights supporter, has conceded that the compromises were necessary by saying: "Unfortunately, enough members of the Senate were not prepared to cope with the threat of a filibuster in order to enact the kind of civil rights bill that was needed."*

The compromises made by people like Humphrey, Anderson and Kennedy, with their generally pro-civil rights records,

* Javits, *Order of Battle, a Republican's Call to Reason,* Atheneum Publishers, New York, 1964, p. 217.

Johnson spoke out in favor of civil rights in the South. "I say to you," he told his southern audiences, "we will protect the Constitutional rights of every American, regardless of race, religion or region." Over and over again he repeated that promise. In Richmond he said, "I did not come down here to promise Virginia exemptions from the obligation to carry out the decision of the Supreme Court [on desegregating schools] but instead brought an invitation to join the nation in extending civil rights. . . . A hundred years of debate among ourselves is enough, I think, don't you?"

In Knoxville, Tennessee, he pledged the Kennedy-Johnson administration to "protect the Constitutional rights of all Americans without regard to the color of their skin." The next week he appeared in Newark, New Jersey, and repeated that statement, explaining: "That was a statement I made in Tennessee last Saturday night, and I say the same thing in New Jersey that I say in Tennessee." In New York City during the campaign he told the American Political Science Association, "I abhor intolerance in any form. Most Americans do. The best thing to do with it is bring it out in the broad sunshine for everyone to see."

Because Johnson was so emphatic in the South and elsewhere on the issue of civil rights, the Republican mistakes in the 1960 campaign were so much welcomed by the Democrats. Johnson's adroit use of the Henry Cabot Lodge promise of a Negro in a Nixon cabinet made the South realize that any administration, Democratic or Republican, would adopt the same stance on civil rights. Some southerners, after listening to Lyndon Johnson in the campaign, even believed a Democratic administration would do less. That was something they found in Johnson's comments and mannerisms, not anything he specifically offered.

As Vice President, Johnson tried to improve his "image" as an advocate of civil rights for Negroes. He often spoke privately with Negro leaders to explain his past record and his work as the chairman of the President's Committee on Equal Employment Opportunity. But his past record remained under suspicion and not too many persons were interested in the President's committee on jobs. If that committee was accomplishing anything, it was due to the interest of the President and Robert Kennedy, or so it was widely believed. The Vice President made many public speeches espousing civil rights, particularly to Negro groups. A typical one was a speech at the Gettysburg battlefield in 1963. "The Negro today asks justice," said Johnson. "We do not answer him, and we do not answer those who lie beneath this soil when we reply to the Negro by asking 'Patience.' "

But speeches didn't count for much. All a group had to do to have a Democratic Party official turn up and espouse civil rights was call the speakers' bureau at the Democratic National Committee. In the private councils of the Kennedy administration, however, Johnson took a more activist role in civil rights. Late in 1962, President Kennedy finally was coming around to making good on his promise of requiring that all federally supported housing be opened to both Negroes and whites. This was his famous "stroke of the pen" campaign promise, but he had delayed making that pen stroke for two years because he wanted to placate the southern powers in Congress. After Congress went home in 1962 Kennedy decided to act. Through the Federal Housing Administration, the Veterans Administration, the Urban Renewal Administration, and other programs, the federal government was responsible for the financing of much of the housing market. Although this financing was made possible by tax money collected from all Americans, the federal agencies permitted the exclusion of Negroes from these projects if such an exclusion policy was in keeping with local practices. There had been three results of this federal policy. First, the FHA and the VA had made possible the post-war suburban boom and it was limited almost entirely to whites. With this federal assistance a tight knot had been tied around the Negroes, strangling them in the cities. Second, urban renewal then had come along and destroyed much of the city where the Negro lived, forcing him into a still smaller ghetto so that office buildings and expensive apartments could be built—again for whites only. Finally, in the North, where schools were supposedly desegregated (in contrast to the South, where segregation was acknowledged), the suburban schools became white-only schools and the city schools became predominantly Negro schools.

Because of this background Kennedy's campaign promise to end segregation in federally supported housing was welcomed by Negroes. Its fulfillment was eagerly awaited. By the end of 1962, however, there were growing doubts within the administration that such a stroke of the pen would accomplish anything. The FHA and VA mortgages were accounting for less and less of the housing market. Really to have an impact on the housing situation, it was argued, Kennedy's order should encompass not only federally supported housing but also housing built with conventional mortgages. This meant practically every house or apartment building constructed. To exclude the conventionally financed homes, it was asserted, would be to leave the builders a massive loophole through which they could march to their white-only housing developments. The legal basis for such a sweeping order was the Federal Deposit Insurance Corporation, a federal agency that protected the bank depositor against a run on his bank. Since almost all banks used the facilities of this agency, it was an ideal way of extending the order to all mortgages. Lyndon Johnson was one of the more vigorous exponents of such a sweeping order. In a memorandum to the President he argued that only such a broad order would have any impact on the housing picture. Although Johnson was taking a posture more pro-civil rights than the Kennedy administration in this instance, he could not make any political mileage out of it because he could not announce publicly he disagreed with the President. Kennedy would not go along with such a sweeping order. There was a question of its legality and there also was a question in Kennedy's mind of whether he wanted to make such a brutal challenge to the southern congressional leaders. He would continue to want housing legislation, for example, and the Capitol Hill committees that controlled housing legislation were both chaired by Alabamans. John Kennedy then still believed civil rights could only hurt him politically; he would embrace it when he must, but he would not court it.*

For Lyndon Johnson a pattern on civil rights emerged. He would make the speeches giving strong support to the Negro's cause, but few outside his immediate audience would hear of them and those that did would dismiss his words as the required oratory for a member of the New Frontier. In the closed-door sessions of the administration he would suggest a more activist role for the administration. This approach would eventually become known to the civil rights leaders and would, he hoped, improve his "image." But in the public encounters between the administration and the South over civil rights, Johnson must stay in the background or at least appear to side with the southern powers. Otherwise he risked losing his only power base at the 1964 convention. His growing commitment to civil rights was not yet complete. He had demonstrated this the previous year when he had stayed out of the "Ole Miss" fracas in September of 1962. He demonstrated it again early in 1963 when he refused to join in an attack on the filibuster and was angrily denounced as a "racist."

* Whether Johnson's approach would have been more effective is a matter for conjecture, but it is a fact that Kennedy's approach largely was a failure. The executive order he issued in late 1962 was confined to federally supported housing and did not produce a significant impact on housing patterns.

For years the filibuster had been the foe of the civil rights forces. The filibuster is the right of members of the Senate to talk endlessly—hours, days, weeks, months perhaps—in hopes of stalling action on a bill. The original purpose of the filibuster was to protect a minority in the Senate against what the minority would call the "tyranny of the majority." Northern liberals used the filibuster themselves, but it had become chiefly associated with the southern attempts to block civil rights bills. Usually the threat of a filibuster against civil rights legislation was enough to prevent such bills from coming to a vote. The Senate was divided into three groups on civil rights: the northerners who were very much for, the southerners who were very much against, and the senators from the farm and western states who were not very much interested. Rather than put up with a filibuster by southerners, this last group would make known at the very beginning that it would side with the South in order to avoid the endless wrangling and to get on with the other business of the Senate. This meant the Senate either had to drop the civil rights bill or the northern liberals had to cut it back sharply, as happened in 1957. Stopping a filibuster was considered impossible. A vote of two-thirds of the Senate, sixty-seven members if all one hundred senators were present, was necessary to end a filibuster. A civil rights filibuster never had been ended.*

For some years, liberals like Clinton Anderson, Hubert Humphrey and Jacob Javits had made the filibuster their straw man. If only, they argued, the number of votes necessary to end a filibuster was reduced from two-thirds of the Senate to three-fifths, from sixty-seven to sixty senators, then a southern talkathon could be ended and civil rights legis-

* I am writing here of the attitudes and beliefs existing in 1963 and before. The next year a civil rights filibuster was ended by more than two-thirds of the Senate. The difference was that in 1964 the nation supported the civil rights cause. It had not supported that cause previously.

lation would pass. The southerners, led by Richard Russell, argued that the two-thirds rule must be preserved to save the South from the "tyranny" of the North. It was always a "great" debate. Both sides came onto the Senate floor loaded with lengthy legal arguments and historical precedents. Participants in what was called "the battle of the century" each time it was fought were prepared to spend hours playing Demosthenes on the Senate floor. The battle, however, always was lost by the civil rights advocates. Except, of course, that they had earned new laurels from their constituents for trying. The southerners too enjoyed the fight. They also earned laurels from their constituents for a successful resistance.

The attacks on the filibuster came in January of odd-numbered years, when a new Congress convened and organized itself. The northerners argued that because the Congress was "new," no rules were operative and only a simple majority vote was needed to reduce the two-thirds requirement to three-fifths. The southerners raced to the battle, crying that the Senate was a "continuing" body and the old rules were still operative. They would filibuster any move to cut back on the number of votes needed to end a filibuster—and two-thirds of the Senate was needed to end their filibuster. The argument over whether the Senate was "new" or "continuing" then would go on for weeks.

When the Eighty-eighth Congress convened in January of 1963, northern liberals renewed their attack on the filibuster. Johnson, however, could resolve the conflict quickly. As President of the Senate, his formal title as that body's presiding officer, he could rule at the beginning of a Congress whether the Senate was continuing or new; whether the old rules applied or new rules could be adopted; whether, in effect, sixty-seven or sixty senators would be necessary to end a filibuster, and whether—or so it was argued in January 1963—civil rights legislation would pass that year. His ruling could be challenged from the Senate floor, but only a majority vote was needed to support a Vice Presidential ruling. The ball had been passed to Johnson. He dropped it.

Johnson refused to rule on the question, saying it was the responsibility of the Senate to decide, not the duty of the Vice President. The effect of his inaction was the same as if he had ruled against the liberals. It was also in conflict with the stated intention of Richard Nixon when he was Vice President. Nixon then had indicated that, if asked formally, he would rule the Senate was a new body. Johnson argued that the problem was purely one of parliamentary law. "It is not a question of whether the Vice President is a figurehead or not," Johnson said of himself in the Senate chamber. "It is a question of whether he is going to arrogate to himself power and authority he does not have." Although conceding he had power to enforce rules, Johnson denied he had the right "to assume the authority of a military junta." He then informed the Senate that "as anxious as the Vice President may be at times to choke off debate, this Vice President is never going to choke it off except in accordance with the rules."

Johnson's decision had not been dictated by the White House although it was consistent with the Kennedy administration position then of trying to help the Negro through Executive branch actions while avoiding a fight on civil rights with the southern congressional leaders. It was also the only decision open to Lyndon Johnson of Texas, the former protégé of Richard Russell, the "southern candidate" for the Presidential nomination in 1956 and 1960, the "sippin' and whittlin' " campaigner of the Kennedy-Johnson ticket. Lyndon Johnson had tried picturing himself as a westerner in his last Senate years and as Vice President. He wore the Stetson hats back at the LBJ ranch with aplomb and often spoke of his cattle with the familiarity and interest that other men use in speaking of their cotton crops. And his hill country was more a part of the traditional West than it was a part of the legendary South. Still, Johnson's political heritage came from the South. He could not yet escape it.

He had his defenders. Senator Eugene J. McCarthy of Minnesota, a Democrat, said that Johnson was fulfilling the duties of his office in refusing to make a ruling, and said that "if anybody is on trial it is not the Vice President but the Senate." Those who demand the Vice President make such a ruling, McCarthy insisted, wanted Johnson to "save the Senate from itself." And Senator George D. Aiken of Vermont, a leader of the liberal Republicans in the Senate, said Johnson "is simply trying to perform his duties."

But these were in a minority. Senator Joseph S. Clark of Pennsylvania, a liberal Democrat with many Negro constituents and an old adversary of Lyndon Johnson's, jumped to the attack. "We are not trying to make a dictator out of the Vice President," he said. "Nothing could be farther from our thoughts. All we are trying to do is ask the Vice President to exercise his undoubted authority." Joseph Rauh of the Americans for Democratic Action joined the chorus of criticism. He charged that Johnson "demonstrated once again that his first loyalty is to the southern racists." That was the bluntest and roughest attack of all. The Republicans did not stay out of the fight either. Senator Jacob Javits argued that the Vice Presidency "is not a hollow shell, but a great and vital office. Here is a chance where it could be shown. There comes a time when the chair must recognize he is Vice President of the United States."

These comments were more than practices in oratory. The Javits words signaled that Johnson's failure to act on the filibuster would be a basis for a Republican campaign attack against the Kennedy administration in 1964. The comments by Clark and Rauh indicated that the liberal wing of the Democratic Party was growing increasingly disenchanted with the Kennedy administration's position on civil rights. Although the leaders of this wing of the party could never desert the Democratic banner, they could demonstrate an absence of enthusiasm in the 1964 campaign, creating the possibility of a number of liberals supporting the Republican candidate if he was a liberal on civil rights—such as Nelson A. Rockefeller of New York, then one of the front-runners.

It came to this question: Had Lyndon Johnson, caught between the North he hoped to win and the South he could not afford to lose, become a liability to the Democratic ticket?

Lyndon Johnson has frequently said there comes a time when "a man must push in all his chips." Both he and Kennedy eventually did push in all their chips on the civil rights issue. The moment came in June 1963 after television had shown all America (and much of the world) the brutal treatment that Negroes in Birmingham, Alabama, were receiving from the local authorities. James MacGregor Burns, an early biographer of Kennedy's, once wrote of Kennedy's intellectual approach to the problem of civil rights that "this fear of making too much of a commitment, of going off the intellectual deep end, is locked in Kennedy's character. To him, to be emotionally or ideologically committed is to be captive."* On the night of June 11, 1963, Kennedy appeared on television to announce to the nation that "next week I shall ask the Congress of the United States to act, to make a commitment it has not fully made in this century to the proposition that race has no place in American life or law." Watching him that night convinced one that if John Kennedy's emotional commitment to the cause of civil rights had been lacking before, it no longer was now. He had indeed gone off the "intellectual deep end" and had

* Burns, *John Kennedy: A Political Profile*, Harcourt, Brace & Co., New York, 1959, p. 264.

become "emotionally captive." The black man's cause had become the White House's passion.

So at last had Lyndon Johnson made the same commitment. He made speeches that strongly supported the administration's new position, but that was not the crucial contribution he made. Eleven days after Kennedy had made his television speech to the nation, the President called together a group of civil rights leaders for a White House meeting. This was Saturday, June 22. The purpose of the meeting was to organize a massive lobbying effort for the civil rights bill. Some persons attending the meeting were a little disappointed with the administration's proposals, specifically Kennedy's reluctance to press for an FEPC. They wanted to have Congress add the FEPC to the administration bill, but doing that would require White House approval. When these civil rights people fanned out on Capitol Hill to urge the members of Congress to support not only the administration proposals but also an FEPC, the first question that would be thrown at them by a skeptical member of Congress was whether the White House would go along. If the civil rights people could only shrug, there would be no FEPC. But if they offered a positive "yes," then the members might be willing to make a fight for FEPC.

Joe Rauh, attending the June 22 meeting, wanted to put it directly to Kennedy, to ask his support for an FEPC. Before the question could be asked, however, Kennedy excused himself, turned to Lyndon Johnson and asked him to continue presiding over the session. Kennedy then left the room. Lyndon Johnson never had been Joe Rauh's favorite politician. The ADA had vigorously worked against Lyndon Johnson in 1960, trying to block his ambitions for the Presidential nomination, calling him "a conservative, anti-civil rights, gas-and-oil senator." At that convention, after Johnson's selection as running mate, Rauh denounced the placing of Johnson on the

ticket as "a betrayal."* Rauh had been one of the leaders in
the brief and unsuccessful revolt by the liberals against the
Johnson choice. When the District of Columbia delegation at
that convention, of which Rauh was a member, moved to join
the demonstration for Johnson, Rauh grabbed for the District
standard and wrestled with another man to keep the standard
out of the parade. Then he had capped off his public criticism
of Johnson with the "racists" remark earlier in 1963. Now Joe
Rauh stood to ask his question about the FEPC of Lyndon
Johnson. Rauh was to say later that "I was the worst person
in the world to ask him."

The anticipated answer was that the civil rights leaders
should not attempt to endanger the administration's bill and
its other legislative proposals by going after the "impossible."
The administration believed it would not have the required
Republican support if an FEPC was in the bill. That was the
answer expected from Kennedy. Lyndon Johnson listened po-
litely when Joe Rauh raised the question, giving no indication
he was aware of or cared about the earlier anti-Johnson remarks
made by Rauh. When the question was done, Johnson nodded
and answered: If you can get the votes, go ahead. Rauh and the
civil rights people left that meeting believing they had received
a more favorable response from Johnson than they would have
received from John Kennedy. They now were free to circulate
the message on Capitol Hill that they had the Vice President's
assurance that the White House would go along with an
FEPC, if Congress adds it, despite Kennedy's hesitation in
public. (An FEPC was in the final bill that passed Congress
in 1964.)

* Rauh considered the selection of Johnson in 1960 a personal betrayal as
well as a betrayal of philosophy. In the closing hours of the Kennedy drive
for the Presidential nomination Rauh had lobbied extensively among liberals
for Kennedy, offering the liberals assurances (received from Robert Kennedy
and Kenneth O'Donnell) that Johnson would not be picked for the second
position. After Johnson was named, one of these liberals—a Negro woman
—came to Rauh and spit in his face.

That meeting lacked drama. It was one of many sessions where strategy was plotted, where lobbying efforts were organized, where the administration stand was strengthened and sometimes weakened. It could not match in histrionics much of the debate that would come later in the House and Senate or the intrigue on Capitol Hill as members bartered for votes. Despite the openness and plainness of this meeting, however, it retained a certain glory. The word would spread on Capitol Hill—and to the southerners there—that the old member of the "Club" no longer was interested in making deals with his southern friends. No longer was the Texan pushing for a consensus based on the lowest common denominator as he had done in the past. The gangling young man from the Tenth Congressional District of Texas had come to Washington looking for power and had learned that "to get along, go along" meant that if a southerner was to get along in Washington he must go along with those opposed to civil rights. Now he was cutting out. Lyndon Johnson's commitment on civil rights was complete. No longer would Johnson be bound by his southern political heritage as it seemed he had been just five months earlier when he refused to rule on the filibuster. The change in his political standing was not sudden. It was definite, however. From now on, if the South backed Lyndon Johnson, it must realize that it could no longer count on him to protect his old region from a pro-civil rights administration. The movement of Lyndon Johnson from a southern segregationist to a national politician who would represent the national interest as opposed to a sectional desire was finished. Lyndon Johnson had pushed in all his chips on civil rights.

Why he did at the time was hotly debated by his friends and his enemies. His enemies, of course, said that the Texan was motivated strictly by political expediency, that the South by this time understood Johnson's position within the Kennedy administration and the responsibilities that such a position placed upon the Texan and did not expect more from him. His friends said the process that Johnson announced at the end of the 1957 civil rights fight—"This has been a debate which has opened closed minds"—had reached its climax in the development of Lyndon Johnson into a strong civil rights advocate.

The evidence is that Johnson's friends made a more accurate appraisal than did his enemies. In the summer of 1963 a political question mark hung over the civil rights issue. It was broad enough to cover both the North and the South. Polls showed the South splitting strongly against Kennedy where ordinarily it ran almost three-to-two in favor of a Democratic administration. In the North too there were doubts about being "too strong" on civil rights. The phrase "white backlash" already was coming into vogue. The Kennedy bill, even without the FEPC, was the strongest collection of civil rights proposals ever seriously laid before Congress. They added up to giving the Negro the legal power to move against segregated schools and a segregated way of life. And there was little doubt that the Negro intended to carry his attack not only against the South but also against the North. Many Democratic officials that summer of 1963 considered civil rights a "killing" issue politically. Even Kennedy had his fears that the civil rights issue could defeat him the next year. In the end, it turned out that the American people had been seriously misjudged. They not only were willing to accept the Kennedy bill but through their congressmen insisted that the bill be made stronger. That was a development that would come within the next twelve months; it was not evident when Kennedy, and Johnson with him, tied themselves to what they considered the most dangerous political issue.

But if the appraisal of Johnson's friends is the more accurate, it is not the only explanation. Certainly political expediency entered into the metamorphosis of Lyndon Johnson on civil rights. As a politician he always had responded to his constituency and as that constituency had broadened so had his political positions. Where the line should be drawn between the two explanations is unknown and may never be answered. The American political system concerns itself with results, rarely with motives.

FOUR

Lyndon Johnson long had been concerned about his political base in his home state. If his name on the national ticket in 1964 could not carry Texas, even the Johnson supporters would acknowledge it might be proper for the Democrats to drop him. His popularity obviously was declining from its high point in the late 1950s. This had first become apparent in 1960 when John G. Tower, a Republican, challenged him for his Senate seat. In that election Tower took 42 per cent of the popular vote. Republicans concede that that unusually high vote in 1960 for a member of the GOP was not a vote for Tower, then an obscure college professor, but a protest vote against Lyndon Johnson.

That protest was caused partly by Johnson's choosing to run on the national ticket with a Catholic, pro-civil rights candidate who had graduated from Harvard. "Texas had hardshell Baptists," explained one observer of the Texas political picture. "They combined with the Old South and the feudal barons—the ranchers who believed democracy was okay outside of their ranch, that is. And oil gave them enough money to support their views, which were very parochial. Some Texans who stayed with the Democrats in 1960 said of their buddies who defected: 'You let me look at their bank account and I'll tell you at what point they became Republican.' "

While Johnson's conservative backing was moving away from him, his liberal supporters also were growing increasingly disenchanted. Once Sam Rayburn had been the leader of the liberal faction in Texas and he had been the strong link between that group of Democrats and Johnson. But age and illness had sapped Rayburn's passion and the liberals had begun looking for a new leader. They turned to Ralph Yarborough. A three-time loser for the governorship, Ralph Yarborough was a liberal Democrat who paraded his liberalism, breaking openly with the leaders of his party who backed Eisenhower in 1952 and 1956. When he finally did win the statewide election to the United States Senate in 1957, he was a symbol of the growing strength of the liberal movement in Texas. This was a maverick movement. It would not be roped by the state leaders. Its members showed that in 1961. After Johnson was elected to the Senate in 1960, he resigned to become Vice President and Governor Price Daniel made an interim appointment, William Blakely, a conservative. To hold the office Blakely had to run in a special election in the spring of 1961; it was believed he would be operating from a strategic point because he would be the incumbent. John Tower again entered the Senate race and beat Blakely. Tower's victory was not credited to a Republican resurgence but to the liberal Democrats' staying away from the polls on election day. They chose to see a conservative Republican win rather than a conservative Democrat. It meant the Democratic Party of Texas was out of control.

Johnson was not a conservative. He had supported the national Democratic tickets in 1952 and 1956, even campaigned with Adlai Stevenson in the state. His voting record in the Senate in 1957 and after was as liberal as Yarborough's. But Johnson had cozied up to the business interests of the state, much more so than Yarborough, and was generally identified with the conservative wing. He never made as deep a break with it over the question of support for the national tickets as did Yarborough, for example. Because of Johnson's identification with the conservative Texas "establishment," the liberals in his party made Ralph Yarborough their leader. The irony of Lyndon Johnson's position in Texas was that he was losing his conservative support because he was part of a liberal administration but could not replace it with liberal support because the local liberals in Texas considered him too conservative.

The Vice President's first job in his home state was to make certain that his supporters controlled the state delegation to the 1964 Democratic convention. This delegation would be the start of Johnson's bargaining power at that session, if bargaining power was needed. The opportunity came in May 1962 in a primary election to name the Democratic candidate for governor. Quickly it became obvious that the primary, considered practically tantamount to election, was a test between a Lyndon Johnson man and a Ralph Yarborough man.

John Connally, one of the Johnson men who was brought into the New Frontier, resigned his position as Secretary of the Navy to enter the primary against a field of five other candidates. A former administrative assistant to Johnson when Johnson was in Congress and the manager of Johnson's 1960 drive for the Presidential nomination, John Connally was definitely Lyndon Johnson's "boy." His entire political career had been entwined with Johnson's. Although Connally was a decade younger and somewhat handsomer, he and Johnson were much alike when they stepped on the speaker's stand. It seemed they had adopted each other's mannerisms. More likely Connally had absorbed Johnson's. As Connally spoke, his big chin would thrust outward as if he were daring his opponents to take a swing at him. His fists crashed down on the podium before him. His face contorted into quick smiles as he scored

a point, then flashed into a grimace as he mentioned his opponents. It was like watching Lyndon Johnson; perhaps more
sophisticated, slightly less rough, more controlled, but still
Lyndon Johnson. During that campaign it was said that "if
John is cut up tomorrow, Lyndon will bleed."

Although John Connally could rightly call himself a New
Frontiersman because of his service as Secretary of the Navy,
he preferred describing himself as more moderate than John
Kennedy, even suggesting he was a conservative. He campaigned against such New Frontier staples as federal aid to
education and Medicare. One of his opponents was a young
Houston lawyer named Don Yarborough. Although Don and
Ralph Yarborough were not related by blood, they were alike
in political philosophy. Both were liberals. Don Yarborough
ran in the primary as a supporter of the New Frontier and
described himself as the only New Frontier Democrat in the
field of six primary candidates. It was an accurate description.

Connally started in the primary behind. The conservative
and traditional Democrats were expected to support the incumbent governor, Price Daniel, who was trying for another
two-year term, or divide among the other four candidates, who
ranged from conservative to extreme right wing in their philosophy. But Connally was Johnson's "boy" and the conservative money interests in the state went along with Johnson. As
a result Connally was able to finance a massive television and
billboard campaign which helped push him ahead of the other
five candidates. If being Lyndon Johnson's candidate was good
for raising funds from small groups with big bank accounts, it
was not too good for producing popular support. Except for
the Mexican-Americans in South Texas who remained loyal
to Johnson, the Vice President was considered a political liability among the voters in Texas in 1962. Connally publicly
disassociated himself from Johnson. "When John Connally sits
in that Governor's chair," he cried, "you're going to know

who's Governor of Texas. No man will occupy that chair with me or stand behind me." His campaign brochures showed pictures of Connally with prominent Democrats, even with John Kennedy, but not with Lyndon Johnson. The Vice President stayed out of the open campaigning to dampen down charges that Connally was "Lyndon's tool."

Johnson remained in the background. Connally used the Johnson organization, including the unlimited financing it gave him, the support of the Mexican-Americans who remained in the Johnson camp, plus his own conservative support, to come out ahead in the primary. There was a runoff the next month with Don Yarborough and Connally won that also. The primary contest had produced several results. It showed Texas Democrats still favored a conservative over a liberal. It indicated the political wisdom of public disassociation from both Lyndon Johnson and the New Frontier. And it gave control of the Texas delegation to the 1964 convention to a man who privately was believed completely loyal to Johnson. Lyndon Johnson could count on the party organization if not the voters.

Pulling in the voters was the next job for Lyndon Johnson. The Texan followed an old rule of politics: if you have a competitor for leadership, eliminate him. Johnson was being challenged for the leadership of the Texas Democrats by Ralph Yarborough. The answer then was knock Yarborough out of the race. The senator was up for reelection in 1964 and would face a primary earlier in that year. Johnson's approach was similar to the one used in the gubernatorial primary against Don Yarborough: find another candidate, back him and return Ralph Yarborough to the practice of law. With no leader of their own, the liberals would eventually fall back under the LBJ banner. Lyndon Johnson was, after all, the second half of the Kennedy-Johnson team.

In the summer of 1963 a seat on the Senate Appropriations

Committee opened up because of the death August 10 of Estes Kefauver. This was a prize position for any senator. The appropriations committee decided where and how much money could be spent. A member of that committee could increase his strength by doing favors for other members of the Senate— funneling federal funds into their states—and could collect favors from them later—votes for his own pet projects. Yarborough immediately staked out a claim for the committee seat. He was eligible because of his seniority, but the Democratic Steering Committee voting in secret ballot gave the committee position to Senator William Proxmire of Wisconsin. Proxmire was an ultra-liberal who had made a career out of tilting at the powers who controlled the Senate and it was surprising that those powers responded by giving him such a position of power. They usually are not so generous with their enemies. One of the leaders of the Senate Democrats later explained that Proxmire for some time had been trying to get on the Finance Committee but never had made it. He finally gave up his desire for that committee and switched his interest to Appropriations. "It was Proxmire's persistence that won over Yarborough, even though Yarborough had more seniority than did Proxmire," insisted this Democrat.

Yarborough did not accept this. In Texas he charged that "the lackeys and henchmen of a powerful Texas politician had lobbied with other senators against me. . . . It is more than strange that Texas politicians should work to advance that senator [Proxmire] who is the most bitter foe of Texas petroleum interests and the hardest working advocate of cutting the twenty-seven and one-half per cent depletion allowance." When the people of Texas read that statement of Yarborough's in their newspapers of Sunday, August 25, 1963, there was no doubt any longer that Yarborough and Lyndon Johnson were at war for the control of the state Democratic Party. Johnson's tactics were to strip Yarborough of his power in

Washington and to dramatize that weakness in Texas to make the election of a Johnson man in the 1964 primary that much more possible. Two Democratic members of the House already had been approached about tackling Yarborough in 1964. Yarborough's tactics in return were to charge Lyndon Johnson with sacrificing the best interests of Texas for his own personal ambitions and also to campaign as hard as possible. Yarborough spent fifty of the fifty-two weekends in 1963 campaigning in Texas.

The political situation deteriorated rapidly. The liberals squabbled among themselves. Don Yarborough wanted to take another crack at John Connally in the 1964 gubernatorial primary. Ralph Yarborough wanted Don to stay out that year. Ralph Yarborough figured Don would only split the liberal money and couldn't win anyhow. Also, a race between Don Yarborough and John Connally, Ralph Yarborough feared, might force John Kennedy into the dispute on the side of Lyndon Johnson's candidate and also turn John Kennedy against Ralph Yarborough.

The Democratic conservatives were becoming increasingly angry at Lyndon Johnson, primarily because of his support of the Kennedy civil rights position. Polls in the state were showing the white people in Texas to be five-to-one against the proposed civil rights bill. The Texan could not have it both ways. He had pushed in his chips on the New Frontier and the civil rights issue. He was gaining new support in the North, but he was having trouble within his own state, where the legend of the Old South had not yet completely disappeared. "LBJ," said a newsman who had covered Texas politics for some time, "was in the worst political straits of his career."

To visiting reporters in the fall of 1963 the Texas Republican leaders boasted that Barry Goldwater could take the state by 200,000 votes if the election were held then. Although that estimate was exaggerated, the Republicans were beginning to feel a growing confidence. "There was a general opposition in Texas to JFK's policies," a Republican leader commented later, "and this fell on LBJ, who could not divorce himself from the administration." In October of 1963 a poll taken in the Houston area showed Barry Goldwater more popular there than John Kennedy. The visiting newsmen also heard from Texas Democratic liberals that perhaps "Johnson may have outrun his usefulness on the Democratic ticket."

In September the Houston *Post* tried to give Johnson a boost by commenting editorially: "There's little doubt that Mr. Johnson will again be a candidate for Vice President when John Kennedy runs in 1964. The Washington hatchet corps has done its best to chop the President and the Vice President apart, but they have deep respect for each other; get along well." It was not the Washington hatchet corps doing the chopping, it was the Texas brigade. Liberal Democratic hatchet men figured the dumping of Johnson would finish his political career, end the dominance of the conservative faction within the state party and permit the liberal faction to emerge in control. Republican hatchet men figured dumping Johnson would anger the South and drive it to support a ticket headed by Barry Goldwater, whose views on federal civil rights legislation were more compatible with southern tradition.

The situation was confused and contradictory. It was a classic case of what happens when a state political organization gets out of control. As the leader of the party in the state, Lyndon Johnson was responsible for the confusion. In following the old rule of eliminating competition within an organization, Johnson was ignoring the new realities of politics. A political party was no longer the old-time "club" with a limited membership manipulated by a few people at the top. It was broadening into a vital organism that would dictate to its leaders rather than be dictated to by them. When Johnson, rather than bringing the conservative and liberal factions together, sided with one against the other, the result was chaos. No one was sure of what the party would do. Lyndon Johnson, who always before had managed to have the best of both the conservative and liberal worlds in Texas, now was losing them both. No one was certain of John Kennedy's position. People were confused by the two Yarboroughs. Republicans encouraged the chaos; they could only gain by it.

For some months President Kennedy had considered making a political trip to Texas. In October he met at the White House with Governor Connally, who urged him to make the trip, as did the Vice President. Kennedy tentatively set the second half of November as the time. There would be twenty-five electoral votes at stake in Texas in 1964 and Kennedy wanted to be certain they went Democratic.

FIVE

I N October of 1963 the political future of Lyndon Johnson was already threatened by either the disinterest or
disenchantment of the major powers in the Democratic Party,
the schism within the party in his own state and the general
aloofness of the New Frontier toward him. Then one more
trouble popped up in the form of a sharp, ingratiating young
man who once called himself Bobby Gene Baker but now preferred the more formal Robert G. Baker.

Bobby Baker, as he was usually known, was secretary to the
Democratic majority in the Senate. He had grown into the
position since first coming to the Senate from his native South
Carolina years earlier as a page boy. When Johnson was leader
of the Senate Democrats, Bobby Baker had been his protégé.
Baker did errands for him, counted votes, communicated the
Johnson feelings to recalcitrant members of the Senate. During a roll call vote in the Senate chamber, Baker would stand
at one of the doors to the Senate, telling the incoming Democrats the subject of the vote and the Johnson position. The
two men had a kind of Kennedy-Sorensen relationship. Baker
would walk past Johnson. Johnson would grunt and nod his
head. Baker would nod back. Some mysterious but important
message had passed between them. "They were so close they

could read each other's minds," is how one senator described their relationship in the 1950s.

Johnson had made Baker the secretary to the Democrats and always spoke highly of his aide. "That Bobby Baker is the greatest man who ever worked for me. You watch him. He's going to be governor of South Carolina some day" is how Johnson described his young friend during the 1960 campaign, as remembered by a man who was along on the "LBJ Special" campaign train. Unlike Kennedy and Sorensen, who called it quits at the end of the working day, Johnson and Baker saw each other socially. Two of Baker's children were named Lynda and Lyndon. Johnson was so pleased he gave Baker two white-faced Hereford cattle, which were kept at the LBJ ranch.

Working for Lyndon Johnson never was easy. Despite the temper tantrums of their boss, his constant demands, the long hours, the Johnson assistants were always loyal to him. They stayed with him many years and some of these staff members would later speak of their years with Johnson with love and with an almost-reverent feeling for their former boss. But there was also, mixed in with this respect and reverence, a feeling of fear. They cringed as Johnson drove them mercilessly. One Texan remembered that when Johnson was Senate majority leader his staff members only managed to get a vacation because a sympathetic newspaper reporter embarrassed Johnson into giving them some time off. The reporter wrote a story about the staff members working so hard with no vacation and then made certain Johnson saw the story. Johnson was not quite as difficult an employer as his regular staff thought he was. Once, when the Vice President was touring India with Carl Rowan of the State Department as his public relations man, Johnson wanted to make a statement about Nehru, including a paragraph Rowan wanted taken out. Johnson was not used to "no" men and insisted the paragraph stay in. Rowan was an experienced newsman who believed he knew his trade and insisted the section be deleted. The argument was remembered as hot and heavy. The next day Lyndon Johnson apologized to Rowan and went along with Rowan's advice and deleted the offending paragraph. Johnson thought highly of Rowan for some time after that. But Rowan's assertion of independence was an exception among those people who worked for Lyndon Johnson.

As difficult a job as it was to work for the Texan, no one was better at it than Bobby Baker. He eventually grew from Johnson's "yes" man running errands to a working partner. When the Senate was in session, the two men conferred constantly. Baker would suggest which senator's vote could be had for a slight change in a pending bill and reminded Johnson of past votes of senators. He told senators of their chances of Johnson's granting them a favored committee assignment or of permitting a vote on a favorite bill. It was a powerful position. If Baker had misled Johnson or another senator just slightly, he could change the outcome of a Senate action. Baker played it straight. He was loyal to Johnson, honest with the other senators and never swaggered.

The Democrats liked Baker. He seemed an admirable person. He had earned his law degree at night while holding a full-time job in the Senate during the day. In his earlier years he also had added to his Senate salary by driving a taxicab at night. Everyone respected him for his industriousness. Newspapermen who covered the Senate were particularly fond of him. When he was righthand man for Johnson in the Senate, he was known as one of the few men in Washington who delivered straight stuff. He would tell the reporter what the votes would be, who would win and by how much. He was usually right.

After Johnson left the Senate, Baker began to get more ambitious in a personal way. It is difficult to be near the

Senate without being conscious of money, big money. Many of the senators were rich. Robert Kerr, the oil magnate from Oklahoma with whom Bobby Baker was particularly close, was a fabulously wealthy person who displayed his wealth. Being close to him and others like him in the Senate, it was difficult for a young man who had once had to drive a taxicab at night not to want the kind of money Bob Kerr had. Baker began to branch out into various businesses. He opened a motel in Ocean City, Maryland, and his friends from the Senate and from the Washington press corps were happy to come down and give the motel a well-attended and well-publicized opening. He organized a vending machine company and sold its services to defense contractors. The company obtained some lucrative contracts. Everyone involved in those transactions later denied there was any suggestion that Baker was offering help in obtaining lucrative defense contracts in exchange for the vending machine contracts, nor was there any proof this had been the deal. Starting from scratch, however, Baker's company quickly became one of the biggest in the country.

In the fall of 1963 one of Baker's disgruntled associates brought suit against him. A magazine circulated in the vending machine industry reported the suit and then the newspapers picked up the story. An investigation began that was to involve congressional committees, hundreds of newsmen, the Justice Department, and a federal grand jury—all looking for some evidence of malfeasance on the part of Bobby Baker. His resignation as a Senate employe was quickly accepted.

This was the Billie Sol Estes's scandal all over again, only worse. If Johnson had been protected by the inability of his opponents to link him directly with Billie Sol Estes, there could be no doubt of his ties to Bobby Baker. The question mark that had hovered over him after the Billie Sol Estes case now seemed to settle directly on his shoulders. Bobby Baker definitely had been Johnson's "boy."

As Vice President, Johnson always was concerned about his "image." In Washington he refused to plead for contracts for Texas firms or for the location of federal installations in his home state (although back in Texas he did not object to taking some of the credit when federal funds did come into the state). Johnson did not want the people in the nation's capital to think of him as a "wheeler-dealer." That phrase had been used about him when he was Senate leader to describe his technique in dealing with votes—not with money. But still Johnson's wealth, and he was very wealthy by the time he became Vice President, always had caused a certain amount of suspicion in Washington. If he could in any way be tied to a Bobby Baker deal, a chorus of voices would immediately start up suggesting that all Johnson's money had been made by misusing his position in government.

Born poor, Lyndon Johnson had to borrow $10,000 in 1937 (an advance against his wife's expected inheritance) to finance his first campaign for Congress. By the time he was Vice President twenty-four years later, he and his family had a combined wealth of between five million and ten million dollars. It had come almost exclusively from radio and television broadcasting. No other private industry is so closely regulated and so dependent on the federal government as is the broadcasting industry. It is watched over by the Federal Communications Commission, an independent agency established by Congress, which allots the publicly owned radio and television channels to privately owned companies and then oversees their usage. An FCC decision can destroy or enrich a person.

In 1943 Lady Bird Johnson purchased a money-losing Austin radio station for $17,500. The story is told by friends of the Johnson family of how Mrs. Johnson, after making the purchase, charged into the station offices with a mop and pail. While that may be true, she did not waste too much of her time being a charwoman. The station's difficulties had not stemmed from too much dirt on the floor but from too much interference with the airwaves. The station shared a frequency with a college station and could only operate when the college station was off the air. Also, its broadcasting power had a limited geographical range. The previous owners of the station had tried getting FCC permission to increase the station's power and to operate around the clock on an independent frequency. They were astute businessmen, but they could not persuade the FCC. The wife of the congressman could, however, and quickly did. As soon as Lady Bird Johnson's station was operating full time, it acquired network affiliation and began to earn money.

In 1949 when Johnson became a senator, he joined the Senate Commerce Committee. This committee has more jurisdiction over the FCC than does any body in Washington. It authorizes funds for the agency to operate; it must approve the commission members after the President appoints them and before the Senate confirms them and it writes the legislation under which the FCC operates. In the 1950s the FCC began a series of actions that divided up the financially lucrative television channels to broadcasters across the nation. Mrs. Johnson's company did well in this decision-making process, amazingly well in fact. Because of favorable FCC decisions it gained a monopoly in Austin and did well in other cities when it branched out. There is nothing in the FCC files to indicate Lyndon Johnson ever tried to pressure the agency on behalf of his wife's company and each FCC decision that helped Mrs. Johnson's company could be explained logically as being the correct one. Some of them, however, could easily have gone the other way.

Although the Vice President himself never owned any stock

in his wife's company, he did benefit from having an independent source of income from his wife's money. Being a
member of Congress is expensive. It requires two homes, one
in the congressional district or state and one in Washington.
It requires traveling back and forth between the constituency
and the Capitol. It requires dressing well, contributing to
local charities and entertaining often. This last is more important than is generally realized. A young man in Washington often makes his first important contacts when participating
in Washington's social life. An important personage in Washington also is expected to be generous in his entertaining; it
is part of his job. When Johnson became Vice President, he
gave up his comfortable Georgetown home and purchased
"The Elms" because he needed the larger house for the entertaining he expected his duties would require, particularly of
foreign dignitaries. "The Elms" with its modernization cost
him over $300,000.

Johnson did not enjoy any inference that his wife's company had benefited from his position in Congress. As he told
it to friends, his wife had invested almost all her money into
what had been a losing business, worked diligently and had
made it succeed. As for her "luck" with television, Johnson
argued that his wife was willing to take a chance on television
when it was still a fledgling and chancy industry and that she
should not be punished or reprimanded because she profited
where others had feared to tread with their dollars.

At the FCC there was a little different feeling. Officials
there generally wish that members of Congress would not hold
any interest in radio or television. They do not expect that
members of Congress will try to coerce them into favorable
decisions. But no one can be certain whether an employe of
the agency—be he the lowliest clerk who does the preliminary
work that shapes the decision or an agency chieftain who
formalizes the decision—is influenced by the specter of a

prominent member of Congress looking over his shoulder with great personal interest. It is not an easy situation for the congressman either. If he has independent funds or earns extra money while he is in Congress, it is difficult for him to find any industry or area to invest in that is not, in some way, touched by the federal government and by the laws which the member of Congress either helps pass or opposes.* Congress as an institution has taken no action to help the situation except to decree that a member may refrain from voting on a bill if he feels the personal consideration is too strong. Few members avail themselves of this opportunity.

The situation was worse for newly rich members of Congress like Lyndon Johnson. Americans trust men with inherited wealth such as Franklin Roosevelt and John Kennedy. But Americans are distrustful of persons in public life who amass large wealth quickly, particularly if the wealth is amassed after the person comes to public office. Although the caliber of government officials has risen tremendously since the last century, when votes could often be bought without difficulty and bureaucrats greatly augmented their income with outside "favors," the public still suspects the politician of using his public office for personal gain.

Because of this suspicion Lyndon Johnson was ripe for a charge of being a "wheeler-dealer" with money—not with votes.

Nor did it help Lyndon Johnson that the only taint of scandal touching the Kennedy administration involved either his old associates like Bobby Baker or fellow Texans such as Billie Sol Estes and Fred Korth. Korth, a Fort Worth banker, replaced John Connally as Secretary of the Navy and held the

---

* When John Kennedy became President, he placed his personal fortune in government bonds to avoid the charge of personally benefiting when a company in which he owned stock received a government contract. It was immediately pointed out, however, that as President he could influence the amount of interest paid on his bonds.

job when the Defense Department gave the controversial and lucrative contract for the TFX fighter-bomber airplane to the General Dynamics Corporation. This company was a customer of Korth's old bank. President Kennedy personally defended Korth's integrity. "I have no evidence that Mr. Korth acted in any way improperly in the TFX matter," said the President at his news conference October 31, 1963. Korth resigned his job as Navy Secretary and returned to Texas.

There was a feeling in Washington that was summed up by Senator Thruston B. Morton of Kentucky, who had been the Republican National Committee chairman during the 1960 election. Speaking before a GOP group in late October of 1963, Morton said: "There are some funny things going on in Washington. The Secretary of the Navy has left town rather hurriedly. Lyndon Johnson's boy Bobby Baker resigned. Now I wonder if Lyndon is expecting the purge? I don't think Lyndon expects it, but it may happen." Morton made the comment in the time-honored political tradition of lousing up your opponents, hoping to stir up some trouble between the northern liberal Democrats and the southerners. He himself did not believe that Johnson would be dropped from the 1964 ticket. To do so, he commented privately, would be to make Johnson a "martyr" to the South and make the Democratic losses there in the Presidential election greater than would normally be expected.

There were other views. Reporters know that scandal can topple an administration when nothing else can. They inclined toward the view that Johnson might be the sacrificial lamb if one was needed to prove the purity of the New Frontier. "Mr. President . . . There is talk that Lyndon Johnson will be dumped next year. Senator Thruston Morton used the word 'purged.' Now, sir, assuming that you run next year, would you want Lyndon Johnson on the ticket, and do you expect that he will be on the ticket?" Kennedy paused for a moment, then answered slowly: "Yes, to both of those questions. That is correct." He was caught in the same bind that day, October 31, that he had been caught in when a similar question had been thrown at him in May of 1962. Indicating publicly that he wanted Johnson off the ticket would have begun a mad scramble for the Vice Presidential nomination, probably would have alienated some important southern leaders in Congress and would have created a year of political chaos. For this reason—plus an apparent, even if unintentional, lack of enthusiasm in Kennedy's response when compared to the answer he had given seventeen months earlier —reporters began to fan out over Washington in search of a possible story. They could not find one. John Kennedy, as far as the press could tell, had given no indications that his private thoughts on Johnson were any different from his public comments. And naturally the Democratic leaders followed the President. "It is inconceivable that Vice President Johnson will not be renominated," said Hubert Humphrey to the Associated Press. "He has done a fine job and I am for him." Humphrey apparently had given up his dreams of becoming President or Vice President, settled down to work in the Senate and was beginning to hit his stride as a brilliant legislative leader. There had been some discussion outside White House circles of a Kennedy-Humphrey ticket in 1964.

At about this point Lyndon Johnson received some help from an unexpected quarter. In 1960 the Liberal Party in New York had been reluctant to endorse a Democratic ticket with Lyndon Johnson on it. But in 1963 that same Party was now trying to insure that Johnson would be renominated in 1964. At the 1960 convention, after it was learned that Johnson was Kennedy's choice, a group of labor leaders had met in Walter Reuther's hotel suite. Some of the labor leaders wanted to denounce the ticket, but Reuther was trying to calm them. "A study in controlled anger," according to one participant that Thursday in Los Angeles, "Reuther was not a bomb thrower." He understood the choice of Johnson could not be blocked and any attempts to do so would kill chances for labor-backed legislation in Lyndon Johnson's Senate. One of the labor leaders there who tended toward "bomb throwing" was Alex Rose, president of the United Hatters, Cap and Millinery Workers Union and a vice chairman of the Liberal Party. His opposition to Johnson and that of most of the labor leaders collapsed when Rose took a phone call from David Dubinsky, president of the International Ladies Garment Workers Union and also the first vice chairman of the Liberal Party. Calling from New York, Dubinsky said of the Kennedy-Johnson lineup: "I think it's a good ticket. I think it's a ticket that can win." Dubinsky had known Johnson a long time and believed he had done the best he could in the realm of social welfare legislation. Dubinsky also was a practical politician. He did believe the ticket could beat the Republicans. Now in the fall of 1963 when Johnson again appeared in trouble David Dubinsky returned to his rescue. Johnson was invited to speak at the annual dinner of the Liberal Party in New York. The party members hustled out and oversold the dinner. Instead of the fifteen hundred persons who usually show up at those affairs, two thousand tickets were sold for the Johnson dinner and it had to be moved to a larger hall. The day of the dinner, Dubinsky took the Vice President on a tour of the garment district in New York and introduced him as his special friend. When Dubinsky was asked about the Liberal Party's coolness toward Johnson in 1960, Dubinsky shouted back, "If he wasn't popular then, he's very popular now." The affair was an elaborate demonstration of the Liberal Party's support for the Texan.

Even with David Dubinsky in his corner, Johnson, according to some associates of his at the time, was concerned about his political future. He could not be certain his new devotion to the Negro's cause would earn him the strong support of the civil rights advocates. The situation with the Democratic Party in Texas was coming closer and closer to the explosive point. Johnson could not ask the President for a commitment about his future.

And the talk of Robert Kennedy's being groomed as his older brother's successor continued to float just beneath the surface of talk in Washington, jumping out occasionally to make everyone near Lyndon Johnson stop in embarrassment. The Texan's supporters heard rumors of a Kennedy "cabal" organized to force Johnson off the ticket. The cabal had met late in October with all the Kennedys present except the President. All persons at the session agreed Johnson must be dumped from the 1964 ticket—with one exception, the President's wife, Jacqueline. The story was untrue. Still, it and others like it were the vogue in gossip that month. The President heard them and tried to squelch them. In November he was on an airplane trip and gave a ride to a senator with some experience in Washington. After some idle chatter the senator blurted out the accusation that Robert Kennedy was using his position as Attorney General to "leak" to newsmen information the FBI had gathered connecting Johnson with Billie Sol Estes and Bobby Baker. Robert Kennedy's purpose, the senator charged, was to force the removal of Johnson from the 1964 ticket so that Robert Kennedy could run with his older brother on a Kennedy-Kennedy ticket. The President was aghast. "What you're saying," the President told the senator, "is that my brother is trying to help me by calling the number two man in the administration a crook, something which would blacken my administration as well as alienate the South. And he's doing it so he can run on the ticket with me. There's not enough talk now about too many Kennedys!" The President added: "If he were doing that I'd fire him."

Actually, in the President's official and personal family it was assumed that the 1964 ticket would be Kennedy and Johnson. In April 1963 Robert Kennedy had been asked the question when making a visit to Atlanta, Georgia. He answered there that the ticket would be Kennedy and Johnson and that he also anticipated that the South would be more difficult in 1964 for the Democrats than it had been in 1960, an obvious reference to the civil rights issue. As for his own future Robert Kennedy said he would continue as Attorney General through 1964 and was vague on his plans after that. The Democratic National Committee also anticipated that it would be working for a Kennedy-Johnson ticket. John M. Bailey of Connecticut, the party's national chairman, had publicly predicted it in several speeches and his staff was working in that direction. At the White House the President's personal aides also assumed it would be a Kennedy-Johnson lineup. They saw nothing to indicate that Johnson would leave the ticket. Nor did anyone in the White House circle have any serious suggestions for a replacement; Robert Kennedy's name was not being put forward. There were other reasons that influenced the Kennedy aides to believe the man they still thought of as "Uncle Cornpone" would be around as Vice President for several more years. They considered that when John Kennedy had originally made the offer to Johnson in 1960 it had been for the expected eight years of the Kennedy administration, not just four, even if a specific number of years was not mentioned in the early Thursday morning meeting between Kennedy and Johnson at the 1960 convention. "Jack Kennedy had made a commitment to LBJ and intended to abide by it," said one Kennedy aide sometime later. Another agreed, adding: "Jack Kennedy never fired anybody in his life. He didn't know how. He was not going to start with his Vice President."

The assumption that Johnson would be on the ticket was accepted at the first planning conference on Democratic campaign strategy for the 1964 Presidential election. The meeting was held November 12 at the White House, beginning about four o'clock in the afternoon. Johnson was not present, but then only those who would have an influential voice on the election strategy were. Johnson's role in the 1964 campaign would be much like his role in the 1960 campaign and like his role as Vice President: he would follow others' directives. If he had become an accepted part, he still was not an intimate member of the New Frontier. Nor would he ever be. Most of the discussion that day centered around the convention to be held in Atlantic City the next summer and whether the South should have its delegate strength reduced. The group decided tentatively that Lyndon Johnson should be nominated for the Vice Presidency on Wednesday night of the convention and that John Kennedy should be nominated the next night. This reversed the traditional procedure that had the Presidential candidate nominated first. The switch was contemplated as part of a search to bring some drama to the convention. As one who attended the meeting later said, "Renominating two incumbents is just warmed over potatoes." At previous conventions the Presidential choice had been made first so that the Presidential nominee could then name his choice for a running mate with complete freedom, as Kennedy did in 1960. Only a nominee certain of his choice for a running mate could authorize the running mate's being named first. When that decision was made at the November 12 meeting, those present talked specifically of Johnson's being nominated for the Vice Presidency. No one at that session raised any objections or voiced any doubts that Lyndon Johnson would be the nominee. Among those present were the President, Robert Kennedy and most of the White House contingent of the Irish Mafia who never had been friendly to the Texan.

The strength of Lyndon Johnson had won out. That strength was his ability to persevere. As the men of the Texas hill country stand before the ravages of nature, Johnson had stood before the political hazards of Washington. His toughness was his tenaciousness. The Vice Presidency had been a disappointment to him. He had not been John Kennedy's chief lobbyist on Capitol Hill as he originally planned. He had not been the "one man the President can turn to" as he had hoped. He had been only the shadow of John Kennedy, and a shadow with blurred lines at that. Despite these disappointments, Johnson had held on. When Joe Rauh had described him as a "racist" at the beginning of the year, Johnson had kept his temper and avoided a personal name-calling fracas that would have turned the liberal wing of the Democratic Party even more against him and made an eventual rapprochement with the liberals impossible. When the Kennedy administration made errors, such as the Bay of Pigs episode in 1961, Johnson had not tried to disassociate himself publicly from the responsibility for such acts as did other members of the administration at times. When Johnson had complaints, he generally kept them out of the newspapers. When he ran up against Robert Kennedy, he retreated in silence. When Johnson spoke publicly, he chose his words carefully so as not to embarrass the President. His loyalty to John Kennedy was complete. For Kennedy this was sufficient to cause him to be loyal in return. Lyndon Johnson would be on the ticket again in 1964.

The Kennedy commitment to Johnson, however, could not be complete. Politics forbade that. When an incumbent campaigns to stay in office, he basically wages a defensive campaign. His policies and program, his record of success and failure are public. He must wait for his opponent to stake out the areas of attack and then defend himself. There were several areas, it appeared early in November 1963, where Kennedy might come under attack. With some of these—deficit spending, the alleged Kennedy "attack" on business—it would make little difference who the running mate was. In two other potential areas of attack, however, the identity of the Democratic Vice Presidential candidate could have an impact on the outcome of the election. One was the Bobby Baker investigation and the other was civil rights. It was then too early to know if the Baker investigation would produce anything to embarrass the Vice President. John Kennedy did not believe it would.

As for the impact of the civil rights issue, that depended on whom the Republicans nominated. Although Kennedy looked with a personal eagerness toward a political engagement with Barry Goldwater, a personal friend and a philosophical adversary, Kennedy did not really believe the Arizona Republican would be nominated. He contemplated that the Republicans would nominate someone more in the political center, such as William Scranton of Pennsylvania or perhaps Rockefeller of New York if he could overcome the political handicap of his divorce and remarriage. Such a center candidate would express the same attitudes on civil rights as had Kennedy. "My judgment is," the President said, "based on history, that the Republican Party also will make a clear stand on this issue. I would be surprised if they didn't." The political professionals in the Democratic Party agreed with the Kennedy assessment that the Republican candidate would not be Goldwater, as much as the Democrats would enjoy taking him on. Early in the year an aide at the Democratic National Committee wrote a lengthy memorandum detailing how Goldwater was gaining delegate strength, where he had potential for more delegates and implying he would be the nominee in another nineteen months. The memorandum was filed away and its author scolded for wasting time. If Kennedy was correct, and the Republican candidate was a liberal on civil rights, Lyndon Johnson would then be valuable on the Democratic ticket,

arguing below the Mason-Dixon line that civil rights trans-
cended party lines. That would be the only possible political
tactic in the South and Johnson would be the only possible
person who could convince the South of that without at the
same time costing the Democrats support in the North. Another southerner might do better in the South if he was a
segregationist, but he would hurt Kennedy among Negroes in
the North. A northerner would probably not be listened to in
the South.

But politics is unpredictable. The possibility that Goldwater might capture the candidacy could not be ignored, as
improbable as it was that a major political party would desert
the political center where the votes were. Goldwater was popular in the South. The polls then showed Goldwater beating
Kennedy by 52 to 48 per cent in the South. If Goldwater did
become the nominee, Kennedy would be under pressure to
write off the South entirely, drop Johnson for a running mate
who was a midwestern or far west liberal and concentrate on
picking up strength in that area of the country. Kennedy was
not inclined to go along with this approach. "He wasn't writing
off any part of the country," one of his aides later explained.
Kennedy's inclination was to have Johnson as a counter to
Goldwater, if he was the nominee, in the South.

A significant clue to Johnson's political future was unknown
to him. Ralph Yarborough frequently had complained to John
Kennedy about his patronage problems in Texas. Ever since
his first clash with Johnson over the sixteen appointments in
1961, Yarborough had been trying to eke out more federal
jobs for his supporters. He never had received much encouragement from the White House, but usually there had
been sympathy at least. As 1963 moved toward its close and
the beginning of a Presidential election year, even the sympathy began to wane. The President was indicating more sup-

port for Lyndon Johnson, making clear to Yarborough that the White House regarded Lyndon Johnson as the political boss of the Texas Democrats and would continue to regard him so. Yarborough heard rumors of the impending dumping of Johnson, but he did not believe them.

S I X

*A*ir Force II, its silver wings glinting from the bright
morning sun, touched down at Love Field in Dallas,
Texas, a few moments after eleven thirty o'clock Friday,
November 22, 1963. The Vice President and Mrs. Johnson,
accompanied by several Secret Service agents, came down the
steps from the airplane and shook hands with the local Dallas
officials making up the reception committee. They all chatted
for a few moments and then walked over to where *Air Force I,*
the President's plane, would come to a halt. The President
and Vice President never traveled in the same airplane and
never during parades in the same car. This had disturbed
Lyndon Johnson in the first year of his Vice Presidency, but
he had come to accept it and realize the practice was a valuable one from the standpoint of security. Because it was never
proper that the President be made to wait for anyone, the
Vice President's plane always landed ahead of the President's,
and he waited.

The flight from Fort Worth was less than ten minutes and
shortly the President's plane appeared in the sky, touched
down on the runway and then, at eleven forty, wheeled to a
stop where Lyndon Johnson and the Dallas reception committee were waiting. Inside *Air Force I,* as they were about to

step out into the sunlight, the President and Mrs. Kennedy were in high spirits. David Powers, an old political cohort from John Kennedy's Boston days and the New Frontier's unofficial court jester, stood at the door as the President and his wife disembarked. He told them they looked like "Mr. and Mrs. America" and advised they should not both wave in the same direction because "it would be too much for anyone to receive all that attention at once."

It seemed a day for such pleasant jokes and smiles. This was the second day of the President's two-day political foray into Texas and it was proving successful beyond all expectations. The crowds in Houston and Fort Worth, as would be the crowd here in Dallas, were larger and friendlier than had been anticipated. All the Kennedy-Johnson troubles had seemed to climax in this trip and so far all indications were that they were overcoming them. The first difficulty had been the feud between the two wings of the Democratic Party in Texas. This had played a large part in Kennedy's decision to come to Texas. Those twenty-five electoral votes at stake in the 1964 Presidential election were becoming increasingly pivotal as the GOP continued to gain strength—as indicated by the polls and news stories.

John Kennedy's approach to resolving the feud was different than Lyndon Johnson's had been. Where Johnson had wanted to battle the liberal Democrats by defeating Yarborough in a primary with a hand-picked candidate, Kennedy wanted to compromise the dispute. He would support the conservative John Connally for governor and the liberal Ralph Yarborough for senator in 1964. He would unite the two factions, not split them further. Johnson would go along with this approach. Not only was there no way the Vice President could oppose his President, but also Kennedy was combining this approach with a public demonstration of his support for and his faith in Lyndon Johnson. That Friday night the Kennedys were to be the house guests of the Johnsons at the LBJ ranch. It would be John Kennedy's second visit to the ranch, his first as President, and Mrs. Kennedy's first. Every politician in Texas—and elsewhere—understood that Kennedy would not plan to stay at the LBJ ranch if he were then considering dumping his Vice President in 1964 or if he believed any future Bobby Baker revelations would cause embarrassment.

Although there can be too many unforeseen developments to permit a binding agreement until the very last moment, Kennedy was going as far as he could possibly go in demonstrating his intention of having Lyndon Johnson as his running mate again. The public statements Kennedy had made at his news conferences, first in May 1962 and again in October 1963, were the only answers he could have made to the questions at those times and did not have too much meaning by themselves. But those statements combined with Kennedy's trip to Texas to heal the political feud there and to stay with the Johnsons were an expression of the President's desire for a united Democratic Party in the state with Lyndon Johnson at its head. His White House aides read the events that way also. Not only did they generally agree that Johnson would be on the ticket with Kennedy again in 1964, but most felt that the Texan would be the leading contender—if not the only one—for the Democratic Presidential nomination in 1968.

The rupture in the Texas party did at last look healed that Friday morning. The previous day, when the Presidential motorcade had swept through San Antonio and Houston, Ralph Yarborough carefully avoided riding with Lyndon Johnson. In San Antonio he shared a car with Representative Henry B. Gonzalez and in Houston with Representative Albert Thomas. "It's not that I love Lyndon less," said Yarborough, "but that I love Henry [Gonzalez] more." Gonzalez and Thomas were extremely popular in those cities and every politician wants to be seen with a popular vote-getter in his home ground. Later that day Yarborough had ridden with Johnson, when the motorcade came into Fort Worth from the airport, but it was dark then. That Thursday night the conservative and liberal Democrats remained sharply split. Connally, for example, had arranged a reception for the President in Austin Friday afternoon. He did not want to invite Yarborough, so he limited the guest list to state officials. Yarborough, in turn, released a statement to the press saying: "I desire that my friends take no offense at this. I want everyone to join hands in harmony for the greatest welcome to the President and Mrs. Kennedy in the history of Texas. Besides, Governor Connally is so terribly uneducated governmentally, how could you expect anything else?" By this time the juvenility of the situation had disgusted the Kennedy people. Late Thursday night Kenneth O'Donnell and Larry O'Brien, with some occasional intervention from the President, worked hard on Yarborough to persuade him to end the feud. The Kennedy formula meant Johnson as head of the state party with Connally and Yarborough immediately beneath him and bringing their respective factions behind Johnson and the national ticket. If Yarborough did not agree, there always was the possibility that the President would refuse to support him in the 1964 primary. Yarborough thought he could take on a Johnson candidate without too much difficulty. "That's the kind of opponent you want to have," he said of one of the men approached by Johnson. But Yarborough was less sure that he could win if the President did not back him. Yarborough agreed to the truce and would ride in the Dallas motorcade with the Vice President. Said one person who was involved in the negotiations the previous Thursday evening: "It was all sweetness and light Friday, at least on the surface." It was a troubled truce, but it was a truce.

When the President's plane had landed in Dallas, the President and Mrs. Kennedy, after being greeted by the reception committee, went along the fence shaking hands with well-wishers there. The Vice President and Mrs. Johnson followed behind them, shaking the hands that the Kennedys had missed. While they were politicking, Larry O'Brien was arranging the motorcade. Everyone, it seemed, wanted to ride in an up-front car. As one Texas politician remarked later: "The only rift in Texas was who could stand closest to Kennedy." And this was another reason for considering the trip successful. Despite all the polls and the newspaper stories indicating how badly a Kennedy-Johnson ticket would fare in Texas, the outpouring of the people in the Texas cities visited by the President indicated otherwise and the rush of local politicians to be near Kennedy demonstrated the President's popularity. These local politicians understood the mood of the voters best and they all lined up with Kennedy. "I been telling you all the time Kennedy would sweep Texas," said a Texas member of Congress to one of the Irish Mafia that Friday morning.

The crucial issue in Texas as throughout the South was civil rights and this had been one of the main reasons bringing Kennedy to Texas. There had been so much talk and so many reports of right-wing extremism flourishing in Texas since the 1960 election—fathered by the civil rights trouble and nurtured by conservative oil money—that Kennedy felt obliged to appear himself in the state. He believed that if he could speak to people face-to-face he could convince them of the logic of his approach. It appeared that day that the Texans, while they might complain loudly about civil rights to the pollsters and newsmen, were coming to the point where they would accept it. In Fort Worth that morning Lyndon Johnson had commented to Jack Bell of the Associated Press: "We've got this civil rights thing whipped. They've quit blaming Kennedy for it. They think it's inevitable. I think we're going to be all right in Texas in November."

At eleven fifty the motorcade left Love Field and began

moving through the residential areas outside of Dallas. An earlier threat of rain had disappeared and the officials rode in open cars without tops. The Vice President riding in the motorcade's fourth car, two cars behind the President, commented that the crowds were thin. Mrs. Johnson and Senator Yarborough answered that while that might be true, the crowd obviously was friendly and in good spirits. Riding in the President's car, Governor Connally considered these early crowds "restrained." He said later: "I mean they were not wildly enthusiastic, but they were grown people. There was a mature crowd as we went through some of the residential areas. They applauded and they were obviously very friendly in their conduct." In the car behind the President's, Kenny O'Donnell had a less positive opinion of the crowd lining the suburban streets. "They were mostly white collar," he said later. "The crowd reflected a middle to an upper class type. They were not unfriendly nor terribly enthusiastic. They waved. But were reserved, I thought."

As the motorcade neared downtown Dallas, the nature of the crowd changed. It exploded in a friendliness out of all proportion to what had been expected. A quarter of a million people crushed themselves along the parade route to see the President. They gave tremendous cheers as his car passed by. This is the city that had been considered the hotbed of rightwing extremism. Here three years earlier Lyndon Johnson and his wife had been roughed up and spat upon by a group of overzealous Republicans. Just a month before this Presidential trip Adlai Stevenson also had been treated in the same rough manner. This city had as its congressman the Republican Bruce Alger, who was one of the most conservative members of the House. And Kennedy had done worse in this city in the 1960 election than in any other city in the nation. But the President had not been deterred by these facts. They encouraged him to visit Dallas. If he was being challenged by

right-wing extremism there, he would use the occasion to denounce extremism. In the luncheon speech he had prepared
and which the press already was sending across the nation, he
spoke out against the "other voices [which] are heard in the
land—voices preaching doctrines wholly unrelated to reality,
wholly unsuited to the sixties, doctrines which apparently
assume that words will suffice without weapons, that vituperation is as good as victory and that peace is a sign of weakness."

The voice of Kennedy would be a confident voice among the
strident. He had reason for confidence. After a slow and un-
certain start, the New Frontier was gaining the glow of success. The Cuban confrontation and the limited test ban treaty
had given promise of a turn away from the direction of ulti-
mate war. Domestically, Kennedy was doing well also. His tax
cut bill had passed the House. Because that side of Capitol
Hill was more conservative on money matters than was the
Senate, the House action meant the Senate was certain to follow. Harry F. Byrd of Virginia, the conservative Democrat
who headed the tax-writing Finance Committee in the Senate,
already had conceded to reporters that a bill would pass. Byrd
strongly opposed the bill, but he realized the support for it was
too strong to block. Kennedy was proud of this achievement.
He had spent more than a year educating the American public
to the notion, unique for the United States, that budget defi-
cits should be deliberately sought as a spur to the economy.
The traditional "Puritan ethic" that debt was inherently bad
had been overcome and soon the country would be "moving
again."

The civil rights program also was doing well. In mid-
October the Attorney General had worked out a compromise
acceptable to both liberal Democrats and conservative Republicans. This compromise insured the inevitable passage of
the most sweeping civil rights legislation ever seriously considered by the federal government since the Reconstruction

Era. The bill would include most of the political demands of the civil rights groups. Some of those demands had seemed far beyond the possibility of enactment into law only a few months earlier. And more important, there was strong evidence that once the law was passed, it would be obeyed. Through private and unofficial intercession by the Executive branch many of the establishments that would be covered by the public accommodations section of the proposed bill, its most controversial section, already had agreed voluntarily to desegregate.

There were difficulties remaining. The struggle to keep the next year's budget within reasonable limits had begun. It should not be more than $1.5 billion over the $100 billion mark, Kennedy had directed. The very next week the Senate was taking up a bill to block the sale of American wheat to Russia. The foreign aid program was meeting a greater resistance in Congress than ever before. Perhaps the most serious of the Washington difficulties was taking place that very moment in a secret meeting on Capitol Hill. There an insurance salesman named Don B. Reynolds was telling congressional investigators that with the help of Bobby Baker he had sold Lyndon Johnson a large life insurance policy. Then, Reynolds charged, he had been solicited by Walter Jenkins, an assistant to Johnson, to buy television advertising time on the Johnson family owned television station.

But the major domestic commitments John Kennedy had made and in which he had been joined by Lyndon Johnson appeared near fulfillment. From the point of view of politics in its basic sense, to get reelected, fulfilling the commitment on equal rights had seemed dangerous for both Kennedy and Johnson. Now it appeared this sunny day in Texas that both had overcome the political dangers. The chances were good that the country would back them.

They were still a strange combination, Kennedy and Johnson, after their three-year partnership. Kennedy had started on the road that led him to this point as an adventurer looking for personal fulfillment. When asked about why he liked the job of President, he would answer with the "definition of happiness of the Greeks . . . it is full use of your powers along lines of excellence. I find, therefore, the Presidency provides some happiness." It was for this reason that his biographers often had found a detachment about the man. Kennedy sought the alternative most certain to lead him further to personal fulfillment. But then the moments had come when as President he realized detachment would not do and personal fulfillment was not as important an objective as national obligation. So on several occasions he had risked everything on one toss. Perhaps the most dangerous of the tosses had been the nuclear test ban treaty which he had urged through the Senate just a few weeks earlier and the civil rights legislation he now was fighting for. Once the tosses had been made, however, he was no longer the adventurer using the medium of politics for his personal gratification but had become the true politician using his office daringly for the advancement of the nation.

Kennedy remained a contrast with Johnson because the Texan had not begun his political career seeking personal fulfillment. Instead he had learned as a congressional secretary on Capitol Hill that politics is a means of helping your neighbors and your friends by bringing them federally subsidized electric power to light their homes and water to irrigate their farms, government contracts to provide jobs for their sons and government dollars to feed their hungry. For Johnson politics had not been the area where a political philosophy is developed and advanced. His politics had taught him to think in terms of material gains, not philosophical objectives. That is why Lyndon Johnson had been such a bargainer in Congress. Despite his talk about "pushing in all your chips," Johnson never considered it worthwhile to sacrifice everything on one toss, to risk an entire legislative program with all its benefits on one civil rights bill, for example. Then politics had worked its alchemy on Lyndon Johnson as it had worked it on John Kennedy. If Lyndon Johnson would never be a "philosopher" in a manner satisfying to the liberal intellectuals, he had found that as a national politician he must formulate, endorse and preach a philosophical approach to solving the problems of the nation. He could no longer bargain for the lowest common denominator but he must lead. As Kennedy had learned he must sometimes make strong commitments and accept the political risks that go with them, Lyndon Johnson had realized he must sacrifice some material gains for a long-term objective. He had finally reached the point, twenty-six years after he first cast a vote against civil rights legislation, where he was willing to do that on civil rights. "Our real concern," he had said just eight days before this motorcade, "must be the dignity and integrity of the individual man or woman. Our objective must be the right of each human being to be judged on the basis of merit and not upon accident of ancestry." Like Kennedy he had taken the risk and then found that the danger evaporated as the people agreed to what was right.

And that was why Johnson and Kennedy were such a strange combination this day. More than geography split their origins. Each had a different motivation for coming into politics, but the demands of the political process had joined them. These demands had forced the world of the eastern liberal and sophisticate as represented by Kennedy and the world of the rustic but awakening South as represented by Johnson to join together in a strong and sincere attack on the nation's ugly sore of racial discrimination. It was perhaps more difficult for Johnson than it was for Kennedy because the object of the program then was the South—the homeland of Lyndon Johnson.

The American political system—if it is to work—requires

that people from divergent areas and of different backgrounds join together to promote the common good rather than their regional wishes. The combination of Kennedy and Johnson represented that system's triumph.

The Presidential motorcade now was in the heart of Dallas and the greeting of the people was tumultuous. At the west end of Main Street, the line of cars turned right on Houston Street. It moved one block, creeping along at eleven miles an hour, then turned left onto Elm Street. In the Vice President's car a Secret Service agent named Rufus W. Youngblood noticed the seven-story orange brick Texas School Book Depository building looming ahead on the northwest corner of the intersection of Houston and Elm streets. There was a clock atop the building that indicated the time was twelve thirty P.M.

Two cars ahead, in the President's open Lincoln, Mrs. John B. Connally, the wife of the governor, was thrilled by the size and the spirit of the city's greeting. She could restrain herself no longer. Turning around to John Kennedy, she said: "Mr. President, you can't say Dallas doesn't love you."

A Note on Sources

There are three sources for this book. First is my experience as a reporter in Washington since May of 1958. Second is the published material—books, magazine articles, newspaper stories—about Lyndon Johnson and about the New Frontier. I used this material for general background information and to refresh my own memory. When I quoted from a specific source I attempted to identify the source either in the text or in a footnote.

The third source—and the principal source—is a number of persons who graciously consented to interviews in connection with my researching this book. These persons include prominent members of the New Frontier who were closely associated with John F. Kennedy, members of Lyndon Johnson's staff when he was Senate majority leader and Vice President, members of the United States Congress and other persons, inside and outside of government, who were associated with Lyndon Johnson. I am not identifying them here because I promised them I would not.

On several occasions I wrote Bill D. Moyers, press secretary at the White House, offering to discuss this book (while it was still in preparation) with him or any other persons at the White House. He declined to see me, however.

LEONARD BAKER

Washington, D.C.
February 1966

INDEX

Acheson, Dean, 39
Adams, John, 6, 170
Adenauer, Konrad, 45, 69, 72
Africa, 63–64
Aiken, George D., 225
Albert, Carl, 95–96
Alger, Bruce, 86, 264
Alsop, Stewart, 123, 185
Ambassador to the United Nations, 33, 44
American Federation of Labor, 191–193, 197
American Legion, 35
American Political Science Association, 218
American Veterans Committee, 36
Americans for Democratic Action, 36, 41–42, 106, 107, 184–185, 225, 227
Ames Research Center, 132, 133
Anderson, Clinton P., 214, 215
Anderson, Marian, 8
Appropriations Committee, 19
Armed Services Committee, 18, 19
Astronauts, 129, 134–135, 136
Atomic Energy Commission, 129
Ayres, William H., 94
Ayres-Kitchin bill, 94–95

Bacall, Lauren, 97, 98
Bailey, John M., 253
Baker, Lynda, 242
Baker, Lyndon, 242
Baker, Robert G., 241–245, 248, 266
Balcones Escarpment, 177–178
Barclay, John, 10, 32
Barkley, Alben W., 97, 172–173, 189
Barnett, Ross, 88, 113–116
Bartlett, Charles, 110, 123
Bashir Ahmed, 65–67
Bay of Pigs affair, 44–46
BeLieu, Kenneth E., 41
Bell, Jack, 263
Benson, Ezra Taft, 35
Berlin crisis, 30, 67–77
Birmingham, Alabama, 119, 226
Blakely, William, 233
Blough, Roger, 110
Boggs, Hale, 119
Bohlen, Charles, 74
Bowles, Chester, 42, 47, 55
Braestrup, Peter, 157
Brandt, Willy, 71, 72
Bricker, John, 173
Brown, Edmund G., 163

Bruce, David, 39
Budget busters, 31, 50
Bundy, McGeorge, 120
Burns, James MacGregor, 226
Burr, Aaron, 170
Butler, Paul M., 49
Byrd, Harry F., 265
Byrnes, James, 190

Calhoun, John C., 171
Cannon, Clarence, 19
Carey, James B., 193
Central Intelligence Agency, 44
China, 47
Civil rights, 11–13, 31, 38, 52,
    83–85, 88, 90–92, 112–120,
    146–162, 197–231, 251–252,
    263, 265
  Eisenhower on, 54
  Johnson on, 12–13, 56, 197–231
  Kennedy on, 211, 214, 215,
    219–221, 226–228, 230
Civil Service Commission, 159
Clark, Joseph S., 225, 226
Clay, Lucius, 71, 74, 76
Clifford, Clark, 110
Cohen, Benjamin, 11
Colfax, Schuyler, 171
Committee on Equal Employment
    Opportunity, 43, 98, 146–
    162, 194
Communications Satellite Corpo-
    ration, 133
Congress of Industrial Organiza-
    tions, 191–193, 197
Connally, John B., Jr., 41, 60,
    234–236, 238, 240, 248, 260,
    262, 264
Connally, Mrs. John B., Jr., 269
Conrad, Joseph, 213
Constitution of United States
  Twelfth Amendment, 170
  Twenty-second Amendment, 49

Coolidge, Calvin, 171
Corcoran, "Tommy the Cork," 11
Council of Economic Advisers,
    110
Cuba
  invasion of, 44–46
  missile crisis, 120–123

Daily News (New York), 105
Daley, Richard, 54
Dallas, Texas, 259–269
Daniel, Price, 212, 233, 235
Davis, James C., 150
Dawes, Charles G., 171
Dawson, William L., 38, 39
Day, J. Edward, 40, 41
Declaration of Constitutional Prin-
    ciples, 210–211
Democratic Advisory Council, 50
Democratic National Committee,
    253, 256
Democratic Steering Committee,
    237
DeSapio, Carmine, 189
Dewey, Thomas E., 97, 173, 189
Dillon, Douglas, 40
Dirksen, Everett M., 70
Dixiecrat revolt (1948), 217
Dowling, Walter, 71
Dubinsky, David, 251
Dulles, Allen, 44
Dulles, John Foster, 39

East Germany, 67–77
Eastland, James, 116, 208–209
Eisenhower, Dwight David, 4, 5,
    9, 11–12, 31, 45, 49–50, 61,
    79, 98, 117, 180, 217
  on the Billie Sol Estes affair, 141
  on civil rights, 54
  on the space program, 125–126,
    130–131
  on Vice Presidents, 172

Eisenhower, Mrs. Dwight David, 4
Ervin, Sam, 202–203
Estes, Billie Sol, 59, 139–145
Excom sessions, 121–122

Fair Employment Practices Commission, 200–205, 227–230
Fairbanks, Charles W., 171
Farley, Jim, 13
Farm Home Administration, 59
Faubus, Orval, 118
Federal Bureau of Investigation, 141, 144, 252
Federal Communications Commission, 245–247
Federal Deposit Insurance Corporation, 220
Federal Housing Administration, 219–220
Feild, John G., 155–158
Feldman, Mike, 183
Feldman, Myer, 56
Fleeson, Doris, 170
Fortas, Abe, 11, 148
Freeman, Orville L., 10–11, 41, 42
  in Billie Sol Estes affair, 140–142
Fulbright, J. William, 38–39, 116, 195, 206, 210

Galbraith, John Kenneth, 196
Garner, John Nance, 10, 79–80, 97, 98, 171–173
Gavin, James M., 129
General Dynamics Corporation, 249
George, Walter, 202–203
Glenn, John, 134–136
Glenn, Mrs. John, 135–136
Goldberg, Arthur J., 40, 109, 110, 112, 147, 157, 159, 193

Goldwater, Barry, 212, 238, 239, 256–257
Gone with the Wind (Mitchell), 88
Gonzalez, Henry B., 261
Gore, Albert, 24–27
Governors' Conference, 61
Graham, Philip L., 185
Green, Theodore Francis, 25
Green, William, 54, 189

Hall, Len, 13
Hamilton, Alexander, 37
Hamlin, Hannibal, 171
Harriman, W. Averell, 55
Harvard University, 39, 127
Hayden, Carl, 3, 53
Hays, Brooks, 118
Heller, Walter W., 110
Herald Tribune, 136
Herblock (political cartoonist), 50
Hill, Lister, 202–203
Hillman, Sidney, 190
Hodges, Luther H., 40, 41, 55
House Rules Committee, 29
Houston, Sam, 178
Houston *Post,* 239
Howe, Louis, 13
Humphrey, Hubert H., 26, 52, 57, 163, 185, 214, 215, 250

India, 47
Indochina, 172
International Ladies Garment Workers Union, 251
Irish Mafia, 13–14, 43, 49, 51–52, 57, 118, 167, 181, 254, 263

Jackson, Andrew, 171
Jackson, Henry M., 56, 57, 163, 189
Janson, Donald, 86

Javits, Jacob K., 215, 225
Jefferson, Thomas, 6, 170
Jenkins, Walter W., 105, 266
Jews, 92, 113
John Kennedy: A Political Profile (Burns), 226
Johns, Glover S., Jr., 75–76
Johnson, Andrew, 171
Johnson, Eliza, 178
Johnson, Lucy (Luci), 7
Johnson, Lynda Bird, 7, 45
Johnson, Lyndon Baines
  background of, 177–179, 245
  in Bay of Pigs invasion, 44–46
  Berlin trip, 67–77
  Billie Sol Estes affair, 139–145
  the Bobby Baker affair, 241–245, 248, 266
  on civil rights, 12–13, 56, 197–231
  Committee on Equal Employment Opportunity, 146–162, 194
  compared to Kennedy, 34–37, 266–269
  Cuba crisis, 120–123
  in election of 1960, 80–93
  first goodwill tour, 62–64
  the intellectuals and, 194–197
  with Kennedy in Dallas, 259–269
  on labor, 190–194
  leaves the Senate, 20–28
  as majority leader in the Senate, 9, 22–23, 49–51
  minimum wage bill, 93–95
  Mississippi crisis, 112–119
  on the national government, 36–37
  popularity loss in Texas, 232–240
  on power, 52–53

Johnson, Lyndon Baines (*cont'd.*)
  question of 1964 ticket, 181–187, 249–258
  refusal to enter primaries, 52–53
  regionalism of, 6, 11–13, 48–49, 63–67, 177–179
  space program, 124–137
  in the steel crisis, 109–112
  sworn in as Vice President, 3–10
  tour of southeast Asia, 46–47, 65–66
  wealth of, 245–248
Johnson, Mrs. Lyndon Baines, 3, 7, 15, 63, 85–86, 89, 139, 179, 245–247, 259
Johnson, Rebekah Baines, 9
Johnson, Richard M., 171
Johnson, Sam Ealy, Jr., 35, 200
Jones, Jesse, 8
Justice Department, 106, 113–114

Kefauver, Estes, 111, 208, 237
Kennedy, Caroline, 166
Kennedy, Edward M., 165
Kennedy, John Fitzgerald
  Berlin crisis, 67–77
  in Billie Sol Estes affair, 141, 142
  cabinet of, 31–33, 40
  Catholicism of, 11, 52, 83–85, 90, 92, 116, 164
  on civil rights, 146–162, 211, 214, 215, 219–221, 226–228, 230
  compared to Johnson, 34–37, 266–269
  Cuba crisis, 120–123
  in Dallas, 259–269
  decision making, 44–46
  decision to visit Texas, 240, 260

Kennedy, John Fitzgerald (*cont'd.*)
efforts to influence congress, 28–29
election of 1960, 80–93
as a member of the House of Representatives, 35
men surrounding, 10–11, 13–14, 43, 49, 51–52, 57, 118, 167, 181, 254, 263
minimum wage bill, 93–95
Mississippi crisis, 112–119
on the national government, 36–37
on power, 53–54
on public housing, 219–220
question of 1964 ticket, 105–106, 181–182, 249–258
religious prejudice, 83–85, 90, 92, 116, 164
on Senate Foreign Relations Committee, 6–7
selection of Johnson as running mate, 182–186
space program, 124–127
steel crisis, 109–112
wealth of, 248
Kennedy, Mrs. John Fitzgerald, 15, 135, 252, 260–263
Kennedy, Joseph P., 14, 35, 60
Kennedy, Joseph P., Jr., 156
Kennedy, Robert F., 15, 40–41, 53, 56, 57
Committee on Equal Employment Opportunity, 146–147, 158–162
Cuba crisis, 121
Mississippi crisis, 112–117
as the number two man, 105–108
space program, 134
in the steel crisis, 111
"Kennedy or Nixon: Does It Make

"Kennedy or Nixon," (*cont'd.*)
Any Difference?" (Schlesinger), 195
Kerr, Robert S., 18–19, 32, 128, 145, 168, 244
Khrushchev, Nikita, 67
Kitchin, A. Paul, 94
Kleberg, Richard M., 108
Korth, Fred, 248–249
Krock, Arthur, 170
Ku Klux Klan, 200

Landrum-Griffin labor reform act, 190–192
Laos, 47
Lawrence, David L., 189
Lebanon, Republic of, 64
Lewis, Anthony, 194, 207
Lewis, Ted, 105
Liberal Party (New York), 251–252
Lincoln, Abraham, 37, 44, 171
Little Rock, Arkansas, 117–118
Lockheed Corporation, 151–152, 155
Lodge, Henry Cabot, 39, 83–84, 90, 91, 163, 218
Lovett, Robert A., 39

McCarthy, Eugene J., 225
McCarthy, Joseph, 47
McClellan, John L., 141, 190–191
McCloskey, Matthew, 189
McCormack, John W., 3, 97
McNamara, Robert S., 10–11, 40, 41, 44, 63, 111, 121
in the space program, 129–131
Mansfield, Mike, 17, 20, 23–24, 26–27, 168
Marshall, Burke, 114, 115
Marshall, Thomas R., 171
Massachusetts Institute of Technology, 127

Mattox, W. P., 142
Maverick, Maury, Jr., 178
Meany, George, 192
Medicare, 235
Meredith, James H., 112–114
Mesta, Perle, 61
Mills, Wilbur D., 19
Minimum wage bill, 93–95
Mississippi crisis, 112–119
Mitchell, Margaret, 88
Moon, race for, 130–132
Morton, Thruston B., 249
Moyers, Bill D., 29, 271–272

National Aeronautics and Space Agency, 125, 127
National Association for the Advancement of Colored People, 148
National Cotton Advisory Commission, 140, 142
National Press Club, 36, 97
National Security Council, 43, 97, 120–122
National Youth Administration, 108
N'Doye, Gurtil, 63
Negroes, 12–13, 21, 38, 52, 83–85, 88, 90–92, 112–120, 146–162, 197–231, 251–252, 263, 265
Nehru, Pundit Motilal, 242
New Republic, The, 178
New York Times, The, 17, 86, 123, 157, 170, 194, 207, 213
New York Times Sunday Magazine, The, 76
New Yorker, The (magazine), 180
Nixon, Richard Milhous, 4–7, 39, 40, 52, 79, 122, 167, 172, 184, 217, 224
on civil rights, 148, 149

Nixon, Richard Melhous (cont'd.)
election of 1960, 81, 83–92
on the space program, 130
as Vice President, 98
Nixon, Mrs. Richard Milhous, 4
North Atlantic Treaty Organization (NATO), 62, 63
Nuclear missiles, 120–123

O'Brien, Lawrence F., 10–11, 28, 29, 108, 115, 262, 263
O'Donnell, Kenneth, 10–11, 28, 40, 105, 108, 110, 115, 183–184, 262, 264
Oil industry, 30, 43, 217
Order of Battle, a Republican's Call to Reason (Javits), 215

Pakistan, 63, 65
Peace Corps, 105
Plans for Progress program, 155–156
Post Office Department, 38, 39
Powell, Adam Clayton, 53
Powers, David, 260
Profiles In Courage (Kennedy), 205
Proxmire, William, 237

Racial prejudice, 11–13, 31, 38, 83–85, 88, 90–92, 112–120, 146–162, 197–231, 251–252, 263, 265
Rauh, Joseph L., 197, 225–228, 255
Rayburn, Sam, 8–9, 19, 30, 49–50, 69–70, 93, 94–97, 141, 184, 202, 233
on civil rights, 209, 211
on labor, 191–192
Reedy, George, 29
Regionalism, 6, 11–13, 48–49, 63–67, 177–179

Religious prejudice, 11, 52, 83–85, 90, 92, 116, 164
Reporter, The (magazine), 167
Reuther, Walter, 53, 153, 159, 193, 197, 250–251
Reynolds, Don B., 266
Ribicoff, Abraham, 40, 41, 106
Rice Institute, 126
Rockefeller, Nelson, 64–65, 226, 256
Roosevelt, Franklin D., 8, 51, 97–98, 147, 171–173, 180, 190
  relationship with Vice Presidents, 79–80
  wealth of, 248
Roosevelt, Theodore, 37, 171
Rose, Alex, 193, 251
Rowan, Carl, 242–243
Rozelle, James S., 75
Rusk, Dean, 40, 44, 77, 78, 111, 121, 134, 166
Russell, Richard B., 18, 19, 32, 89, 150–152, 158, 202–203, 223

Salinger, Pierre, 70
Saturday Evening Post, The, 123
Sayre, Francis B., 153, 154
Schlesinger, Arthur M., Jr., 42, 55, 184–185, 195, 196
Scranton, William, 256
Seaborg, Glenn T., 129
Senate Antitrust Subcommittee, 111
Senate Appropriations Committee, 236–237
Senate Commerce Committee, 246
Senate Foreign Relations Committee, 6–7, 38, 195
Senegal, 62, 63
Shepard, Alan, 134–135
Shriver, Sargeant, 39, 40, 105

Shriver, Mrs. Sargeant, 105
Slavery, 200
Sorensen, Theodore C., 11, 41–42, 44, 56, 110, 112, 115, 183, 241, 242
South Vietnam, 46, 47
Southeast Asia, 46–47, 65–66
Southern Manifesto, 210–211
Space Act of 1958, 124–125
Space Council, 125–137
Space program, 124–137
Spain, 63
Sparkman, John, 208, 210
Sputnik I, 124
Stassen, Harold E., 79
Steel crisis, 109–112
Stevenson, Adlai E., 44, 90, 123, 180, 181, 208, 233, 264
Supersonic transports, 133–134
Symington, Stuart, 57, 163

Taft-Hartley labor bill, 36, 189–190
Talmadge, Herman, 158
Taxes, 30–31, 43, 217
Taylor, Hobart, Jr., 158, 162
Texas Democratic Party, 26, 142–143
Texas School Book Depository, 269
Texas State Agricultural and Conservation Committee, 142
Thomas, Albert, 127, 261
Thousand Days, A (Schlesinger), 184–185
Time (magazine), 167
Tower, John G., 86–87, 232, 233
Troutman, Robert, 154–158
Truman, Harry S., 7, 45, 51, 61, 90, 97–98, 128, 173, 189–190, 196

Udall, Stewart L., 41

Union of Soviet Socialist Republics, 120–123, 131, 266
  space program, 124–125
  wheat sales to, 30
United Auto Workers, 53, 153, 197
United Hatters, Cap and Millinery Workers Union, 250
United States Steel Corporation, 109–112
Urban Renewal Administration, 219

Van Buren, Martin, 6
Vance, Cyrus R., 41
Veterans Administration, 219–220
Vinson, Carl, 19, 93, 94, 151, 202

Waging Peace (Eisenhower), 172
Wallace, George, 88, 113, 116
Wallace, Henry A., 80, 173, 190

Warren, Earl, 7, 97, 189
Washington Post, The, 50, 183, 185
Watkins, Tom, 114
Ways and Means Committee, 19
Webb, James E., 128–133
White backlash, 230
Wicker, Tom, 213
Wiesner, Jerome B., 127–129
Williams, Mennen, 42, 55
Wilson, Woodrow, 171

Yarborough, Don, 235, 236, 238
Yarborough, Ralph, 25–26, 96, 141, 142–143, 169, 212, 257–258, 260–262, 264
  as the liberal leader, 233–234, 236–238
  on Texas jobs, 58–59
Youngblood, Rufus W., 269

DATE